NEWMAN THE THEOLOGIAN

A READER

NEWMAN THE THEOLOGIAN

A Reader

IAN KER

Collins

Collins Religious Publishing
8 Grafton Street, London W1X 3LA

Collins Dove
PO Private Bag 200
Burwood, Victoria 3125

Collins New Zealand
PO Box 1
Auckland

Collins Canada
100 Lesmill Road
Don Mills
Ontario MDB 2T5

© 1990 Ian Ker
First published 1990
ISBN 0 00 599208 7

Typesetting by BP Integraphics Ltd., Bath
Printed in Great Britain at The Bath Press, Avon

CONTENTS

ABBREVIATIONS OF NEWMAN'S WORKS

Newman collected his works in a uniform edition of 36 volumes (1868–81). Until his death in 1890 he continued making minor textual changes in reprints of individual volumes in this edition, of which all the volumes from 1886 were published by Longmans, Green, and Co. of London. References are usually to volumes in the uniform edition published after 1890 by Longmans, which are distinguished from other editions by not including publication details in brackets after the title.

Apo.	*Apologia pro Vita Sua*, ed. Martin J. Svaglic (Oxford: Clarendon Press, 1967)
Ari.	*The Arians of the Fourth Century*
Ath. i, ii	*Selected Treatises of St. Athanasius*, 2 vols.
AW	*John Henry Newman: Autobiographical Writings*, ed. Henry Tristram (London and New York: Sheed and Ward, 1956)
Call.	*Callista: A Tale of the Third Century*
Campaign	*My Campaign in Ireland, Part I*, ed. W. Neville (privately printed, 1896)
CS	*Catholic Sermons of Cardinal Newman*, ed. at the Birmingham Oratory (London: Sheed and Ward, 1957)
Cons.	*On Consulting the Faithful in Matters of Doctrine*, ed. John Coulson (London: Geoffrey Chapman, 1961)
DA	*Discussions and Arguments on Various Subjects*
Dev.	*An Essay on the Development of Christian Doctrine*
Diff. i, ii	*Certain Difficulties felt by Anglicans in Catholic Teaching*, 2 vols.
Ess. i, ii	*Essays Critical and Historical*, 2 vols.
GA	*An Essay in Aid of a Grammar of Assent*, ed. I. T. Ker (Oxford: Clarendon Press, 1985)
HS, i, ii, iii	*Historical Sketches*, 3 vols.

Idea	*The Idea of a University*, ed. I. T. Ker (Oxford: Clarendon Press, 1976)
Jfc.	*Lectures on the Doctrine of Justification*
LD	*The Letters and Diaries of John Henry Newman*, ed. Charles Stephen Dessain et al., vols. i–vi (Oxford: Clarendon Press, 1978–84), xi–xxii (London: Thomes Nelson, 1961–72), xxiii–xxxi (Oxford: Clarendon Press, 1973–7)
LG	*Loss and Gain: The Story of a Convert*
MD	*Meditations and Devotions of the late Cardinal Newman* (London: Longmans, Green, and Co., 1893)
Mir.	*Two Essays on Biblical and on Ecclesiastical Miracles*
Mix.	*Discourses addressed to Mixed Congregations*
NO	*Newman the Oratorian: His Unpublished Oratory Papers*, ed. Placid Murray, O.S.B. (Dublin: Gill and Macmillan, 1969)
OS	*Sermons preached on Various Occasions*
PS i–viii	*Parochial and Plain Sermons*, 8 vols.
Phil. N. i, ii	*The Philosophical Notebook of John Henry Newman*, ed. Edward Sillem, 2 vols. (Louvain: Nauwelaerts, 1969–70)
Prepos.	*Present Position of Catholics in England*
SD	*Sermons bearing on Subjects of the Day*
SE	*Stray Essays on Controversial Points* (privately printed, 1890)
SN	*Sermon Notes of John Henry Cardinal Newman, 1849–1878*, ed. Fathers of the Birmingham Oratory (London: Longmans, Green, and Co., 1913)
TP i	*The Theological Papers of John Henry Newman on Faith and Certainty*, ed. Hugo M. de Achaval, SJ, and J. Derek Holmes (Oxford: Clarendon Press, 1976)
TP, ii	*The Theological Papers of John Henry Newman on Biblical Inspiration and on Infallibility*, ed. J. Derek Holmes (Oxford: Clarendon Press, 1979)
TT	*Tracts Theological and Ecclesiastical*
US	*Fifteen Sermons preached before the University of Oxford*
VM i, ii	*The Via Media*, 2 vols.
VV	*Verses on Various Occasions*

INTRODUCTION

1

NEWMAN'S ANGLICAN THEOLOGY

During his lifetime John Henry Newman (1801–90) was a figure of considerable controversy, both as an Anglican and as a Roman Catholic. Nor did controversy cease with his death. On the one hand, the protagonists on both sides of the Modernist crisis within the Catholic Church at the beginning of this century were happy to label Newman as the father of Modernism. On the other hand, the apparent triumph of Ultramontanism at the First Vatican Council and the papal condemnation of Anglican Orders six years after Newman's death did not help to encourage sympathy within the Church of England for the celebrated convert to Rome. In recent decades, however, the rise of the ecumenical movement and the changes wrought in the Roman Catholic Church by the Second Vatican Council have considerably altered the perception of Newman on both the Anglican and the Catholic sides. Not only is Newman now seen as one of the pioneers of ecumenism and a kind of bridge-figure between Canterbury and Rome, but he is often hailed as "the Father of the Second Vatican Council". Increasingly, too, the study of his writings, together with the publication of a mass of unpublished materials, in particular most of the vast corpus of his letters, have greatly enhanced Newman's stature as one of those comparatively few Christian thinkers whose name may be mentioned in the same breath as the Fathers of the Church.

Newman's long life, which spans almost the entire nineteenth century is divided almost equally into two halves by his conversion to Roman Catholicism in 1845. But although the essential continuity between his Anglican and Catholic periods is very striking, still it is not inappropriate to consider his Anglican theology separately from his Catholic theology. After all, Newman's decisive contribution to the theology of Tractarianism, which so transformed the Church of England, is clearly distinguishable and distinct from his seminal contribution to the development of modern Catholic ecclesiology. For in spite of the connexions, there is a difference of approach and emphasis which reflects the very different preoccupations that influenced his thought in two very dissimilar ecclesial situations.

FORMATIVE INFLUENCES

Newman was brought up as an ordinary member of the Church of England in an unremarkable religious atmosphere. His parents belonged to what their son was later to call "the national religion of England" or "Bible Religion", which "consists, not in rites or creeds, but mainly in having the Bible read in Church, in the family, and in private".[1]* He himself, Newman tells us in his autobiography, the *Apologia pro Vita Sua*, had been "brought up from a child to take great delight in reading the Bible", particularly by his grandmother and aunt in whose house he had stayed as a little boy. At the same time he "had no formed religious convictions" till he was fifteen.[2] For it was during the summer and autumn of 1816 that he underwent the first of the two great religious conversions of his life. He had had to stay on at his boarding school at Ealing after the summer term ended because the family had been forced to leave their home in London after the failure of the bank in which his father was a partner.

Left, then, at school by himself during the long summer holidays ("my friends gone away"), he "was terrified at the heavy hand of God which came down upon me". It was not simply that his life had been turned upside down by his father's disaster; he was now afflicted by the first of the "three great illnesses" of his life. Years later he referred to it as the "first keen, terrible one, when I was a boy of 15, and it made me a Christian with experiences before and after, awful, and known only to God".[3] At the end of his life he confessed he found it "difficult to realize or imagine the identity of the boy before and after August 1816;" as he looked back over seventy years, he could only see "another person".[4] When he recollected the crisis four or five years after the event, he discerned "the wisdom and goodness of God" in the troubles that had come upon him, which allowed "room" for particular "influences" to be brought to bear – those of "an excellent man, the Revd Walter Mayers . . . one of the classical masters, from whom [I] received deep religious impressions . . .

*Numbered footnotes are on pp. 278 ff.

4

Calvinistic in character, which were to [me] the beginning of a new life".[5] Mayers himself had only been "converted" two years previously, shortly after receiving Holy Orders.

A year before, at the age of fourteen, Newman had been rather enjoying reading objections to Christianity in writers like Thomas Paine. His general frame of mind was that he wanted "to be virtuous, but not religious. There was something in the latter idea I did not like. Nor did I see the *meaning* of loving God".[6] But now he "fell under the influences of a definite Creed, and received into my intellect impressions of dogma, which, through God's mercy, have never been effaced or obscured". It was not only "the conversations and sermons" of Mayers ("who was the human means of this beginning of divine faith in me"), but, more important, there was "the effect of the books which he put into my hands, all of the school of Calvin". From one of them he learned the Calvinist doctrine of "final perseverance", namely that "the regenerate cannot fall away", a belief which "gradually faded away" when he was twenty-one, but which tended to influence him on the lines of certain "childish imaginations", that is to say "in isolating me from the objects which surrounded me, in confirming me in my mistrust of the reality of material phenomena, and making me rest in the thought of two and two only absolute and luminously self-evident beings, myself and my Creator". The most important writer Mayers introduced him to was Thomas Scott, the famous Evangelical commentator on the Bible, "who made a deeper impression on my mind than any other, and to whom (humanly speaking) I almost owe my soul". Scott's autobiography *The Force of Truth* showed how he had "followed truth wherever it led him, beginning with Unitarianism, and ending in a zealous faith in the Holy Trinity. It was he who first planted deep in my mind that fundamental truth of religion". Significantly, Newman was also struck by "the minutely practical character of his writings. They show him to be a true Englishman, and I deeply felt his influence; and for years I used almost as proverbs . . . 'Holiness rather than peace', and 'Growth the only evidence of life'."[7]

Profoundly influences as he was by Evangelicalism, Newman had not been converted, as he soon became aware, "in that special way which it laid down as imperative". In 1821 he acknowledged in his journal that his own "feelings" had been "different from any account I have ever read". A few years later he noted that his "feelings" had not been "*violent*" in the prescribed Evangelical manner, "but a returning to, a renewing of, principles, under the power of the Holy Spirit, which I had *already* felt, and in a measure acted on, when young". He had not in fact had "those special Evangelical experiences, which like the grip of the hand or other prescribed signs of a secret society, are the sure token of a member"; for he had not undergone "the evangelical process of conversion" with "its stages of conviction of sin, terror, despair, news of the free and full salvation, joy and peace, and so on to final perseverance".[8]

There were two other developments in those crucial months of 1816, both of enormous significance for the future. First,

I read Joseph Milner's Church History, and was nothing short of enamoured of the long extracts from St. Augustine, St. Ambrose, and the other Fathers which I found there. I read them as being the religion of the primitive Christians; but simultaneously with Milner I read Newton on the Prophecies, and in consequence became most firmly convinced that the Pope was the Antichrist predicted by Daniel, St. Paul, and St. John. My imagination was stained by the effects of this doctrine up to the year 1843; it had been obliterated from my reason and judgment at an earlier date . . .

These two very different works "produced a deep impression" on him, "each contrary to each, and planting in me the seeds of an intellectual inconsistency which disabled me for a long course of years".[9]

In 1822, at the age of twenty-one, Newman was elected to a coveted fellowship at Oriel College, at the time the most academically prestigious of the Oxford colleges. Two years later he took Holy Orders in the Church f England and began pastoral work in a working-class parish. It was during this time that he "underwent a great change in [my] religious opinions". To begin with, there was the intellectual "atmosphere" of the Oriel Common Room, which was "neither high Church nor low Church, but . . . characterized by its spirit of moderation and comprehension". Its leading lights, figures like Edward Copleston, Richard Whately, John Davison, Edward Hawkins, and Thomas Arnold, were objects of suspicion to "the old unspiritual high-and-dry, then in possession of the high places of Oxford", who "pronounced them unsafe". Like other Evangelicals, Newman was 'grateful for that liberality of mind which was in such striking contrast with the dominant high-Church'. Because of his parochial duties he had to stay in Oxford in vacation time, as did Edward Hawkins, then Vicar of St Mary's, the University Church. In the long vacation, when all the other fellows were away, they were thrown into each other's company. Newman learned from Hawkins ("a man of most exact mind") intellectual rigour: "He was the first who taught me to weigh my words, and to be cautious in my statements". Theologically, Newman was deeply influenced by a university sermon which Hawkins had preached on tradition, to the effect that the Bible "was never intended to teach doctrine, but only to prove it, and that, if we would learn doctrine, we must have recourse to the formularies of the Church". But Hawkins influenced him more directly and personally by criticizing the first sermon he ever wrote, which "divided the Christian world into two classes, the one all darkness, the other all light". Newman maintained the usual Evangelical distinction between "nominal" Christians and "real" Christians who had experienced true conversion. Hawkins argued that it was "impossible for us in fact to draw such a line of demarcation", that people were "not either saints or sinners" but somewhere in between, that there were differences of degree not of kind. To prove his point, Hawkins lent him a book which showed how St. Paul did not divide Christians into two categories, "the converted and unconverted", but addressed them all as believers with the gift of the Holy Spirit, however much he might rebuke them for their actual behaviour. It was this book which "was successful in the event beyond anything else, in routing out" Newman's "evangelical doctrines". He had not, then, been in Orders long before he "had taken the first step towards giving up the evangelical form of Christianity; however, for a long while certain shreds and tatters of that doctrine hung about [my] preaching, nor did [I] for a whole ten years altogether sever [myself] from those great religious societies and their meetings, which then as now were the rallying ground and the strength of the Evangelical body'.

The "teaching of facts" also played an important part: he found from working in a parish that Evangelicalism did not "work", that "it was unreal", and "not a key to the phenomena

7

of human nature, as they occur in the world". Although, he later readily recognized, Evangelical "teaching had been a great blessing for England", for "it had brought home to the hearts of thousands the cardinal and vital truths of Revelation, and to [myself] among others", still, "much as [I] owed" to it, "[I] never had been a genuine evangelical". True, Evangelicalism had "converted" him to "a spiritual life" (although his conversion had not followed the classic Evangelical pattern), but "considered as a system and in what was peculiar to itself", it "had from the first failed to find a response in [my] own religious experience, as afterwards in his parochial'.[10] Having to write sermons forced him to "systematize and complete" his ideas, and he found that he taken "almost on trust" a number of doctrines from Evangelical writers which did not seem to be supported by Scripture. In particular, he began to give up "the doctrine of imputed righteousness" in favour of the traditional church doctrine of Baptismal regeneration, the rejection of which had come to be the hallmark of the true Evangelical but which Newman had never felt easy about dismissing: how otherwise, he had once asked Mayers, could unbaptized babies who died be saved?[11] Finally, there was an aspect of Newman's mind "which seemed to intimate from the first that the ethical character of Evangelical Religion could not lastingly be imprinted upon it", and that was his "great attraction" both to the Classics (whom, like the ancient Fathers, he valued "as being in a certain sense inspired moralists and prophets of truths greater that they knew") and to the Fathers themselves. Had it not been for his love of the patristic writings, he would no doubt have embraced a "cold Arminian doctrine" which was "the characteristic aspect, both of the high and dry Anglicans of that day and of the Oriel divines". But "the permanent effect" of reading as a schoolboy Milner's *Church History* had been that "the first centuries were [my] *beau idéal* of Christianity", and an "imaginative devotion" to the Fathers "saved [me] from the danger" of taking "refuge in the flats" of the high-and-dry and Latitudinarian theologies on "leaving the crags and precipices of Luther and Calvin".[12]

Yet another influence leading him away from Evangelicalism was brought to bear during the summer of 1825, when at the end of June he began reading Joseph Butler's classic *Analogy of Religion* (1736). It helped place "[my] doctrinal views on a broad philosophical basis, with which an emotional religion could have little sympathy".[13] Butler insisted on the similarities between the works of God as shown in nature and as revealed in revelation, arguing that the objections which can be made against Christianity are analogous to those which can be made against theism. In retrospect, it is obvious how deeply the idea of analogy influenced Newman both as an intellectual principle and as a mode of argument, strongly affecting him not only as a thinker but also as a writer. However, in the *Apologia* he merely points out the religious significance of "the very idea of an analogy between the separate works of God", which "leads to the conclusion that the system which is of less importance is economically or sacramentally connected with the more momentous system, and of this conclusion the theory, to which I was inclined as a boy, viz. the unreality of material phenomena, is an ultimate resolution".[14]

Under the influence of the intellectualism of the Oriel Common Room, Newman was, he later admitted, "beginning to prefer intellectual excellence to moral". Not only was he "drifting in the direction of the Liberalism of the day", but he was even guilty of using "flippant language against the Fathers" in a couple of published articles, thus exemplifying "a certain disdain for Antiquity" which had been "growing" on him. He was, however, "rudely awakened" from this "dream at the end of 1827 by two great blows", a nervous breakdown and the death of his beloved youngest sister Mary.[15]

During the summer of 1828 Newman started to read the Fathers systematically, beginning with the early Apostolic Fathers, for "as I moved out of the shadow of that liberalism which had hung over my course, my early devotion towards the Fathers returned".[16] Not all the influences at Oriel moreover were of a theologically liberal nature. In *The Christian Year* (1827) of John Keble (who resigned his fellowship at Oriel a year after Newman was elected a fellow) he found the same sacramental idea ('though recast in the creative mind of my new master') that he had already learned from Butler's *Analogy*, namely that "material phenomena are both the types and the instruments of real things unseen".[17] As a result of a growing friendship with one of the younger Oriel fellows, Richard Hurrell Froude, he also began to delight "in the notion of an hierarchical system, of sacerdotal power, and of full ecclesiastical liberty".[18] In other words, having abandoned Evangelicalism and after flirting briefly with liberalism, Newman's views were becoming increasingly "high church". And the more he read the Fathers, the more Catholic his theology was becoming. The opportunity to devote himself more fully to his patristic studies came in 1830 when the Provost of Oriel refused to entrust any more students to him after a row over the college tutorial arrangements. Freedom from teaching duties meant that Newman had much more time for the study of the writings of the Fathers. The controversy between the Provost and Tutors of Oriel was not without significant educational interest, but it had much more momentous, albeit unforeseen, implications of a religious nature. "Humanly speaking", Newman later reflected, the Oxford or Tractarian Movement "never would have been, had he not been deprived of his Tutorship, or had Keble, not Hawkins, been Provost".[19]

REVELATION AND DOGMA*

Newman did not see his first book, *The Arians of the Fourth Century* (1833), as simply a piece of historical and theological research: in writing it he was "resisting the innovations of the day, and attempting to defend the work of men indefinitely above me (the Primitive Fathers) which is now assailed".[20]

For although *The Arians* may be primarily a historical work, its author's own theological preoccupations are never far from the surface. Like contemporary religious liberalism, Arianism, unlike earlier heresies, was originally "a sceptical rather than a dogmatic teaching", aiming "to inquire into and reform the received creed, rather than to hazard one of its own", and as such enjoying all the advantages of "the assailant" over "the party assailed" in "finding" rather than "solving objections".[21] In disputing the orthodox creed, the Arians, too, were guilty of misapplying human reason to the mysteries of revelation. Moreover, their objections to using "words not found in Scripture, in confessions of faith" was of the very essence of the

*For texts, see below p. 67.

"principle of liberalism".[22] As for doctrinal "comprehensive-ness", Newman declares bluntly: "If the Church would be vigor-ous and influential, it must be decided and plain-spoken in its doctrine . . . To attempt comprehensions of opinion . . . is to mis-take arrangements of words, which have no existence except on paper, for . . . realities; and ingenious generalizations of dis-cordant sentiments for that practical agreement which alone can lead to co-operation". While it is only realistic to realize that "there are no two opinions so contrary to each other, but some form of words may be found vague enough to comprehend them both", comprehensiveness is impractical because it is unreal: "We may indeed artificially classify light and darkness under one term or formula; but nature has her own fixed courses . . . However plausible may be the veil thus thrown over hetero-geneous doctrines, the flimsy artifice is discomposed so soon as the principles beneath it are called upon to move and act". But comprehensiveness is, in fact, harmful to the Church, because of its unreal substitution of "words for things", in the form of "statements so faintly precise and so decently ambi-guous, as to embrace the greatest number of opinions possible, and to deprive religion, in consequence, of its austere and com-manding aspect".[23]

The alternative to comprehensiveness is not necessarily dog-matism. We should notice how at the outset of his theological writing Newman maintains a careful and characteristic balance between opposing extremes. Far from dogmatic formularies being desirable for their own sake, he insists that "freedom from symbols and articles is abstractedly the highest state of Christian communion, and the peculiar privilege of the primitive Church", for "technicality and formalism are, in their degree, inevitable results of public confessions of faith", and "when confessions do not exist, the mysteries of divine truth, instead of being exposed to the gaze of the profane and uninstructed, are kept hidden in the bosom of the Church, far more faithfully than is otherwise possible". It were better for both liberals and Evan-gelicals if there were no formulated dogmas, for they "are daily wrested by infidels to their ruin", while "on the other hand, much of that mischievous fanaticism is avoided, which at present abounds from the vanity of men, who think that they can explain the sublime doctrines and exuberant promises of the Gospel, before they have yet learned to know themselves and to discern the holiness of God". For these reasons, "and again from tenderness both for the heathen and the neophyte, who were unequal to the reception of the strong meat of the full Gospel, the rulers of the Church were dilatory in applying a remedy, which nevertheless the circumstances of the times imperatively required. They were loath to confess, that the Church had grown too old to enjoy the free, unsuspicious teaching with which her childhood was blest ..."[24] Throughout his life Newman was to keep the balance between insisting on the necessity of dogmatic formulations and yet allowing for their inherent limitations.

His awareness of the inadequacy of human language to express dogma came from his understanding of the early Church's principle of "economy", the treatment of which is perhaps the most interesting aspect of the book. The principle of economy meant that even that most fundamental of Christian dogmas, the doctrine of the Trinity, could be seen as only "the shadow, projected for the contemplation of the intellect, of the Object of scripturally-informed piety: a representation, economical; necessarily imperfect, as being exhibited in a foreign medium, and therefore involving apparent inconsistencies or mysteries". The "systematic" dogma could be "kept in the background in the infancy of Christianity, when faith and obedience were vigorous", and only "brought forward at a time when, reason being disproportionately developed, and aiming at sovereignty in the province of religion, its presence became necessary to expel an usurping idol from the house of God". From the individual believer's point of view, to make explicit what was implicit was not necessarily desirable: "so reluctant is a well-constituted mind to reflect on its own motive principles, that the correct intellectual image, from its hardness of outline, may startle and offend those who have all along been acting upon it". But having indicated how undesirable dogmatic formulations are, Newman immediately proceeds to show how necessary they are; for the fact that "we cannot restrain the rovings of the intellect, or silence its clamorous demand for a formal statement concerning the Object of our worship", means paradoxically that the earlier insistence that "intellectual representation should ever be subordinate to the cultivation of the religious affections" actually demands the "intellectual expression of theological truth", not only because it "excludes heresy", but because it "directly assists the acts of religious worship and obedience".[25]

Newman's enthusiasm for the Alexandrian doctrine that all religion comes from God – "There never was a time when God had not spoken to man, and told him to a certain extent his duty" – is striking. He agrees that "the Church of God ever has had, and the rest of mankind never have had, authoritative documents of truth, and appointed channels of communication with Him ... but all men have had more or less the guidance of Tradition, in addition to those internal notions of right and wrong which the Spirit has put into the heart of each individual". And he calls this "vague and uncertain family of religious truths, originally from God, but sojourning without the sanction of miracle, or a definite home, as pilgrims up and down the world, and discernible and separable from the corrupt legends with which they are mixed ... the *Dispensation of Paganism*". Arguing that this kind of economy is to be found in the Old Testament (in the figures, for example, of Job and Balaam), he claims that "there is nothing unreasonable in the notion, that there may have been heathen poets and sages, or sibyls again, in a certain sense divinely illuminated, and organs through whom religious and moral truth was conveyed". The practical conclusion is that the Christian apologist or missionary should "after St. Paul's manner, seek points in the existing superstitions as the basis of his own instructions, instead of indiscriminately condemning and discarding the whole assemblage of heathen opinions and practices", thus "recovering and purifying, rather than reversing the essential principles of their belief". What was then a radical approach, whether from a Catholic or Protestant point of view, stands in typically marked contrast to Newman's less than open attitude to "deliberate heretics and apostates", towards whom such "economy" is not to be shown. As always for Newman, superstition was far preferable to scepticism, for "he who believes a little, but encompasses that little with the inventions of men, is undeniably in a better condition than he who blots out from his mind both the human inventions, and that portion of truth which was concealed in them".[26]

*

13

Two years after the commencement of the Oxford or Tractarian Movement in 1833, Newman wrote *Tract 73* of the *Tracts for the Times*. It was republished later under the title "On the Introduction of Rationalistic Principles into Revealed Religion". Newman defines rationalism as an "abuse" of reason, "that is, a use of it for purposes for which it never was intended, and is unfitted".

To rationalize in matters of Revelation is to make our reason the standard and measure of the doctrines revealed; to stipulate that those doctrines should be such as to carry with them their own justification; to reject them, if they come in collision with our existing opinions or habits of thought, or are with difficulty harmonized with our existing stock of knowledge.

He is careful, however, not to exclude a legitimate use of reason in religious inquiry, and the sharp juxtaposition of the ways in which it is appropriate to employ reason with illegitimate instances of rationalism is very characteristic of the kind of intellectual tension that characterises Newman's thought:

As regards Revealed Truth, it is not Rationalism to set about to ascertain, by the use of reason, what things are ascertainable by reason, and what are not; nor, in the absence of an express Revelation, to inquire into the truths of Religion, as they come to us by nature; nor to determine what proofs are necessary for the acceptance of a Revelation, if it be given; nor to reject a Revelation on the plea of insufficient proof; nor, after recognizing it as divine, to investigate the meaning of its declarations, and to interpret its language ... This is not Rationalism; but it is Rationalism to accept the Revelation, and then to explain it away; to speak of it as the Word of God, and to treat it as the word of man; to refuse to let it speak for itself; to claim to be told the *why* and the *how* of God's dealings with us ... and to assign to Him a motive and a scope of our own; to stumble at the partial knowledge of what He may give us of them; to put aside what is obscure, as if it had not been said at all; to accept one half of what has been told us, and not the other half; to assume that the contents of Revelation are also its proof; to frame some gratuitous hypothesis about them, and then to garble, gloss, and colour them, to trim, clip, pare away, and twist them, in order to bring them into conformity with the idea to which we have subjected them.

14

For Newman, the moral basis of rationalism is obvious enough: "The Rationalist makes himself his own centre, not his Maker". This "narrow and egotistic temper of mind", he fears, is "the spirit" that is pervasive in the modern world: "Instead of looking out of ourselves, and trying to catch glimpses of God's workings, from any quarter, – throwing ourselves forward upon Him and waiting on Him, we sit at home bringing everything to ourselves, enthroning ourselves in our own views, and refusing to believe anything that does not force itself upon us as true". The result is that "the idea of Mystery" is "discarded", and religion takes on a subjective rather than objective character. The blame is laid squarely on Evangelical Christianity, which directs "its attention to the heart itself, not to anything external to us, whether creeds, actions, or ritual", and which "is really a specious form of trusting man rather than God", and so "in its nature Rationalistic". In a postscript which he added in 1836, Newman explained the theology of Schleiermacher, which had just come to his attention, as the typical "result of an attempt of the intellect to delineate, philosophise, and justify that religion (so called) of the heart and feelings, which has long prevailed".

It is a measure of his genius that even in the middle of his furious struggle against anti-dogmatic liberalism, Newman avoids losing his balance and falling into the opposite kind of rationalism, an over-systematic approach to revelation. He is saved from this by a profound sense of the mystery of Christianity and by an idea of mystery completely distinct from any kind of mere vagueness. "Considered as a Mystery", revelation, he says, "is a doctrine enunciated by inspiration, in human language, as the only possible medium of it, and suitably, according to the capacity of language; a doctrine *lying hid* in language, to be received in that language from the first by every mind, whatever be its separate power of understanding it ...". The necessity of verbal formulations, then, is taken for granted, but the inevitable inadequacy of language is also recognized, as well as the limitations of human thought. There is a brilliant exposition of how mystery is not only compatible with but is involved in the very idea of revelation:

No revelation can be complete and systematic, from the weakness of the human intellect; *so far as* it is not such, it is mysterious ... A Revelation is religious doctrine viewed on its

15

illuminated side; a Mystery is the selfsame doctrine viewed on the side unilluminated. Thus Religious Truth is neither light nor darkness, but both together; it is like the dim view of a country seen in the twilight, with forms half extracted from the darkness, with broken lines, and isolated masses. Revelation ... is not a revealed system, but consists of a number of detached and incomplete truths belonging to a vast system unrevealed, of doctrines and injunctions mysteriously connected together ...[27]

THE "VIA MEDIA"*

Newman always dated the beginning of the Oxford Movement to the Assize Sermon which John Keble preached on 14 July 1833 from the pulpit of the University Church of St Mary the Virgin on the subject of "National Apostasy". The occasion for the protest was the bill to abolish ten sees of the established Anglican Church of Ireland and impose a tax on the higher clerical incomes to pay for the upkeep of the churches, in place of the extremely unpopular church rates levied on the largely Catholic population. There is certainly ample irony in the fact that this attempt by a British government to conciliate and do justice to Irish Catholics should have set in train the events which would lead to a Catholicizing of the Church of England as well as to many secessions to Rome, including that of the greatest Anglican of the century and the man who became the undisputed leader of the Movement, John Henry Newman. However, for those first Tractarians the real issue was not the question of justice to Ireland but the supremely important matter of the independence of the Church and its divine authority. As Newman always insisted, Tractarianism began as a protest against Erastianism, that is, state control of the Church. Of course as the Movement progressed, it gradually became a concerted effort to recover or restore the Catholic character of a Church which claimed to be the successor of the medieval Church which had been in communion with Rome.

Newman himself soon became not only the master strategist of an ecclesiastical campaign but also the leading theologian of

*For texts, see below p. 81.

a religious movement. The more he studied the Fathers, the more Catholic his theology became; and the more Catholic his theology, the greater the need to distinguish Anglicanism from Roman Catholicism. If the Anglican Church was, as the Tractarians claimed, a branch of the Catholic Church, of which the Roman and Orthodox Churches were two other main branches, then the Church of England was not a Protestant church, as most English people and their religious leaders thought, but a Catholic church, although it had been "reformed" at the Reformation. The difficulty of distinguishing this "Anglo-Catholicism" both from Roman Catholicism and from Protestantism became Newman's principal theological task, and out of the attempt came his most original theology as an Anglican. The fact, which Newman never denied, was that since the eighteenth century the Church of England had seen herself, with a few exceptions, as essentially a Protestant state church. But this, claimed Newman and his fellow Tractarians, was not her true self at all. However, the more they studied the early Church, from which the Church of England had descended, and the more Catholic they discovered the true self of their Church to be, the more imperative it became to show why the Church of England was justified in her separation from and "protest" against the Church of Rome. From a personal point of view they had no alternative, as to their contemporaries they were hardly more than Roman Catholic fifth columnists in a Protestant Church.

In 1834 Newman wrote two *Tracts from the Times* on the so-called "Via Media" to show that Anglicanism lay between Rome and the Protestantism of the Reformation. An exchange of published letter with a French priest in 1834–5 helped him to formulate his views of the "Via Media", which would receive its classic expression in his *Lectures on the Prophetical Office of the Church viewed relatively to Romanism and Popular Protestantism* (1837).[28]

The theology of the Church which Newman was to develop during the next forty years begins and ends with the *Prophetical Office*, for the lengthy preface he wrote for the third edition of 1877 constitutes his last and greatest contribution to ecclesiology. He commences the 1837 work by pointing out that "Roman Catholics having ever insisted upon" the Church "and Protestants having neglected it, to speak of the Church at all, though it is mentioned in the Creed, is thought to savour of Rome". Therefore, those "who feel its importance, and yet are not Romanists, are bound to show why they are not Romanists, and how they differ from them", both "in order to remove the prejudice with which an article of the Creed is at present encompassed; and on the other hand to prevent such persons as have right but vague ideas concerning it, from deviating into Romanism because no other system of doctrine is provided for them". Leaving aside the "directly political and ecclesiastical" aspects of the Church, his own object is to formulate "a correct theory" of the "Prophetical Office" of the Church, such as "popular Protestantism" does not even attempt, while Rome provides "an untrue one". What, in fact, is demanded by the theory of the "Via Media" as "the nearest approximation to that primitive truth which Ignatius and Polycarp enjoyed, and which the nineteenth century has virtually lost"?[29]

The Protestant insistence on "the Bible as the only standard of appeal in doctrinal inquiries" inevitably leads to the conclusion that "truth is but matter of opinion", for "the Bible is not so written as to force its meaning upon the reader", nor does it "carry with it its own interpretation". Those who think that Christians must draw their faith from Scripture "hold an unreal doctrine, and ... to be consistent, they must ... either cease to think orthodoxy necessary, or allow it to be taught them".[30] True, the Anglican, unlike the Roman Catholic, argues that the "creed can be proved entirely ... from the Bible" – but "we take this ground only in controversy, not in teaching our own people or in our private studies". None of the various denominations which claim to derive the Christian faith from the Bible alone actually "embraces the whole Bible, none of them is able to interpret the whole, none of them has a key which will revolve through the entire compass of the words which lie within. Each has its favourite text, and neglects the rest". As for Anglo-Catholics, "we rely on Antiquity to strengthen such intimations of doctrine as are but faintly, though really, given in Scripture" – unlike Protestantism, which "considers it a hardship to have anything clearly and distinctly told it in elucidation of Scripture doctrine, an infringement of its right of doubting, and mistaking, and labouring in vain".[31]

Roman Catholics, on the other hand, appeal to Tradition as well as Scripture, maintaining that it was impossible to commit to writing all that the Apostles taught – "No one you fall in with on the highway, can tell you all his mind at once; much less could the Apostles ... digest in one Epistle or Treatise a systematic view of the Revelation made to them'. The New Testament, they argue, is "an incomplete document", without "harmony or consistency in its parts" and without any "code of commandments" and "list of fundamentals". Analogy and imagery are brilliantly employed to suggest the Catholic idea of Tradition:

> It is latent, but it lives. It is silent, like the rapids of a river, before the rocks intercept it. It is the Church's unconscious habit of opinion and sentiment; which she reflects upon, masters, and expresses, according to the emergency. We see then the mistake of asking for a complete collection of the Roman Traditions; as well might we ask for a complete catalogue of a man's tastes and thoughts on a given subject. Tradition in its fulness is necessarily unwritten ... and it cannot be circumscribed any more than a man's countenance and manner can be conveyed to strangers in any set of propositions.

Newman agrees that it is certainly the case that "we receive through Tradition both the Bible itself, and the doctrine that it is divinely inspired", as do most Protestants, who "believe in the divinity of Scripture precisely on the ground on which the Roman Catholics take their stand on behalf of their own system of doctrine, viz. because they have been taught it".[32] The fact is that Christians "derive their faith" not from Scripture but from Tradition.[33] And it is not the concept of Tradition that Anglo-Catholics object to, but the fact that Rome "substitutes the authority of the Church for that of Antiquity", merely keeping the Fathers "around her to ask their advice when it happens to agree with her own", but otherwise superseding them "because they are hard of hearing, are slow to answer, are circuitous in their motions, and go their own way to work". True Tradition is attested to by "Catholicity, Antiquity, and consent of Fathers", and how far this test is met "must be decided by the same principles which guide us in the conduct of life ... which lead us to accept Revelation at all, for which we have but probability to show at most".[34] Certainly, while "Private Judgment" may interpret Scripture to a considerable extent as it pleases, it cannot "so deal with Antiquity" – for "History is a record of facts'', and the Fathers ''are far too ample to allow'' selective interpretation.[35]

The key distinction that Newman tries to make between two different kinds of Tradition is the most significant part of the book, attempting as it does to preserve the centrality of Tradition without damage to the uniqueness of Scripture. He divides Tradition into ''Episcopal Tradition'', which is derived from the Apostles, and ''Prophetical Tradition'', which consists of the interpretation of the Revelation, a ''body of Truth, pervading the Church like an atmosphere'', and ''existing primarily in the bosom of the Church itself, and recorded in such measure as Providence has determined in the writings of eminent men''. It is this latter kind of Tradition which Newman claims may be ''corrupted in its details'', so that the doctrines which develop out of it ''are entitled to very different degrees of credit''. The decrees of the Council of Trent may reasonably claim to be ''Apostolic'', and yet ''they are the ruins and perversions of Primitive Tradition''.[36]

This view of ''Prophetical Tradition'' is in keeping with ''the Tradition of the Fathers'', which ''witnesses'' not only ''to its own inferiority to Scripture'', but also to the fact that ''Scripture is the record'' and ''the sole records of saving truth''.[37] And this ''fundamental faith'' or ''doctrine of the Apostles'' was what the ''Ancient Church'' taught before ''it broke up into portions, and for Catholic agreement substituted peculiar and local opinions'' – although it ''still remains to us, and to all Christians all over the world''.[38] Given that ''the Church Catholic'' must be ''indefectible in faith, we have but to inquire what that common faith is, which she now holds everywhere as the original deposit'', and we shall find it is those ''fundamental or essential doctrines ... which are contained in the Creed'' – which ''has become almost sacred from being the chief remains left us of apostolical truth; as the likeness of a friend, however incomplete in itself, is cherished as the best memorial of him, when he has been taken from us''.[39] As for the ''Catholic Church'' of the early centuries, she was now only the ''Church Catholic'' because of the loss of ''Unity ... the sacramental channel through which ... purity of doctrine'' is ''secured to the Church'', and because, consequently, ''the separate branches of the Church do disagree with each other in the details of faith''.[40]

JUSTIFICATION*

Like the *Prophetical Office*, the *Lectures on the Doctrine of Justification* (1838) originated in a controversial correspondence, this time with the Evangelical newspaper the *Christian Observer*, which had challenged the Tractarians to say how they were able to accept those parts of the Book of Common Prayer which seemed to be clearly Protestant and not Catholic in their meaning. Newman took up the challenge and wrote two lengthy letters to the paper in January and March 1837; he ended his reply by admitting, pointedly, that he had not treated the most crucial subject of all, that of justification by faith, the doctrine which formed the theological basis of the Reformation.[41]

Newman begins the *Lectures on Justification* by saying that they were originally intended to show that "certain essential Christian truths, such as Baptism Regeneration and the Apostolical Ministry", are not in fact "incompatible with the doctrine of justifying faith".[42] It was in fact another attempt to steer a "Via Media" between Protestantism and Romanism, between the "erroneous" idea of justification by "faith only" and the "defective" theory of "justification by obedience". These two "rigid" and "extreme" views are both partially right, for the idea that "we are absolutely saved by obedience, that is, by *what we are*, has introduced the proper merit of good works; that we are absolutely saved by faith, or by *what Christ is*, the notion that good works are not conditions of our salvation".[43]

Newman argues that Lutheran theology assumes that "justifying faith" will always be "lively" and "lead to good works"; but it is quite possible to believe fully that one has been saved by Christ "without any fruit following": "Trusting faith is not necessarily living faith." The explanation that the "life of faith" must be "love" is rejected by Luther on the ground that this would be "to deny the innate life and power of faith as such, and to associate another principle with it as a joint instrument in justification".[44] Instead, it is claimed that justifying faith is defined "not by what *it is*, but by what it *does*", for it is "trust *in Christ*, and it differs from all other kinds of faith in that towards

*For texts, see below p. 84.

which it reaches forward and on which it rests". Such a faith hardly "admits of a definition", but derives "its character" and "its form" from the "Object of the faith ... which makes the faith what it is". Newman criticizes the evasiveness of the explanation: "They seem to allow that faith *is* in itself something more than trust, though men may be unable to say what it is more".[45] It is claimed that faith "*sees* the purchased redemption, and therefore must be able to *take* and *apply* it": in other words, "it *apprehends* Christ; a suitable, or rather convenient term as vaguely including both ideas, of accepting the message and receiving the gift, without making the distinction between them".[46] To the Roman and Anglican objection that "the thought of Christ may be possessed by those who have not Christ, and therefore that it is in no sense the form of characteristic principle of justifying faith; rather that love ... is the true form, the discriminating mark and moulding principle under which belief is converted into Faith and made justifying", Luther's answer is that such a doctrine "makes our thought centre on ourselves ... fixes our faith on that love with which it is supposed to be instinct, instead of its mounting up worthless, rude, and unformed, to receive subsistence, fashion, and acceptableness in Christ".[47] It was his "wish to extirpate all notions of human merit" and "to give peace and satisfaction to the troubled conscience" that accounts for his vehement insistence on a doctrine which arose "from his opposition to the Roman doctrine concerning good works".[48] Faith also in his view "is the instrument by which Christ's Righteousness becomes ours", for "He is our Righteousness, in the sense of His obedience being the substitute for ours in the sight of God's justice", with the result that "every believer has at once a perfect righteousness, yet not his own", which "precludes all boasting" because "it is not his own", and "all anxiety" because "it is perfect": "The conscience is unladen, without becoming puffed up".[49] The "doctrine of faith as the instrument, and Christ's righteousness as the form, of justification" is supposed "to secure us against self-contemplation" and all forms of self-reliance, as well as destroying "the state of doubt about our justification which must ever attend the belief that it depends in our graces and works".[50] The fact that faith makes Christ's fulfilment of the moral laws ours as well "places us above the Law". It is true that Christians will obey the moral law and be "fruitful in good works", but only "naturally" as a result of faith, and not out of a sense of duty or conscience.[51]

Newman now turns "to consider the opposite scheme of doctrine, which is not unsound or dangerous in itself, but in a certain degree incomplete, – truth, but not the whole truth", in so far as it must not be "detached and isolated", as "in the Roman schools", from "other truths". This is the traditional view that "justification consists in love, or sanctity, or obedience", and that to be justified is not just to be counted righteous but actually to be made righteous – "not a change merely in God's dealings towards us, like the pale and wan sunshine of a winter's day, but ... the possession of Himself".[52] Like the Arians, Protestants "entrench themselves in a few favourite texts", but unlike the "one or two texts only, detached from their context" of Lutheranism, the whole of Scripture testifies to this "actual inherent righteousness" which is "not a shadow but a substance, not a name but a power, not an imputation but an inward work".[53] As usual for Newman, there is one decisive consideration: "it is what the rival doctrine is not, a real doctrine, and contains an intelligible, tangible, practical view which one can take and use."[54] By contrast, the Protestant "idea of faith" is damned as "a mere theory", from which it follows that "their whole theology is shadowy and unreal":

The one view then differs from the other as the likeness of a man differs from the original. The picture resembles him; but it is not he. It is not a reality, it is all surface. It has no depth, no substance; touch it, and you will find it is not what it pretends to be ... I wish to deal with things, not with words. I do not look to be put off with a name or a shadow. I would treat of faith as it is actually found in the soul; and I say it is as little an isolated grace, as a man in a picture. It has depth, a breadth, and a thickness; it has an inward life which is something over and above itself; it has a heart, and blood, and pulses, and nerves, though not upon the surface ... Love and fear and obedience are not really posterior to justifying faith for even a moment of time, unless bones or muscles are formed after the countenance and complexion. It is as unmeaning to speak of living faith, as being independent of newness of mind, as of solidity as divisible from body, or tallness from stature, or colour from the landscape. As well might it be said

23

that an arm or a foot can exist out of the body, and that man is born with only certain portions, head and heart, and that the rest accrues afterwards, as that faith comes first and gives birth to other graces.

In short, just as "the presence of the soul changes the nature of the dust of the earth, and makes it flesh and blood ... so love is the modelling and harmonizing principle on which justifying faith depends, and in which it exists and acts".[55] There is no need to argue that the Protestant theory of justification by faith is false; it is enough for Newman to have shown that it is unreal.

Are the Protestant and the Roman the only ways of understanding justifications? Newman thinks not, for two reasons: first, the classical Anglican divines contrive to combine both approaches in their view of the subject; second, he has is own individual understanding of the matter, which is only original to the extent that it is a rediscovery of what has been forgotten or lost.

According to Newman, the word "justifying" means literally "counting righteous", but includes *under* its meaning "making righteous".[56] By "calling righteous what is not righteous till He calls it so", God not only declares we are justified, but "He *justifies* us".[57] After all, it would be "a strange paradox to say that a thing is not because He says it is".[58] Rather, it is characteristic of God's word in Scripture that it "effects what it announces".[59] Justification, then, means both God's "*justifying*" and man's "*being justified*", just as "work" means "both the doing and the thing done"; and while Protestants generally use it in the first active sense, and Roman theologians employ it in the second passive sense, in the standard Anglican writers there is no attempt to separate "the seal and the impression, justification and renewal".[60]

In the last analysis of what "our state of justification ... consists in", Newman dismisses both the archetypal Protestant and Roman answers as superficial and unsatisfactory. If "the inward principle of acceptance" is held to be faith, then "the question arises, what gives to faith its acceptableness?" And the answer must be that the reason why faith rather than unbelief is "acceptable" is because the former has "a something in it" which the latter does not, namely, "God's grace". And so we are driven to the conclusion that "the having that grace or that presence, and not faith, which is its result, must be the real token, the real state of a justified man". Conversely, "if we say that justification consists in a supernatural quality imparted to the soul by God's grace, as Roman writers say, then in like manner, the question arises" whether "this renovating principle" does not necessarily involve "grace itself, as an immediate divine power or presence". But if so, "then surely the possession of that grace is really our justification, and not renewal, or the principle of renewal". It can thus be shown, "by tracing farther back the lines of thought on which these apparently discordant views are placed", how they in fact "converge" in "an inward divine presence or grace, of which both faith and spiritual renovation are fruits". Having, incisively and penetratingly, cut through the apparently impenetrable thicket of a controversy deeply rooted in a late medieval scholastic theology of grace which had lost touch with Scriptural and patristic sources, Newman can now put forward a solution to the age-old problem which transcends both the rival positions and whose brilliant originality lies simply in the rediscovery of the central New Testament doctrine of the "indwelling" of the Holy Spirit: "The presence of the Holy Ghost shed abroad in our hearts, the Author both of faith and of renewal, this is really that which makes us righteous, and ... our righteousness is the possession of that presence." Justification, then, "is wrought by the power of the Spirit, or rather by His presence within us", while "faith and renewal are both present also, but as fruits of it".[61] The "connection" between "justification and renewal" is that they are "both included in that one great gift of God, the indwelling of Christ [through the Holy Spirit] in the Christian soul", which constitutes "our justification and sanctification, as its necessary results" – "And the one cannot be separated from the other except in idea, unless the sun's rays can be separated from the sun, or the power of purifying from fire or water."[62] Faith, on the other hand, as the "correlative" to God's grace, is first the "condition" and then the "instrument" of justification; while "love is the modelling and harmonizing principle on which justifying faith depends, and in which it exists and acts".[63]

It would be impossible not to pay special attention to the most powerful and striking final lecture, "On Preaching the Gospel", where Newman maintains that Protestantism – "having fallen, after the usual manner of self-appointed champions and reformers, into the evil which it professed to remedy" – is itself guilty of the very charge of "*legalism*" which it wrongly makes against "Catholic Truth". It charges that just as "Judaism interposed the Mosaic Law between the soul and Christ . . . so the Christian Church, Ancient and Catholic, also obscures the right and true worship of Him . . . by insisting on Creeds, on Rites, and on Works".[64] In so far, Newman agrees, as Roman theology, for instance, "makes itself co-extensive with the Gospel Dispensation" and "keeps pace with what is infinite and eternal, and exhausts the Abyss of grace, such a system is certainly open to the objection".[65] But doctrinal statements, which are negative rather than positive, are necessary and useful as "landmarks" and summaries of belief, "intended to forbid speculations, which are sure to spring up in the human mind, and to anticipate its attempts as systematic views by showing the ultimate abyss at which all rightly conducted inquiries arrive, not to tell us anything definite and real, which we did not know before, or which is beyond faith of the most unlearned".[66] As just as bigotry is "making the statement itself our end', so superstition 'is the substitution of human for divine means of approaching God", but "a rite is not properly superstitious, unless it is such self-worship".[67]

By refusing "what has been actually given", Protestantism was "sure to adopt what had not been given". Thus Protestants "congratulate themselves on their emancipation from forms and their enlightened worship, when they are but in the straight course to a worse captivity, and are exchanging dependence on the creature for dependence on self". Ironically, "they substitute faith for Christ", and "so regard it, that instead of being the way to Him, it is in the way". Pithily, Newman presses home the point: "they make is a something to rest in . . . they alter the meaning of the word, as the Jews altered the meaning of the word Law . . . they have brought into the Gospel, the narrow, minute, technical, nay, I will say carnal and hollow system of the Pharisees." With contemporary Evangelicals in mind, he explains:

a system of doctrine has risen up during that last three centuries, in which faith or spiritual-mindedness is contemplated and rested on as the end of religion instead of Christ ... And in this way religion is made to consist in contemplating ourselves instead of Christ; not simply in looking to Christ, but in ascertaining that we look to Christ, not in His Divinity and Atonement, but in our conversion and our faith in those truths. Instead of preaching Christ, the "fashion of the day" is "to preach conversion", to tell people "to be sure they look at Christ, instead of simply holding up Christ to them", and "to tell them to have faith, rather than to supply its Object" – with the result that "faith and ... spiritual-mindedness are dwelt on as *ends*, and obstruct the view of Christ". It would be as if one were to "affect people by *telling* them to weep or laugh'. Rather than feeling "spontaneously, as the consequence of the objects presented to them", people "will feel this and that", because they are told to "feel it". This explains "the absence of ... composure, unobtrusiveness, healthy and unstudied feeling, variety and ease of language, among those who are thus converted, even when that conversion is sincere".[68] There follows a splendidly sarcastic denunciation of the slavery of self-preoccupation:

Poor miserable captives, to whom such doctrine is preached as the Gospel! What! is *this* the liberty wherewith Christ has made us free, and wherein we stand, the home of our own thoughts, the prison of our own sensations, the province of self ... This is nothing but a specious idolatry ...[69]

Referring to Luther's condemnation of "the conscience-stricken Catholics of his day", Newman remarks tersely and satirically, "surely it is better not to have Christ and to mourn, than to let Him go and to think it gain."[70] Protestants picture faith "as a sort of passive quality which sits amid the ruins of human nature, and keeps up what may be called a silent protest, or indulges a pensive meditation over its misery"; whereas

True faith is what may be called colourless, like air or water; it is but the medium through which the soul sees Christ; and the soul as little really rests upon it and contemplates it, as the eye can see the air. When, then, men are bent on holding it (as it were) in their hands, curiously inspecting, analysing ... they are obliged to colour and thicken it, so that it may be seen and touched. That is, they substitute for it something or other ... which they may hang over, and doat upon. They

27

rather aim at experiences ... within them, than at Him that is without them.

Such "being the difference", Newman concludes, "between true faith and self-contemplation, no wonder that where the thought of self obscures the thought of God, prayer and praise languish, and only preaching flourishes".[71] Yet another brilliant aphorism sums up the argument: "To look at Christ is to be justified by faith; to think of being justified by faith is to look from Christ and to fall from grace." The reader is left with the great paradox:

[Luther] found Christians in bondage to their works and observances; he released them by his doctrine of faith; and he left them in bondage to their feelings ... For outward signs of grace he substituted inward; for reverence towards the Church contemplation of self. And ... whereas he preached against reliance on self, he introduced it in a more subtle shape; whereas he professed to make the written word all in all, he sacrificed it in its length and breadth to the doctrine which he had wrested from a few texts.

The moral with which Newman draws to a close the lecture is that this is "what comes of fighting God's battles in our own way"; for just as the Pharisees, who "were more careful of their Law than God who gave it", and Judas, who "was concerned at the waste of the ointment, which might have been given to the poor", were "bad men" who "professed to be more zealous ... than the servants of God", so "in a parallel way Protestants would be more spiritual".[72] It was an arresting irony with which to conclude his final, most sustained repudiation of what he scathingly called earlier

this modern, this private, this arbitrary, this unscriptural system, which promising liberty conspires against it; which abolishes Christian Sacraments to introduce barren and dead ordinances; and for the real participation of the Son, and justification through the Spirit, would, at the very marriage feast, feed us on shells and husks, who hunger and thirst after righteousness! It is a new gospel, unless three hundred years stand for eighteen hundred; and if men are bent on seducing us from the ancient faith, let them provide a more specious error, a more alluring sophism, a more angelic tempter, than this. It is surely too bold an attempt to take from our hearts the power, the fulness, the mysterious presence of Christ's most holy death and resurrection, and to soothe us for our loss with the name of having it.[73]

In conclusion, we may say that the *Lectures*, although hardly eirenic in intention or tone, can now be seen to be a pioneering classic of genuine "ecumenical" theology; that is, to the extent that they offer not a compromise between two apparently opposed positions, but rather a wholly new perspective which actually changes the nature of the problem. This kind of approach, whereby opposing positions are undercut by being circumvented, was to be used later very fruitfully by Newman in tackling highly sensitive problems of Catholic ecclesiology. Here it is employed to solve a crucial point of contention between Protestants and Roman Catholics, and as such suggests its considerable potential value as a method in ecumenical theology, to which Newman's book is an early, outstanding contribution. Indeed, while the *Essay on the Development of Christian Doctrine* is no doubt the most influential and seminal of his theological writings, the *Lectures on Justification* is arguably his most profound and subtle theological work.

DEVELOPMENT OF DOCTRINE*

In the *Apologia*, Newman states that he had already recognized the principle of doctrinal development in his first book, *The Arians of the Fourth Century*. Certainly, in the early years of the Tractarian Movement there is more than one explicit reference to the development of doctrine. Thus, in a private letter of 1834, Newman writes that "the greater part of the theological and ecclesiastical system, which is implicitly contained in the writings and acts of the Apostles ... was developed at various times according to circumstances".[74] And in one of the *Tracts for the Times* of the same year, he says that the "articles of faith" which "are necessary to secure the Church's purity, according to the rise of successive heresies and error", were "all hidden, as it were, in the Church's bosom from the first, and brought out into form according to the occasion".[75] Again, in the *Apologia*,

---

*For texts, see below p. 123.

he points out that in an article published in 1836 he had clearly acknowledged the Roman Catholic answer to objections that the Church of Rome "has departed from Primitive Christianity", namely, that such apparent departures may be seen as "developments of gospel truth" which are also to be found in Anglicanism, since "The Anglican system itself is not found complete in those early centuries".[76]

But it was not until the last of his *Oxford University Sermons* (1843), "The Theory of Developments in Religious Doctrine", preached in 1843, that Newman turned his full attention to the problem of doctrinal development. It was by no means simply a question of academic interest. Rather, for Newman, it was, as far as his continuing membership in the Church of England was concerned, literally a matter of life and death. The Tractarian claim for the Anglican Church was that it possessed the "note" of "Apostolicity", that is, that it only taught the doctrines of the original Apostolic Church, as opposed to the Roman Catholic Church, which clearly possessed the "note" of "Catholicity" or universality, but which also appeared to have added a number of dogmas (such as Transubstantiation) to the Christian faith. What, however, if these "new" doctrines were in fact, as Roman Catholics claimed, authentic developments from, rather than additions to, primitive Christianity?

In the summer of 1839 Newman had suffered a severe shock while studying the Monophysite heresy of the fifth century: he thought his "stronghold was Antiquity",[77] but suddenly the argument from "Apostolicity" seemed to be threatened by the picture presented by history, which appeared to suggest that it was Rome not Canterbury which enjoyed the "note of Apostolicity" as well as that of "Catholicity". There were other blows to come during the six ensuing years that ended in Newman's leaving the Church of England and joining the Roman Catholic Church. But in the end the issue narrowed down to the question of the development of doctrine: were specifically Roman Catholic doctrines illegitimate accretions and additions, or were they authentic developments from scriptural and apostolic doctrines? Why were those doctrines, which Anglicans shared with Roman Catholics but which were sometimes less clearly to be found in Scripture and the Fathers, not also accretions and additions?

Newman's idea in his *Lectures on the Prophetical Office* of a "Prophetical Tradition" existing within the Church had allowed in principle for developments taking place as a normal occurrence; but in his 1843 sermon he went even further, saying that developments were not simply explanations of doctrines already formulated but further doctrines implied by and arising out of these original dogmas.

In his lengthy sermon, the most brilliant of the *University Sermons* and one of the most original and penetrating of his writings, Newman applies to the problem of doctrinal development a key epistemological distinction he had already made in one of the earlier *University Sermons* on the difference between "Implicit and Explicit Reason". The differentiation is crucial to his whole idea of the development of doctrine. Thus he insists in "The Theory of Developments in Religious Doctrine" that, "naturally as the inward idea of the divine truth ... passes into explicit form by the activity of our reflective powers, still such an actual delineation is not essential to its genuineness and perfection", so that a "peasant may have such a true impression, yet be unable to give any intelligible account of it". Indeed, the "impression made upon the mind need not even be recognized" by the person "possessing it". Such "unperceived impressions" are commonplace in life: thus people may not even be "conscious" of "an idea" of which they are actually "possessed". Nor is the "absence, or partial absence, or incompleteness of dogmatic statements" any "proof of the absence of impressions or implicit judgments, in the mind of the Church. Even centuries might pass without the formal expression of a truth, which had been all along the secret life of millions of faithful souls."[78]

As we have seen, Newman's rejection of dogmatic liberalism does not lead him into the trap of fundamentalism. Dogmatic statements are "necessary only because the human mind cannot reflect ... except piecemeal" upon "the one idea which they are designed to express", but they are only expressions of "aspects" of the "idea" and "can never really be confused with the idea itself, which all such propositions taken together can but reach, and cannot exceed", and indeed to which they "are never equivalent" – for "dogmas are, after all, but symbols of a Divine fact, which, far from being compassed by those very propositions, would not be exhausted, nor fathomed, by a thousand." Newman now goes on to give a classic statement of the relation of dogma to personal faith, which once again offers an alternative to the formalism of "orthodoxy" on the one hand and the feelings of emotional Evangelicalism on the other:

That idea is not enlarged, if propositions are added, not impaired if they are withdrawn: if they are added, this is with a view of conveying that one integral view, not of amplifying it. That view does not depend on such propositions: it does not consist in them; they are but specimens and indications of it. And they may be multiplied without limit. They are necessary, but not needful to it, being but portions or aspects of that previous impression which has at length come under the cognizance of Reason and the terminology of science ... [These] propositions imply each other, as being parts of one whole; so that to deny one is to deny all, and to invalidate one is to deface and destroy the view itself. One thing alone has to be impressed on us by Scripture, the Catholic idea, and in it they all are included. To object, then, to the number of propositions, upon which an anathema is placed, is altogether to mistake their use; for their multiplication is not intended to enforce many things, but to express one ...

The error of "doctrinal innovators", he adds, is "to go away with this or that proposition of the Creed, instead of embracing that one idea which all of them together are meant to convey; it being almost a definition of heresy, that it fastens on some one statement as if the whole truth" – which "is a proof that it does not really hold even that very statement for the sake of which it rejects the others". Heresy, then, is something fundamentally *unreal*, whereas "Realizing is the very life of true developments; it is peculiar to the Church, and the justification of her definitions." As for the objection that dogmas cannot "convey ... knowledge of the Divine Nature itself", Newman is more than ready to admit that they "convey no true idea of Almighty God, but only an earthly one, gained from earthly figures, provided it be allowed, on the other hand, that the senses do not convey to us any true idea of matter, but only as idea commensurate with sensible impressions". For "earthly figures and images" can only give us "an approximation to the truth". For that matter, the very "diversities of language" in the world are a hindrance to "communicating ideas", given the infinite complexity of ideas. Understanding between individuals is often difficult because of the lack of "a common measure or economy to mediate between them".[79]

By the end of 1844 Newman was practically certain that the Church of England, far from being a branch of the Catholic Church, was in fact in schism and that the Roman Catholic Church was identical with the Catholic Church of the Fathers. There was only one obstacle to acting on his belief, as he explains in the *Apologia*: "My difficulty was this: I had been deceived greatly once; how could I be sure that I was not deceived a second time? I thought myself right then: how was I to be certain that I was right now?" Obviously, however, he could not continue to entertain indefinitely such "vague misgivings", and so "I came to the conclusion of writing an Essay on Doctrinal Development; and then, if, at the end of it, my convictions in favour of the Roman Church were not weaker, of taking the necessary steps for admission into her fold." In fact, he never completed the book: "Before I got to the end, I resolved to be received, and the book remains in the state in which it was then, unfinished."[80] Newman was received into the Roman Catholic Church on 9 October 1845, and before the year was out of the *Essay of the Development of Christian Doctrine* was published.

The book, then, which is certainly Newman's most famous and seminal work of theology was left unfinished on his becoming Catholic. It is worth emphasizing the word "essay" in the title, as it would certainly be unhelpful to approach a book which is anyway incomplete as though it were a systematic treatise propounding a formal theory. It is true that it was written on a "view", which Newman says "has at all times, perhaps, been implicitly adopted by theologians", that is, "the Theory of Development of Doctrine". But he prefers to regard it simply as "an hypothesis to account for a difficulty", The "difficulty" being that Christianity has apparently undergone so many changes and variations over the centuries that the question arises whether there has been any "real continuity of doctrine" since the time of the Apostles. [81] It would be hardly possible for Newman to have a systematic theory of development, since he does not regard the actual doctrinal developments which have taken place as being in any way systematic.

The development ... of an idea [like Christianity] is not like an investigation worked out on paper, in which each successive advance is a pure evolution from a foregoing, but it is carried on through and by means of communities of men and their leaders and guides; and it employs their minds as its instruments, and depends upon them, while it uses them.[82]

The *Development of Christian Doctrine* can arouse anticipations that are bound to be disappointed if its essentially unsystematic character is not appreciated. Most obviously, the seven "Notes" which Newman proposed to distinguish developments from corruptions have been criticized as unconvincing and uncomprehensive. But Newman sounds more diffident than dogmatic when he introduces them (I venture to set down ...'[83]), and it is noteworthy how in the revised edition he substitutes the vaguer, less definite word ("Notes") for the more rigorous "Tests" of the original first edition. They are not intended to be necessarily in themselves definitive and comprehensive criteria.

In the *Essay* Newman is not attempting to "prove" anything, in the strict sense of that word. Rather, he is concerned with two pictures he has before his mind's eye, that of the modern Roman Catholic Church and that of the early Church. Are these two apparent very dissimilar pictures in fact portraits of one and the same Church? The appeal to the reader is fundamentally to see or recognize a likeness which the author has seen. In other words, to regard the book as a theoretical work is to miss the role which the imagination plays and which, given the nature of Newman's philosophy of the mind, we should expect it to play. Indeed, the appeal is far more to the imagination than to the intellect. It is, of course, obvious that Roman Catholicism is lineally descended from primitive Christianity, but the point for Newman is clinched by the imaginative realization that modern Catholicism is "the nearest ... to say the least, to the religious sentiment, and what is called *ethos*, of the early Church, nay, to that of the Apostles and Prophets ... [who were] saintly and heroic men ... more like a Dominican preacher, or a Jesuit missionary, or a Carmelite friar, more like St. Toribio, or St. Vincent Ferrer, or St. Francis Xavier, or St. Alphonso Liguori, than to any individuals, or to any classes of men, that can be found in other communions."[84] And there are several highly rhetorical passages identifying the early with the contemporary Roman Catholic Church.

The reader is invited to "see" the resemblance and to recognize the nineteenth-century Church of Rome as the Church of the apostles and martyrs. This is apologetic writing with a special emphasis on the imagination. Nor should it cause surprise when we think of Newman's own conversion: how in the fateful summer vacation of 1839 as he was reading about the Monophysite controversy he experienced his first serious doubt about Anglicanism:

My stronghold was Antiquity; now here, in the middle of the fifth century, I found, as it seemed to me, Christendom of the sixteenth and the nineteenth centuries reflected. I saw my face in that mirror, and I was a Monophysite. The Church of the *Via Media* was in the position of the Oriental communion, Rome was, where she now is; and the Protestants were the Eutychians.[85]

A couple of months later Newman received another shock, although this time it struck his auditory rather than his visual imagination. His attention had been drawn to an article on the Donatist schism and its relevance to Anglicanism. At first, the intellectual force of the analogy did not at all impress Newman; the two ecclesial situations seemed quite different.

But my friend ... pointed out the palmary words of St. Augustine, which were contained in one of the extracts made in the Review, and which had escaped my observation. "Securus judicat orbis terrarum."* He kept repeating these words again and again, and, when he was gone, they kept ringing in my ears. "Securus judicat orbis terrarum"; they were words which went beyond the occasion of the Donatists: they applied to that of the Monophysites ... They decided ecclesiastical questions on a simpler rule than that of Antiquity; nay, St. Augustine was one of the prime oracles of Antiquity; here then Antiquity was deciding against itself. What a light was hereby thrown upon every controversy in the Church! ...

The words which sounded so loudly in Newman's ears stimulated, of course, a series of intellectual reflections, but they also cast a new light on church history, placing old problems in a

---

*Newman's own (free) translation was: "The universal Church is in its judgments secure of truth."

different, fresh perspective. This passage, one of the most powerful in all of his writings and worthy of that traumatic moment, concludes with an acknowledgment of the incalculable power of the imagination:

> Who can account for the impressions which are made on him? For a mere sentence, the words of St. Augustine, struck me with a power which I never had felt from any words before. To take a familiar instance, they were like the "Turn again Whittington" of the chime; or, to take a more serious one, they were like the "Tolle, lege, – Tolle, lege," of the child, which converted St. Augustine himself. "Securus judicat orbis terrarum!" By those great words of the ancient Father, interpreting and summing up the long and varied course of ecclesiastical history, the theory of the *Via Media* was absolutely pulverized.

It was true, Newman tells us, that "After a while, I got calm, and at length the vivid impression upon my imagination faded away," but still he "had seen the shadow of a hand upon the wall." However, although he now "determined to be guided, not by my imagination, but by my reason," this was not because he rejected the validity of the imagination, but because he knew that the mind consists of more than the imagination.[86] In his *Lectures on Certain Difficulties felt by Anglicans in submitting to the Catholic Church* (1850), Newman recounts how it was "the living picture" which the study of "history presents to us" that opened his eyes to the identity of the Church of the Fathers with the Roman Catholic Church. But this was only possible because of his ability to "see" the historical analogy: "That ancient history is not dead, it lives ... we see ourselves in it, as in a glass, and if the *Via Media* was heretical then, it is heretical now." Naturally, it was impossible to prove an analogy like this to somebody else; it had to be "seen".[87]

The *Essay* may be more of an apologetic than a strictly systematic work, but it remains of great theological interest, not least because, as has been said, it is "the almost inevitable starting point for an investigation of development of doctrine".[88] However, it is also of great theological significance by virtue of its exemplifying the philosophy of the mind which Newman had adumbrated in the *Oxford University Sermons*. For it is not only the imagination which plays a crucial part in a theological inquiry, which Newman, as usual, sees as inseparable from the study of history. No less important is the concept of implicit as opposed to explicit knowledge.

It has been claimed in a standard history of the theology of development that according to the *Essay* the original Christian revelation was given partly in feelings such as could hardly be developed into new doctrines which were not also an addition to revelation, since dogmatic propositions can hardly be deduced from wordless experiences.[89] But if so, then for Newman developing doctrine is really synonymous with continuing revelation; in which case his theology is certainly not Catholic as the Church teaches that God's revelation was completed once and for all in Christ. As Newman himself put it pithily in a private letter, "the Church does not know more than the Apostles knew".[90] However, such an interpretation of Newman's thought assumes that if the apostolic Church was not "conscious" of later dogmas, then she could not have been cognizant of them. But the problem disappears once we understand that Newman meant that the Church had an implicit but not explicit knowledge of later doctrinal formulations. As he explained in "The Theory of Developments in Religious Doctrine", "It is no proof that persons are not possessed, because they are not conscious, of an idea".[91] Since he is not a systematic thinker or writer, Newman's terminology tends to be informal and there is no doubt that he occasionally does use the word "feelings", as in this sentence: ". . . St Justin or St. Irenaeus might be without any digested ideas of Purgatory or Original Sin, yet have an intense feeling, which they had not defined or located, both of the fault of our first nature and the responsibilities of our nature regenerate". But the immediately preceding sentence makes it perfectly clear that this feeling is not intended to be non-cognitive: ". . . the holy Apostles would without words know all the truths concerning the high doctrines of theology, which controversialists after them have piously and charitably reduced to formulae, and developed through argument".[92] What was implicitly believed becomes explicitly professed, as Newman expounds in the following passage which he quotes from the sermon on development, and which he introduces by commenting that in theology the mind develops "the solemn ideas, which it has hitherto held implicitly and without subjecting them to its reflecting and reasoning powers'':

The mind which is habituated to the thought of God, of Christ, of the Holy Spirit, naturally turns with a devout curiosity to the contemplation of the object of its adoration, and begins to form statements concerning it, before it knows whither, or how far, it will be carried. One proposition necessarily leads to another, and a second to a third; then some limitation is required; and the combination of these opposites occasions some fresh evolutions from the original idea, which indeed can never be said to be entirely exhausted. This process is its development, and results in a series, or rather body, of dogmatic statements, till what was an impression on the Imagination has become a system or creed in the reason.

... As God is one, so the impression which He gives us of Himself is one ... It is the vision of and object ... Creeds and dogmas live in the one idea which they are designed to express, and which alone is substantive ...[93]

The last paragraph shows how modern Newman's theology of revelation is in its ''personalist'' as opposed to ''propositional'' emphasis. But the whole passage surely makes it quite clear that Newman is concerned with an intuitive knowledge which is far more like ''seeing'' than ''feeling''.

Finally, any doubt is removed by a paper Newman wrote on the development of doctrine in 1868, where he makes it plain that the ''idea'' the apostolic Church received was definitely known, although implicitly rather than explicitly:

the apostles had the *fullness* of revealed knowledge, a fullness which they could as little realise to themselves, as the human mind, as such, can have all its thought present before it at once. They are elicited according to the occasion. A man of genius cannot go about with his genius in his hand: in an Apostle's mind great part of his knowledge is from the nature of the case latent or implicit ...

Indeed, the ''idea'' which the Church has received is cognitive enough to be called a ''Divine philosophy'' –

not a number of formulas ... but a system of thought ... in such sense that a mind that was possessed of it, that is, the Church's mind, could definitely and unequivocally say whether this part of it, as traditionally expressed, meant this or that, and whether this or that was agreeable to, or inconsistent with it in whole or in part. I wish to hold that there is nothing which the Church has defined or shall define but what an Apostle, if asked, would have been fully able to answer and would have answered, as the Church has answered, the one answering by inspiration, the other from its gift of infallibility . . .

As an analogy, Newman sites the situation of someone who has complete knowledge of Aristotle's philosophy, and yet who cannot have "before his mind" every thought and saying of Aristotle, any more than Aristotle himself could have had "a host of thoughts present" to his mind "at once".

The philosophy, as a system, is stored in the *memory* . . . and is brought out according to the occasion. A learned Aristotelian is one who can answer any whatever philosophical questions in the way that Aristotle would have answered them. If they are questions which could not occur in Aristotle's age, he still answers them . . . In one respect he knows more than Aristotle; because, in new emergencies after the time of Aristotle, he *can* and *does* answer what Aristotle would have answered, but for the want of the opportunity did not. There is another point of view in which he seems to have the advantage of Aristotle, though it is no real superiority, viz that, from the necessities of the interval between Aristotle and himself, there has been the growth of . . . a scientific vocabulary, which makes the philosophy easier to remember, easier to communicate and to defend . . .

So, for example, St. Paul could hardly have understood what was meant by the "Immaculate Conception", but "if he had been asked, whether or not our Lady had the grace of the Spirit anticipating all sin whatever, including Adam's imputed sin, I think he would have answered in the affirmative". The "living idea", then, of Christianity, or what Newman as a Roman Catholic calls "the deposit of faith",

is in such sense committed to the Church or to the Pope, that when the Pope sits in St. Peter's chair, or when a council is collected round him, it is capable of being presented to their minds with that fullness and exactness . . . with which it habitually, not occasionally, resided in the minds of the Apostles; – a vision of it, not logical, and therefore consistent with errors of reasoning and of fact in the enunciation, after the manner of an intuition or an instinct.[94]

2

NEWMAN'S CATHOLIC THEOLOGY

After he became a Catholic, Newman repeatedly repudiated any suggestion that he was a theologian or that he was qualified to write on theological subjects. Compared with his profound knowledge of Scripture and the Fathers his familiarity with St. Thomas Aquinas and the scholastic tradition was much more modest. And yet, more through force of circumstances than deliberate choice on his part, he was gradually led to develop an ecclesiology which in important ways anticipates the great Constitution on the Church of the Second Vatican Council (1962–5) and which remains highly relevant to some of the most sensitive theological problems of the post-conciliar Catholic Church.

The Church which Newman joined in 1845 was a Church made in the image of the Council of Trent. It was still effectively the Church of the Counter-Reformation, and from our historical vantage point we can see that this Tridentine Catholicism was to reach its apogee at the First Vatican Council with the definition of papal infallibility (1870), before giving way finally to the more scriptural and patristic model of the Church that was rediscovered at the Second Vatican Council. The religious and theological movement called "Ultramontanism" had begun as a protest against state control of the local church, but it is one of the great ironies of ecclesiastical history that its appeal to the external authority of Rome as a way of gaining religious freedom from the shackles of the state eventually led to an agitation to override local ecclesial autonomy by strictly curtailing the rights of the episcopate in favour of the centralizing authority of the Holy See. As this kind of extreme Ultramontanism gathered force, so, in reaction, there grew up a recognizably liberalizing Catholicism, which included many, like Newman, who would have proudly claimed to be Ultramontanes in the original sense of the word. However, there was a more extreme kind of liberal Catholicism which included some like the great German church historian, Ignaz von Döllinger, who would leave the Roman

Catholic Church after the First Vatican Council, but from which Newman carefully distanced himself, sympathetic though he was to the antipathy of liberal Catholics to the exaggerated papalism of the extreme Ultramontanes. In England the chief organ of the liberal Catholics became the *Ramblet* magazine, of which Lord Acton was the proprietor and Richard Simpson the editor. Newman was sympathetic to the aims and purposes of the magazine but critical of its methods and tone. And when tension with the English bishops reached such a pitch that it looked as if the magazine might be officially condemned, Newman was an obvious, if unwilling, compromise candidate for the post of editor. This highly unwelcome, albeit temporary, appointment was to lead to Newman's first piece of theological writing as a Catholic.

LAITY*

It was Newman's experience as Rector of the Catholic University of Ireland (an appointment he held from 1851 to 1858) that first really opened his eyes to the way in which the hierarchical Church of his day regarded the laity. Indeed, it was his frustrated desire to involve laymen closely in the affairs of the university that was one of the principal reasons why in the end he resigned and returned to England.

His reluctant acceptance of the editorship of the *Rambler* in March 1859 led to his writing in the May issue a piece on a recent pastoral letter by the English hierarchy on education, in which he ventured to suggest that the bishops should ask the laity's opinion on educational matters, particularly since they had been "consulted" before the recent definition of the doctrine of the Immaculate Conception. In reply to a letter of protest from a scandalized seminary professor, Newman wrote:

> To the unlearned reader the idea conveyed by "consulting" is not necessarily that of asking an opinion. For instance, we speak of consulting a barometer about the weather. The barometer does not give us its opinion, but ascertains for us a fact ... I had not a dream of understanding the word ... in the sense of *asking an opinion*.[95]

*For texts, see below p. 199.

In conversation with his bishop, who was concerned about the offending passage, Newman remarked, with characteristic pragmatism, that "the Church would look foolish" without the laity.[96] Before resigning his editorship on the bishop's advice, he decided to deal more fully with the place of the laity in the Church. The result was the famous article "On Consulting the Faithful in Matters of Doctrine".

He begins by again defending his use of the word "consult", which he says in ordinary English " includes the idea of inquiring into a matter of *fact*, as well as asking a judgment". Thus, for example, a "physician consults the pulse of his patient; but not in the same sense in which his patient consults *him*". It is in the former sense that the Church "consults" or "regards" the faith of the laity before defining a doctrine. For, although the laity's "advice, their opinion, their judgment on the question of definition is not asked", nevertheless, "the matter of fact, viz. their belief, *is* sought for, as a testimony to that apostolical tradition, on which alone any doctrine whatsoever can be defined."[97] The reason, then, why the laity is consulted is "because the body of the faithful is one of the witnesses to the fact of the tradition of revealed doctrine, and because their *consensus* through Christendom is the voice of the Infallible Church". There are "channels of tradition", through which "the tradition of the Apostles, committed to the whole Church ... manifests itself variously at various times", none of which "may be treated with disrespect", even though the hierarchy has sole responsibility for "discerning, discriminating, defining, promulgating, and enforcing any portion of that tradition."[98] He himself, he explains, is "accustomed to lay great stress on the *consensus fidelium*" in order to compensate for the lack of testimony from bishops and theologians in favour of defined points of doctrine. At the time of the definition of the Immaculate Conception, Bishop Ullathorne had referred to the faith of the laity as a "reflection" of the teaching of the Church, and Newman comments with dry irony: "Reflection; that is, the people are a *mirror*, in which the Bishops see themselves. Well, I suppose a person may *consult* his glass, and in that way may know things about himself which he can learn in no other way".[99]

He now proceeds to his celebrated historical example drawn from that period of the early Church's history which he had studied so deeply and intensely as an Anglican. In spite of the fact that the fourth century was the age of great doctors and saints, who were also bishops, like Athanasius, Ambrose, Chrysostom, and Augustine, "nevertheless in that very day the divine tradition committed to the infallible Church was proclaimed and maintained far more by the faithful than by the Episcopate". During the Arian heresy, "in that time of immense confusion the divine dogma of our Lord's divinity was proclaimed, enforced, maintained, and (humanly speaking) preserved, far more by the "Ecclesia docta" than by the "Ecclesia docens" ... the body of the episcopate was unfaithful to its commission, while the body of the laity was faithful to its baptism". The importance of the illustration is shown by the fact that it occurred so early in the history of the Church and involved the very identity of Christ. Newman boldly concludes by saying that "there was a temporary suspense of the functions" of the teaching Church, the unpalatable truth being that the "body of Bishops failed in their confession of the faith". The danger of the present time, when the hierarchy was so faithful and orthodox, was that the role of the laity would be neglected – but "each constituent portion of the Church has its proper functions, and no portion can safely be neglected". The article ends with an almost defiant challenge:

I think certainly that the *Ecclesia docens* is more happy when she has ... enthusiastic partisans about her ... than when she cuts off the faithful from the study of her divine doctrines ... and requires from them a *fides implicita* in her word, which in the educated classes will terminate in indifference, and in the poorer in superstition.[100]

THE MAGISTERIUM AND THEOLOGIANS*

A controversial issue had elicited from Newman his first contribution to theology as a Catholic. His next major essay in ecclesiolgy was also the fruit of controversy. This time the controversy was with an Anglican critic, Charles Kingsley, whose famous outburst in a magazine review had impugned the integrity both of Newman and of Catholic priests in general.[101]

*For texts, see below p. 205.

The result was his autobiography *Apologia pro Vita Sua* (1864), in which Newman attempts to justify and explain his conversion. However, the fifth and final chapter, which serves as a general defence of Catholicism, constitutes one of Newman's most significant theological writings. It is aimed not so much at Kingsley and opponents of Catholicism as at the two extreme wings of the Church, the Ultramontanes and the liberal Catholics.

Defending the Catholic belief in the Church's infallibility, Newman calls it a "power" ... happily adapted to be a working instrument ... for smiting hard and throwing back the immense energy of the aggressive, capricious, untrustworthy intellect". There follows a severely uncompromising exposition of the Church's authority "viewed in its fulness" and "viewed in the concrete, as clothed and surrounded by the appendages of its high sovereignty ... a supereminent prodigious power sent upon earth to encounter and master a giant evil.

This unequivocal statement of faith provokes the obvious objection that "the restless intellect of our common humanity is utterly weighed down" by such an authority, "so that, if this is to be the mode of bringing it into order, it is brought into order only to be destroyed". This leads to the counter-claim that in fact the "energy of the human intellect ... thrives and is joyous, with a tough elastic strength, under the terrible blows of the divinely-fashioned weapon, and is never so much itself as when it has lately been overthrown". The resolution of the conflict lies in the remarkable argument that far from being mutually contradictory, authority and reason need each other precisely because, paradoxically, each is actually sustained by conflict with the other.

... it is the vast Catholic body itself, and it only, which affords an arena for both combatants in that awful, never-dying duel. It is necessary for the very life of religion ... that the warfare should be incessantly carried on. Every exercise of Infallibility is brought out into act by an intense and varied operation of the Reason, both as its ally and as its opponent, and provokes again, when it has done its work, a re-action of Reason against it; and, as in a civil polity the State exists and endures by means of the rivalry and collision, the encroachments and defeats of its constituent parts, so in like manner Catholic Christendom is no simple exhibition of religious absolutism, but presents a continuous picture of Authority and Private Judgment alternately advancing and retreating as the ebb and flow of the tide: – it is a vast assemblage of human beings with wilful intellects and wild passions, brought together into one by the beauty and the Majesty of a Superhuman Power, – into what may be called a large reformatory or training-school, not as it into a hospital or into a prison, not in order to be sent to bed, not to be buried alive, but (if I may change my metaphor) brought together as if into some moral factory, for the melting, refining, and moulding, by an incessant, noisy process, of the raw material of human nature, so excellent, so dangerous, so capable of divine purpose.[102]

The infallible authority, Newman insists, ''is a supply for a need, and it does not go beyond that need'', for its purpose is ''not to enfeeble the freedom or vigour of human thought in religious speculation, but to resist and control its extravagance''. Having begun by freely admitting the wide powers enjoyed by ecclesiastical authority, he now emphasizes both the narrow limits of infallibility in defining as explicit doctrine what is already implicit in revelation, and also its rare occurrence (normally by a ''Pope in Ecumenical Council'). But, more important, he recognizes what '' *is* the great trial to the Reason'', namely, that the Church claims jurisdiction over a wide area of ''secular matters which bear upon religion''. These disciplinary rather than doctrinal judgements are not, however, infallible – but they do claim obedience (although not faith). Again, ''because there is a gift of infallibility in the Catholic Church'', it does not necessarily follow that ''the parties who are in possession of it are in all their proceedings infallible''. Indeed, ''I think history supplies us with instances in the Church, where legitimate power has been harshly used''. The unequivocal assertion of the Church's legitimate authority is thus sharply qualified by these reminders of its limits and limitations. But the apparent discrepancy is resolved by the consideration that it does not ''follow that the substance of the acts of the ruling power is not right and expedient, because its manner may have been faulty''. In fact, Newman remarks tartly, ''high authorities act by means of instruments'', and ''we know how such instruments claim for themselves the name of their principals, who thus get the credit of faults which really are not theirs".[103]

What emerges in the argument that follows is not a kind of compromise position between the conservative and liberal Catholics of the day; but rather the idea that truth is attained not in spite of but through the conflict of opposites, which forces the crucial shift of perspective that allows the dilemma to be seen in a new light and so to be resolved.

Newman begins by reinforcing the case for authority and the need for submission. Despite all abuses, he insists that history shows that ecclesiastical authority has been "mainly in the right, and that those whom they were hard upon were mainly in the wrong". For example, Origen (whose name "I love") "was wrong" and "his opponents were right". And yet – "who can speak with patience of his enemy and the enemy of St. John Chrysostom, that Theophilus, bishop of Alexandria? who can admire or revere Pope Vigilius?" The contradiction is resolved by a completely fresh perspective, at once enlightening and provocative:

In reading ecclesiastical history, when I was an Anglican, it used to be forcibly brought home to me, how the initial error of what afterwards became heresy was the urging forward some truth against the prohibition of authority at an unseasonable time. There is a time for every thing, and many a man desires a reformation of an abuse, or the fuller development of a doctrine, or the adoption of a particular policy, but forgets to ask himself whether the right time for it is come: and knowing that there is no one who will be doing any thing towards its accomplishment in his own lifetime unless he does it himself, he will not listen to the voice of authority, and he spoils a good work in his own century, in order that another man, as yet unborn, may not have the opportunity of bringing it happily to perfection in the next. He may seem to the world to be nothing else than a bold champion for the truth and a martyr to free opinion, when he is just one of those persons whom the competent authority ought to silence; and, though the case may not fail within that subject-matter in which that authority is infallible, or the formal conditions of the exercise of that gift may be wanting, it is clearly the duty of authority to act vigorously in the case.

Again, Newman argues, the proof that infallibility has not crushed intellectual freedom in the Church is that it is "individuals, and not the Holy See, that have taken the initiative, and given the lead to the Catholic mind, in theological inquiry". "Indeed", he points out with a certain irony, "it is one of the reproaches against the Roman Church, that it has originated nothing, and has only served as a sort of *remora* or break in the development of doctrine. And it is an objection which I really embrace as a truth; for such I conceive to be the main purpose of its extraordinary gift". The historical examples that follow are unrelentingly negative. The fact is that "the Church of Rome possessed no great mind in the whole period of persecution". There was not a single doctor till St. Leo, who anyway taught only "on point of doctrine". Not even Pope St. Gregory has a place in the history of theology. The greatest Western theologian, St. Augustine, belonged, like the best early Latin theologians, to the African Church. Western theology, in fact, was formed to a considerable extent by heterodox theologians such as Tertullian and Origen and Eusebius, with the result that actual heretical "questionings" became "salutary truths". Even Ecumenical Councils were guided by the "individual reason" of a mere presbyter like Malchion, or a young deacon like Athanasius. At Trent, too, particular theologians "had a critical effect on some of the definitions of dogma". The real, albeit hidden, conclusion is that history gives little support to the Ultramontane idea that Rome is a kind of oracle of truth.[104]

The claim that history shows how little authority has interfered with the freedom of theologians is not a merely historical point. For Newman is not only protesting against the present by means of the past; he is also stating with great deliberateness his considered view on the crucial balance to be maintained between theology and the teaching authority of the Church. He begins by referring pointedly to the medieval Church which tended to be idealized by so many Catholics of his time:

There never was a time when the intellect of the educated class was more active, or rather more restless, than in the middle ages. And then again all through Church history from the first, how slow is authority in interfering! Perhaps a local teacher, or a doctor in some local school, hazards a proposition, and a controversy ensues. It smoulders or burns in one place, no one interposing; Rome simply lets it alone. Then it comes before a Bishop; or some priest, or some professor in some other seat of learning takes it up; and then there is a second stage of it. Then it comes before a University, and it may be condemned by the theological faculty. So the controversy process year after year, and Rome is still silent. An appeal perhaps is next made to a seat of authority inferior to Rome; and then at last after a long while it comes before the supreme power. Meanwhile, the question has been ventilated and turned over and over again, and viewed on every side of it, and authority is called upon to pronounce a decision, which has already been arrived at by reason. But even then, perhaps the supreme authority hesitates to do so, and nothing is determined on the point for years; or so generally and vaguely, that the whole controversy has to be gone through again, before it is ultimately determined.

Newman, even at this point, when his own personal interest is almost palpable, refrains from outright criticism of the abuse of authority in the contemporary Church. But, for all his restraint, his point is only too obvious.

It is manifest how a mode of proceeding, such as this, tends not only to the liberty, but to the courage, of the individual theologian or controversialist. Many a man has ideas, which he hopes are true, and useful for his day, but he is not confident about them, and wishes to have them discussed. He is willing, or rather would be thankful, to give them up, if they can be proved to be erroneous or dangerous, and by means of controversy he achieves his end. He is answered, and he yields; or on the contrary he finds that he is considered safe. He would not dare to do this, if he knew an authority, which was supreme and final, was watching every word he said, and made signs of assent or dissent to each sentence, as he uttered it. Then indeed he would be fighting, as the Persian soldiers, under the lash, and the freedom of his intellect might truly be said to be beaten out of him.

But even now he is ready to undermine his own indignation with the frank qualification that "when controversies run high" then "an interposition may . . . advisably take place; and again, questions maybe of that urgent nature, that an appeal must, as a matter of duty, be made at once to the highest authority in the Church''. However, the insistent emphasis on the universal character of the Church that follows barely conceals an unfavourable allusion to the Italian monopoly of the Holy See.

> ... the multitude of nations which are within the fold of the Church will be found to have acted for its protection, against any narrowness, on the supposition of narrowness, in the various authorities at Rome, with whom lies the practical decision of controverted questions ... Then, again, such national influences have a providential effect in moderating the bias which the local influences of Italy may exert on the See of St. Peter. It stands to reason that ... Rome must have in it an element of Italy; and it is no prejudice to the zeal and devotion with which we submit ourselves to the Holy See to admit this plainly ... Catholicity is not only one of the notes of the Church, but ... one of its securities.[105]

What emerges from these last pages of the *Apologia* is not, of course, anything in the nature of a systematic theology of the magisterium. But then, the implication of the argument is that there is an important sense in which it is inappropriate to seek any kind of blueprint for the relation between authority and freedom in the Church. The point of Newman's carefully balanced dialectic is that it is impossible either to describe or to prescribe exactly how this aspect of the Church's life is lived or ought to be lived. No theory can cover every case. What can be done is to set out some guidelines: first, to stress the importance of both authority and freedom; second, to emphasize the creative value of an interaction which inevitably involves tension; third, to modify and qualify the legitimate claims of authority; fourth, to show how it is precisely conflict which may force open the new perspective that allows the resolution of a difficulty; fifth, to distinguish carefully between the theological and teaching offices in the Church; sixth, to suggest practical ways in which justice may be done to the rights of both the magisterium and the theologians; and, finally, to plead for that catholicity of the Church, which gives due recognition to local national churches, but without prejudice to the ultimate jurisdiction of Rome.

PAPAL INFALLIBILITY*

The rising tide of Ultramontanism reached its high point in 1870 with the definition of the infallibility of the pope at the First Vatican Council. Newman was an "inopportunist': although he had accepted the essential doctrine as part of tradition when he became a Catholic, he thought that formally to define the dogma without a great deal more historical and theological study and to impose it as an article of faith on a Church that was not ready for it was premature. The more extreme Ultramontane theory of the almost limitless infallibility of the papacy was of course dismissed out of hand by Newman, who never doubted the Council would be protected from teaching any such exaggerated doctrine. This turned out to be the case. And Newman had no difficulty in accepting the comparatively limited and moderate definition which was finally passed. Although he had deplored the methods of the very vocal pressure group which had lobbied for a definition that he thought was quite unneccessary since no heresy was involved and had more to do with ecclesiastical politics than the faith, nevertheless in time he came to feel it must somehow be providential. At least it was now manifestly clear where the supreme authority in the Church lay, and that could only be beneficial in the event of another heresy threatening the Church. But at the same time Newman accurately predicted the practical effect the definition would have on the Church in terms of "creeping infallibility". From the ecclesiological point of view he regretted that the Council had not placed the dogma within the wider context of the Church as a whole. However, he correctly predicted that there would be another Council whose teaching would place that of the Vatican Council in its proper perspective – which is exactly what the Second Vatican Council did in the most important of its "Constitutions", that on the Church (*Lumen Gentium*, as it is usually called).

In October 1874 the Liberal statesman William Gladstone published an article in which he maintained that since the Vatican Council "no one can become her [the Roman Catholic Church's]

*For texts, see below p. 23.

convert without renouncing his moral and mental freedom, and placing his civil loyalty and duty at the mercy of another''. Newman saw his opportunity to speak out against extreme Ultramontanism by replying to Gladstone. With the publication on 5 November of Gladstone's pamphlet *The Vatican Decrees in their bearing on Civil Allegiance: A Political Expostulation*, which was popular in tone and became a best-seller, Newman saw that it was imperative that a moderate Catholic voice should be heard. His own answer, another lengthy pamphlet, was addressed in the form of a letter to the leading Catholic layman in England, the Duke of Norfolk.

In *A Letter to the Duke of Norfolk* (1875), Newman tries to steer a middle course between the two extreme positions on the question of papal infallibility. In dissociating himself both from the Ultramontanes and from the irreconcilable opponents of the Vatican Council definition, he adds a new important consideration to the general point he had made in the *Aplogia* about the interdependence of the magisterium and theology. At the very beginning of the *Letter* he emphasizes a point he had already made with some force, before the definition, in a letter of March 1870, where he pointed out that even the pronouncements of an infallible Pope would still require interpretation. The same was true of a Council's definitions, which – just as ''lawyers explain acts of Parliament'' – had to be explained by theologians. Obvious as the fact might be, the conclusion to be drawn from it had serious consequences for the fantasies of extreme Ultramontanism. ''Hence, I have never been able to see myself that the ultimate decision rests with any but the general Catholic intelligence''. This realistic theology of ''reception'' also meant that the whole Church ratified a definition as ''authentic'', although Newman was careful to emphasize that the ''subsequent reception'' did not actually enter into the ''necessary conditions'' of a dogmatic decision.[106]

In the earlier private letter he also noted that abstract definitions could not ''determine particular fact': the doctrine, for example, that there was no salvation outside the Church did not apply to people in ''invincible ignorance''.[107] For ''it does not follow, because there is no Church but one, which has the Evangelical gifts and privileges to bestow, that therefore no one can be saved without the intervention of that one Church''. And it was "possible to belong to the soul of the Church without belonging to the body". Other teachings of the Church admitted of exceptions in practice, like the condemnations in theory of mixed education and usury. In the case of usury, moreover, as in that of the doctrine of absolute predestination, distinctions had been drawn between different connotations of the words in question, which had led to the serious modification, even suspension, of the abstract teaching. Such changes and qualifications in the Church's official teaching "show what caution is to be observed" in interpreting her pronouncements. But, on the other hand, because general doctrines cannot be divorced from concrete circumstances and contexts, it did not follow that condemnations of "the very wording" of particular doctrinal deviations in books may not be infallible, since otherwise "neither Pope nor Council could draw up a dogmatic definition at all, for the right exercise of words is involved in the right exercise of thought".[108]

He continued to insist after the definition that "the voice of the Schola Theologorum, of the whole Church diffusive" would "in time make itself heard", and that "Catholic instincts and ideas" would eventually "assimilate and harmonize" it into the wider context of Catholic belief.[109] As time went on, too, theologians would "settle the force of the wording of the dogma, just as the courts of law solve the meaning and bearing of Acts of Parliament".[110] While it was hardly more than common sense that ultimately the only way in which the solemn declarations of Councils and Pope could be authenticated was by the acceptance and recognition by the Church that they were indeed what they purported to be, nevertheless their interpretation involved necessarily the technicalities of theological science: the meaning of dogmatic statements was not self-evident, but they were "always made with the anticipation and condition of this lawyer-like, or special-pleader-like, action of the intellect upon them".[111] All human statements required interpretation. In defining doctrines, Popes and Councils enjoyed an "active infallibility", but more was involved in the infallibility of the Church than that, since a *"passive infallibility"* belonged to the whole Catholic people, who had to determine the force and meaning of these doctrinal definitions, although the chief responsibility for this lay with the theologians, whose discussions and investigations assured a clear distinction between "theological truth" and "theological opinion", which was essential for preventing "dogmatism". The differences between theologians maintained "liberty of thought", whilst their consensus on points of dogma was "the safeguard of the infallible decisions of the Church".[112] Infallibility (itself a comparatively recent term) resided in its fullness in the whole Church (although this had always been assumed and never formally defined).

In his treatment of the role of theology, Newman repeats and develops the points he had already made in private correspondence. He does not hesitate to say that the "definite rules" and "traditional principles of interpretation" needed for interpreting dogmatic statements are "as cogent and unchangeable" as the definitions themselves.[113] Central to this process, he claims, is the "principle of minimizing",[114] whereby theologians explain "in the concrete" a pronouncement of the teaching authority, "by strict interpretation of its wording, by the illustration of its circumstances, and by the recognition of exceptions, in order to make it as tolerable as possible, and the least of a temptation, to self-willed, independent, or wrongly educated minds." After all, he insists, the virtue of faith is "so difficult," and "so difficult is it to assent inwardly to propositions, verified to us neither by reason nor experience, but depending for their reception on the word of the Church as God's oracle, that she has ever shown the utmost care to contract, as far as possible, the range of truths and the sense of propositions, of which she demands this absolute reception.[115] This "legitimate minimizing" takes advantage on the one hand of the "intensely concrete character of the matters condemned" in "negative" pronouncements, and on the other hand of the abstract nature of "affirmative" definitions of doctrine ("excepting such as relate to persons'), which "admit of exceptions in their actual application".[116] These principles have to be applied to the definition of papal infallibility, the scope of which is carefully limited to deliberate and actual definitions of faith and morals, which are referable either to revelation or to the moral law, and which are intended to be authoritative teachings, binding on the whole Church as pertaining to salvation. In the event, however, of "a false interpretation" of the infallibility definition, then "another Leo will be given us for the occasion". The reference is to Pope St Leo's Council of Chalcedon, which, "without of course touching the definition" of the preceding Council of Ephesus, "trimmed the balance of doctrine by completing it".[117] The warning is an exact prophecy both of the theology of "creeping infallibility" that came in the wake of the First Vatican Council, and of the Second Vatican Council, which Pope John XXIII convoked nearly a hundred years later.

At the heart of *A Letter to the Duke of Norfolk* is the celebrated treatment of the sovereignty of conscience. Newman, of course, had often written on conscience as the basis of religious belief. But here he discusses the individual believer's conscience in its relation to ecclesiastical authority. He first defines conscience as the law of God "as apprehended in the minds of individual men" – which, "though it may suffer refraction in passing into the intellectual medium of each ... is not therefore so affected as to lose its character of being the Divine Law, but still has, as such, the prerogative of commanding obedience". On this view of conscience it is "the voice of God", whereas the world regards it as little more that "a creation of man". Far from being "a long-sighted selfishness" or "a desire to be consistent with oneself", Newman declares in ringing tones that "Conscience is the aboriginal Vicar of Christ, a prophet in its informations, a monarch in its peremptoriness, a priest in its blessings and anathemas, and, even though the eternal priesthood throughout the Church could cease to be, in it the sacerdotal principle would remain and would have a sway". In earlier times "its supremacy was assailed by the arm of physical force", but "now the intellect is put in operation to sap the foundations of a power which the sword could not destroy". The secularized idea of conscience merely concerns "the right of thinking, speaking, writing, and acting" as one sees fit, "without any thought of God at all". Paradoxically, it has become "the very right and freedom of conscience to dispense with conscience". In effect, conscience "has been superseded by a counterfeit", namely, "the right of self-will".[118]

Were the Pope himself to "speak against Conscience in the true sense of the word, he would commit a suicidal act. He would be cutting the ground from under his feet". Indeed, continues Newman, "we shall find that it is by the universal sense of right

55

and wrong, the consciousness of transgression, the pangs of guilt, and the dread of retribution, as first principles deeply lodged in the hearts of men, it is thus and only thus, that he has gained his footing in the world and achieved his success". It is the "championship of the Moral Law and of conscience" which is "his *raison d'être*", and the "fact of his mission is the answer to the complaints of those who feel the insufficiency of the natural light; and the insufficiency of that light is the justification of his mission". Newman emphasizes the precarious nature of the moral sense, which "is at once the highest of all teachers, yet the least luminous; and the Church, the Pope, the Hierarchy are ... the supply of an urgent demand". But if revelation is the fulfilment of natural religion, it is in no sense "independent of it': "The Pope, who comes of Revelation, has no jurisdiction over Nature".[119]

Turning to the crucial question of the relation of the individual conscience to authority, Newman begins by laying down that since "conscience is not a judgment upon any speculative truth, any abstract doctrine, but bears immediately ... on something to be done or not done", it "cannot come into direct collision with the Church's or the Pope's infallibility; which is engaged on general propositions, and in the condemnation of particular and given errors". Here[120] Newman means by conscience not what moral theologians call "habitual" conscience, that is, the conscience which entertains general moral norms and principles, but rather what they mean by "actual" conscience, that is, the judgment that this particular thing here and now is to be done or not done (always, of course, in the light of the relevant moral principles). In other words, my "habitual" conscience on the one hand tells me that lying is wrong, but on the other hand my "actual" conscience has to decide whether this particular statement qualifies as a lie, as opposed, for example, to an evasion, and also whether if it is a lie it is justifiable to prevent a greater evil. Or again, my "habitual" conscience may tell me that indiscriminate bombing is wrong but my "actual" conscience has to decide whether this particular bombing raid counts as an instance of indiscriminate bombing and, if so, whether the prevention of a greater evil may justify it. Even in the case of the most (apparently) unexceptionable moral rules, like, for example, "torturing innocent children is always wrong", the "actual" conscience has still to decide whether this particular action counts as torture or as justifiable punishment. And so, Newman argues, because "actual" conscience is "a practical dictate", *direct* conflict is possible "only when the Pope legislates, or give particular orders, and the like". However, "a Pope is not infallible in his laws, nor in his commands, nor in his acts of state, nor in his administration, nor in his public policy". After all, St Peter was not infallible at Antioch when St. Paul disagreed with him, nor was Liberius when he excommunicated Athanasius. However, the "dictate" of conscience, "in order to prevail against the voice of the Pope, must follow upon serious thought, prayer, and all available means of arriving at a right judgment on the matter in question". The onus of proof, then, lies on the individual conscience: "Unless a man is able to say to himself, as in the Presence of God, that he must not, and dare not, act upon the Papal injunction, he is bound to obey it, and would commit a great sin in disobeying it".[121] The bold admission about the fallibility off the first Pope in no way excludes a rigorous emphasis on loyalty and obedience to a legitimate superior. But on the other hand, to obey a papal order which one seriously thinks is wrong would be a sin – even if one is culpably mistaken (a person may be to blame for having a false conscience, but not for acting in accordance with it). In the last analysis, conscience, however misguided, is supreme; and Newman concludes the discussion with the famous declaration on the ultimate sovereignty of conscience:

> I add one remark. Certainly, if I am obliged to bring religion into after-dinner toasts, (which indeed does not seem quite the thing) I shall drink – to the Pope, if you please – still, to Conscience first, and to the Pope afterwards.[122]

THE TRIPLE OFFICE OF THE CHURCH*

Newman's *Lectures on the Prophetical Office* had been his first ecclesiological work and it is fitting that his last contribution to ecclesiology is the famous Preface of 1877 to his new edition of the *Prophetical Office*. It also contains his final reflections on the problem of the corruption of the Church. In a letter he says that he had "long wished" to write an essay "on the conflicting

*For texts, see below p. 248.

interests, and therefore difficulties of the Catholic Church, because she is at once, first a devotion, secondly a philosophy, thirdly a polity''. At present, as at other times, it was clear that ''the philosophical instinct'' had been eclipsed by the other two aspects. The French Revolution had destroyed the great theological schools of Europe, as Newman often pointed out, while the dominance of Ultramontanism meant that stress fell on authority and devotion at the expense of theological inquiry and investigation.

In the Preface Newman explains that his object is to provide an answer to one of the two important and plausible objections to the Roman Catholic Church which he had reproduced from Anglican writers in those lectures forty years ago. In the *Development of Doctrine* he had already dealt with ''the contrast which modern Catholicism is said to present with the religion of the Primitive Church''. Now he proposes to consider ''the difference which at first sight presents itself between its formal teaching and its popular and political manifestations''. It is no mere academic problem for him, as he will be ''explaining, as I have long wished to do, how I myself get over difficulties which I formerly felt''. And far from these difficulties decreasing since his own conversion, ''It is so ordered on high that in our day Holy Church should present just that aspect to my countrymen which is most consonant with their ingrained prejudices against her''.[123]

Newman's simple answer to the problem is that ''such an apparent contrariety between word and deed, the abstract and the concrete, could not but take place'', since the Church's ''organization cannot be otherwise than complex, considering the many functions which she has to fulfil''. By way of analogy, he points out how difficult it is for one and the same person to perform different public and private situations. The Church is the mystical body of Christ, who ''is Prophet, Priest and, King; and after His pattern, and in human measure, Holy Church has a triple office too; not the Prophetical alone and in isolation, as [the *Lectures on the Prophetical Office*] virtually teach, but three offices, which are indivisible, though diverse, viz. teaching, rule, and sacred ministry''. It follows that Christianity ''is at once a philosophy, a political power, and a religious rite: as a religion, it is Holy; as a philosophy, it is Apostolic; as a political power, it is imperial, that is, One and Catholic. As a religion, its special centre of action is pastor and flock; as a philosophy, the Schools; as a rule, the Papacy and its Curia''. Although the Church has always exercised the three offices,

> they were developed in their full proportions one after another, in a succession of centuries; first, in the primitive time it was recognized as a worship, springing up and spreading in the lower ranks of society ... Then it seized upon the intellectual and cultivated class, and created a theology and schools of learning. Lastly it seated itself, as an ecclesiastical polity, among princes, and chose Rome for its centre.

The three different offices are based on different principles, use different means, and are liable to different corruptions:

> Truth is the guiding principle of theology and theological inquiries; devotion and edification, of worship; and of government, expedience. The instrument of theology is reasoning; of worship, our emotional nature; of rule, command and coercion. Further, in man as he is, reasoning tends to rationalism; devotion to superstition and enthusiasm; and power to ambition and tyranny.

The difficulty of combining all three offices is well illustrated by the question, ''What line of conduct, except on the long, the very long run, is at once edifying, expedient, and true?'' Certainly, the gift of infallibility protects the Church from error not only directly in teaching but also ''indirectly'' in ''worship and political action also'; however, ''nothing but the gift of impeccability granted to her authorities would secure them from all liability to mistake in their conduct, policy, words and decisions''. The problem of exercising these three very different functions ''supplies the staple of those energetic charges and vivid pictures of the inconsistency, double-dealing, and deceit of the Church of Rome''.[124]

Without attempting to deny the corruptions of the Church, Newman is anxious to correct his mistake in the *Prophetical Office* in blaming them on Catholic theology, by pointing out that ''ambition, craft, cruelty, and superstition are not commonly the characteristic of theologians'', whereas the alleged corruptions in fact ''bear on their face the marks of having a popular or a political origin'', and ''theology, so far from encouraging them, has restrained and corrected such extravagances as have been committed, through human infirmity, in the exercise of the regal and sacerdotal powers". Indeed, he adds almost dramatically, religion is never "in greater danger than when, in consequence of national or international troubles, the Schools of theology have been broken up and ceased to be". He then gives the reason for this in some of the most weighty words he ever wrote:

I say, then, Theology is the fundamental and regulating principle of the whole Church system. It is commensurate with Revelation, and Revelation is the initial and essential idea of Christianity. It is the subject-matter, the formal cause, the expression, of the Prophetical Office, and, as being such, has created both the Regal Office and the Sacerdotal. And it has in a certain sense a power of jurisdiction over those offices, as being its own creations, theologians being ever in request and in employment in keeping within bounds both the political and popular elements in the Church's constitution, – elements which are far more congenial than itself to the human mind, are far more liable to excess and corruption . . .[125]

Ever mindful of the need to keep a balance, Newman promptly qualifies his high praise: "Yet theology cannot always have its own way; it is too hard, too intellectual, too exact, to be always equitable, or to be always compassionate . . . ." Sometimes even a theologian in his writings has to "let his devout nature betray itself between the joints of his theological harness". Popular religion may, for example, reject a more accurate translation of the Bible because to "the devotional mind what is new and strange is as repulsive, often as dangerous, as falsehood is to the scientific. Novelty is often error to those who are unprepared for it, from the refraction with which it enters into their conceptions." People's "imaginations" have to become accustomed to religious changes, whereas "when science crosses and breaks the received path of Revelation", religious people are criticized if "they show hesitation to shift at a minute's warning their position, and to accept as truths shadowy views at variance with what they have ever been taught and have held". The modern idea is that it is "a great moral virtue to be fearless and thorough in inquiry into facts", whereas the "pursuit of truth in the subject-matter of religion . . . must always be accompanied by the fear of error".[126] Elsewhere, Newman says: "What the genius of the Church cannot bear is, changes in thought being hurried, abrupt, violent – out of tenderness to souls, for unlearned and narrowminded men get unsettled and miserable. The great thing is to move all together and then the change, as geological changes, must be very slow". In another letter, however, he emphasizes the role of theology in preparing the Church for changes – "it is the arena on which questions of development and change are argued out . . . it prepares the way, accustoming the mind of Catholics to the idea of the change". Because theology also, he explains in the same letter, "protects" dogma by "forming a large body of doctrine which must be got through before an attack can be made on the dogma", without theology "the dogma of the Church would be the raw flesh without skin – nay or a tree without leaves – for, as devotional feelings clothe the dogma on the one hand, so does the teaching of [theology] on the other".[127]

The distinction between theology and popular religion, Newman argues, may be traced to the Gospel itself, and he cites the case of the woman with the haemorrhage who hoped to be cured by touching the cloak of Jesus, who "passed over the superstitious act" and healed her because of her faith. In fact, he praised her for "what might, not without reason, be called an idolatrous act". Actually the Gospels show that the "idolatry of ignorance" is not regarded on a level with other idolatries (of wealth, for example), which, however, are not normally "shocking to educated minds". Jesus constantly insisted on the necessity of faith – "but where does He insist on the danger of superstition?" However, the fact remains that this and other incidents in the Gospels "form an aspect of Apostolic Christianity very different from that presented" by the Epistles of St. Paul. "Need men wait for the Medieval Church in order to make their complaint that the theology of Christianity does not accord with its religious manifestations?" Does "a poor Neapolitan crone, who chatters to the crucifix" do anything inherently more superstitious than the woman with the haemorrhage? Given "the ethical intelligence of the world at large", Newman remarks that he would wonder "whether that nation really had the faith, which is free in all its ranks and classes from all kinds and degrees of what is commonly considered superstition". There is no reason to be surprised if the Catholic Church, in the face of popular religion, finds it difficult "to make her Sacerdotal office keep step with her Prophetical''. This applies obviously to the cult of the angels and saints, which, ''though ever to be watched with jealousy by theologians, because of human infirmity and perverseness . . . has a normal place in revealed Religion''. For monotheism implies beings inferior to God but superior to human beings, that are able to bridge ''the vast gulf which separates Him from man''. And so polytheism is only ''a natural sentiment corrupted''. The Church's mission is not ''to oppose herself to impulses'' which are ''both natural and legitimate'', though previously ''the instruments of sin, but to do her best, by a right use, to moderate and purify them''. The fact that she has not always been successful simply shows that ''there will ever be a marked contrariety between the professions of her theology and the ways and doings of a Catholic country''. Moreover, the Church allows much more freedom in devotion, which is ''of a subjective and personal nature'', than in doctrine. This contrast is accentuated if ''ecclesiastical authority takes part with popular sentiment against a theological decision''. A very early example would be the occasion at Antioch when St. Peter stopped associating with converts from paganism because of pressure from converts from Judaism, a lapse for which he was rebuked by St. Paul. However, Paul himself was ready to conform to Jewish customs when necessary, and the principle of ''accommodation'' – though it may be misapplied, as perhaps in the case of the Jesuit Missionaries' adoption of Chinese customs – has always been practiced by Christians since the earliest time. [128]

The theological office of the Church, then, may find itself in opposition to both the so-called political and pastoral offices. But equally, the political office may come into conflict with the other two offices. This office is, in fact, essential if the Church is to preserve her independence and freedom of action – as is illustrated by the Orthodox Church, ''which has lost its political life, while its doctrine, and its ritual and devotional system, have little that can be excepted against''. Like ''a sovereign State'', the Church has ''to consolidate her several portions, to enlarge her territory, to keep up and to increase her various populations in this ever-dying, ever-nascent world, in which to be stationary is to lose ground, and to repose is to fail''. So important is this aspect of the Church that a point of theology may at times actually be ''determined on its expediency relatively to the

Church's Catholicity", that is, "by the logic of facts, which at times overrides all positive laws and prerogatives, and reaches in its effective force to the very frontiers of immutable truths".[129] The interests of the Church may override apparently decisive theological arguments, as when Pope St Stephen decided that heretical baptisms were after all valid (a view later accepted by theologians).

The essay concludes with the reflection that "whatever is great refuses to be reduced to human rule, and to be made consistent in its many aspects with itself". There should be no cause for surprise, then, if the Church "is an instance of the same law, presenting to us an admirable consistency and unity in word and deed, as her general characteristic, but crossed and discredited now and then by apparent anomalies".[130] These exceptions may prove the rule, but it is important to stress once again that Newman is only concerned with a general rule: he is not writing the kind of systematic theology which would provide a blueprint for the Church's constitution. Indeed, it is precisely because the Church is a living body that it is not possible to draw an exact diagram of her internal workings. And it is especially difficult to describe at all schematically that conflict which is for Newman an integral part of the Church's life, the creative tension between her three offices. As in the last chapter of the *Apologia*, guidelines and general principles are offered, but always on the understanding that the necessary demarcations and limitations are drawn pragmatically rather than theoretically, realistically rather than ideally. There had been a change since those early days when the problem was whether the theory of the "Via Media" actually fitted the existing Church it was supposed to delineate. There was no difficulty now about the reality of the Church: the question rather was to find a "view" (to use Newman's favourite word) which would account for the apparently discordant, even apparently incompatible, features of a very complex, because living, Church.

———

It would be wrong to complete this brief study of Newman's theology without recognizing that his theological contribution is much larger than any account of his specifically theological works can suggest. Far less a professional theologian than a Christian thinker, practically everything he wrote is of theological significance. It is not surprising that his unsystematic, richly varied work has often suggested that he belongs more to the world of patristic than to that of modern theology. "St. Bernard is called the last of the Fathers because in him dogma and piety and literature are still one ... Newman, who leaves later developments on one side, took over where St. Bernard left off, and perhaps should be allowed to succeed to his title".[131]

SELECTED TEXTS

1

REVELATION AND DOGMA*

THE ARIANS OF THE FOURTH CENTURY

The Arians of the Fourth Century was Newman's first book. Originally commissioned in 1831 to contribute a history of Church Councils to a new theological library, Newman first conceived of a three-volume work dealing consecutively with the Councils of the East, the West, and Trent. But the first volume turned out to be much narrower in scope than had been intended. Rejected by the editors of the projected theological library as unsuitable for their purposes and too specialized for the general reader, the book was completed in 1832 and published in 1833. Newman was never very happy with either the contents or the style of the book, but he never repudiated the substance of the work, which he thought had merit and originality in parts. The extracts given here have been chosen for their theological rather than historical significance. They are taken from chapters I ("The Church of Alexandria') and II ("On the Principle of the Formation and Imposition of Creeds').

CHAPTER I
THE CHURCH OF ALEXANDRIA

If I avow my belief, that freedom from symbols and articles is abstractedly the highest state of Christian communion, and the peculiar privilege of the primitive Church, it is not from any tenderness towards that proud impatience of control in which many exult, as in a virtue: but first, because technicality and formalism are, in their degree, inevitable results of public confessions of faith; and next, because when confessions do not exist, the mysteries of divine truth, instead of being exposed to the gaze of the profane and uninstructed, are kept hidden in the bosom of the Church, far more faithfully than is otherwise possible; and reserved by a private teaching, through the channel

*See also above, p. 10.

of her ministers, as rewards in due measure and season, for those who are prepared to profit by them; for those, that is, who are diligently passing through the successive stages of faith and obedience. And thus, while the Church is not committed to declarations, which, most true as they are, still are daily wrested by infidels to their ruin; on the other hand, much of that mischievous fanaticism is avoided, which at present abounds from the vanity of men, who think that they can explain the sublime doctrines and exuberant promises of the Gospel, before they have yet learned to know themselves and to discern the holiness of God, under the preparatory discipline of the Law and of Natural Religion. Influenced, as we may suppose, by these various considerations, from reverence for the free spirit of Christian faith and still more for the sacred truths which are the objects of it, and again from tenderness both for the heathen and the neophyte, who were unequal to the reception of the strong meat of the full Gospel, the rulers of the Church were dilatory in applying a remedy, which nevertheless the circumstances of the times imperatively required. They were loth to confess, that the Church had grown too old to enjoy the free, unsuspicious teaching with which her childhood was blest; and that her disciples must, for the future, calculate and reason before they spoke and acted.

... St. Paul evidently connects the true religion with the existing systems which he laboured to supplant, in his speech to the Athenians in the Acts, and his example is a sufficient guide to missionaries now, ... but are we able to account for his conduct, and ascertain the principle by which it was regulated? I think we can; and the exhibition of it will set before the reader another doctrine of the Alexandrian school, which it is as much to our purpose to understand and which I shall call *the divinity of Traditionary Religion*.

We know well enough for practical purposes what is meant by Revealed Religion; viz. that it is the doctrine taught in the Mosaic and Christian dispensations, and contained in the Holy Scriptures, and is from God in a sense in which no other doctrine can be said to be from Him. Yet if we would speak correctly, we must confess, on the authority of the Bible itself, that all knowledge of religion is from Him, and not only that which the Bible has transmitted to us. There never was a time when

God had not spoken to man, and told him to a certain extent his duty. His injunctions to Noah, the common father of all mankind, is the first recorded fact of the sacred history after the deluge. Accordingly, we are expressly told in the New Testament, that at no time He left Himself without witness in the world, and that in every nation He accepts those who fear and obey Him. It would seem, then, that there is something true and divinely revealed, in every religion all over the earth, overloaded, as it may be, at times even stifled by the impieties which the corrupt will and understanding of man have incorporated with it. Such are the doctrines of the power and presence of an invisible God, of His moral law and governance, of the obligation of duty, and the certainty of a just judgment, and of reward and punishment, as eventually dispensed to individuals; so that Revelation, properly speaking, is an universal, not a local gift; and the distinction between the state of Israelites formerly and Christians now, and that of the heathen, is, not that we can, and they cannot attain to future blessedness, but that the Church of God ever has had, and the rest of mankind never have had, authoritative documents of truth, and appointed channels of communication with Him. The word and the Sacraments are the characteristic of the elect people of God; but all men have had more or less the guidance of Tradition, in addition to those internal notions of right and wrong which the Spirit has put into the heart of each individual.

This vague and uncertain family of religious truths, originally from God, but sojourning without the sanction of miracle, or a definite home, as pilgrims up and down the world, and discernible and separable from the corrupt legends with which they are mixed, by the spiritual mind alone, may be called the *Dispensation of Paganism* ... And further, Scripture gives us reason to believe that the traditions, thus originally delivered to mankind at large, have been secretly re-animated and enforced by new communications from the unseen world; though these were not of such a nature as to be produced as evidence, or used as criteria and tests, and roused the attention rather than informed the understandings of the heathen. The book of Genesis contains a record of the Dispensation of Natural Religion, or Paganism, as well as of the patriarchal. The dreams of Pharaoh and Abimelech, as of Nebuchadnezzar afterwards, are instances of the dealings of God with those to whom He did not vouchsafe a written revelation. Or should it be said, that these particular cases merely come within the range of the Divine supernatural Governance which was in their neighbourhood, – an assertion which requires proof, – let the book of Job be taken as a less suspicious instance of the dealings of God with the heathen. Job was a pagan in the same sense in which the Eastern nations are Pagans in the present day. He lived among idolaters, yet he and his friends had cleared themselves from the superstitions with which the true creed was beset; and while one of them was divinely instructed by dreams, he himself at length heard the voice of God out of the whirlwind, in recompense for his long trial and his faithfulness under it. Why should not the book of Job be accepted by us, as a gracious intimation given us, who are God's sons, for our comfort, when we are anxious about our brethren who are still "scattered abroad" in an evil world; an intimation that the Sacrifice, which is the hope of Christians, has its power and its success, wherever men seek God with their whole heart? – If it be objected that Job lived in a less corrupted age than the times of ignorance which followed, Scripture, as if for our full satisfaction, draws back the curtain farther still in the history of Balaam. There a bad man and a heathen is made the oracle of true divine messages about doing justly, and loving mercy, and walking humbly; nay, even among the altars of superstition, the Spirit of God vouchsafes to utter prophecy. And so in the cave of Endor, even a saint was sent from the dead to join the company of an apostate king, and of the sorceress whose aid he was seeking. Accordingly, there is nothing unreasonable in the notion, that there may have been heathen poets and sages, or sibyls again, in a certain extent divinely illuminated, and organs through whom religious and moral truth was conveyed to their countrymen; though their knowledge of the Power from whom the gift came, nay, and their perception of the gift as existing in themselves, may have been very faint or defective ...

If this doctrine be scriptural, it is not difficult to determine the line of conduct which is to be observed by the Christian apologist and missionary. Believing God's hand to be in every system, so far forth as it is true (though Scripture alone is the depositary of His unadulterated and complete revelation), he will, after St. Paul's manner, seek some points in the existing superstitions as the basis of his own instructions, instead of indiscriminately condemning and discarding the whole assemblage of heathen opinions and practices; and he will address his hearers, not as men in a state of actual perdition, but as being in imminent danger of "the wrath to come," because they are in bondage and ignorance, and probably under God's displeasure, that is, the vast majority of them are so in fact; but not necessarily so, from the very circumstance of their being heathen. And while he strenuously opposes all that is idolatrous, immoral, and profane, in their creed, he will profess to be leading them on to perfection, and to be recovering and purifying, rather than reversing the essential principles of their belief. (*Ari.* 36–7, 79–84)

CHAPTER II
ON THE PRINCIPLE OF THE FORMATION AND IMPOSITION OF CREEDS

Before the mind has been roused to reflection and inquisitiveness about its own acts and impressions, it acquiesces, if religiously trained, in that practical devotion to the Blessed Trinity, and implicit acknowledgement of the divinity of Son and Spirit, which holy Scripture at once teaches and exemplifies. This is the faith of uneducated men, which is not the less philosophically correct, nor less acceptable to God, because it does not happen to be conceived in those precise statements which presuppose the action of the mind on its own sentiments and notions. Moral feelings do not directly contemplate and realize to themselves the objects which excite them. A heathen in obeying his conscience, implicitly worships Him of whom he has never distinctly heard. Again, a child feels not the less affectionate reverence towards his parents, because he cannot discriminate in words, nay, or in idea, between them and others. As, however, his reason opens, he might ask himself concerning the ground of his own emotions and conduct towards them; and might find that these are the correlatives of their peculiar tenderness towards him, long and intimate knowledge of him, and unhesitating assumption of authority over him; all which he continually experiences. And further, he might trace these characteristics of their influence on him to the essential relation itself, which involves his own original debt to them for the gift of life and reason, the inestimable blessing of an indestructible, never-ending existence. And now his intellect contemplates the object of those affections, which acted truly from the first, and are not purer or stronger merely for this accession of knowledge. This will tend to illustrate the sacred subject to which we are directing our attention.

As the mind is cultivated and expanded, it cannot refrain from the attempt to analyze the vision which influences the heart, and the Object in which that vision centres; nor does it stop till it has, in some sort, succeeded in expressing in words, what has all along been a principle both of its affections and of its obedience. But here the parallel ceases; the Object of religious veneration being unseen, and dissimilar from all that is seen, reason can but represent it in the medium of those ideas which the experience of life affords (as we see in the Scripture account, as far as it is addressed to the intellect); and unless these ideas, however inadequate, be correctly applied to it, they re-act upon the affections, and deprave the religious principle. This is exemplified in the case of the heathen, who, trying to make their instinctive notion of the Deity an object of reflection, pictured to their minds false images, which eventually gave them a pattern and a sanction for sinning. Thus the systematic doctrine of the Trinity may be considered as the shadow, projected for the contemplation of the intellect, of the Object of scripturally-informed piety: a representation, economical; necessarily imperfect, as being exhibited in a foreign medium, and therefore involving apparent inconsistencies or mysteries; given to the Church by tradition contemporaneously with those apostolic writings, which are addressed more directly to the heart; kept in the background in the infancy of Christianity, when faith and obedience were vigorous, and brought forward at a time when, reason being disproportionately developed, and aiming at sovereignty in the province of religion, its presence became necessary to expel an usurping idol from the house of God.

If this account of the connexion between the theological system and the Scripture implication of it be substantially correct, it will be seen how ineffectual all attempts ever will be to secure the doctrine by mere general language. It may be readily granted that the intellectual representation should ever be subordinate to the cultivation of the religious affections. And after all, it must be owned, so reluctant is a well-constituted mind to reflect on its own motive principles, that the correct intellectual image, from its hardness of outline, may startle and offend those who have all along been acting upon it. Doubtless there are portions of the ecclesiastical doctrine, presently to be exhibited, which may at first sight seem a refinement, merely because the object and bearings of them are not understood without reflection and experience. But what is left to the Church but to speak out, in order to exclude error? Much as we may wish it, we cannot restrain the rovings of the intellect, or silence its clamorous demand for a formal statement concerning the Object of our worship. If, for instance, Scripture bids us adore God, and adore His Son, our reason at once asks, whether it does not follow that there are two Gods; and a system of doctrine becomes unavoidable; being framed, let it be observed, not with a view of explaining, but of arranging the inspired notices concerning the Supreme Being, of providing, not a consistent, but a connected statement. There the inquisitiveness of a pious mind rests, viz., when it has pursued the subject into the mystery which is its limit. But this is not all. The intellectual expression of theological truth not only excludes heresy, but directly assists the acts of religious worship and obedience; fixing and stimulating the Christian spirit in the same way as the knowledge of the One God relieves and illuminates the perplexed conscience of the religious heathen. – And thus much on the importance of Creeds to tranquillize the mind; the text of Scripture being addressed principally to the affections, and of a religious, not a philosophical character.

Nor, in the next place, is an assent to the text of Scripture sufficient for the purposes of Christian fellowship. As the sacred text was not intended to satisfy the intellect, neither was it given as a test of the religious temper which it forms, and of which it is an expression. Doubtless no combination of words will ascertain an unity of sentiment in those who adopt them; but one form is more adapted for the purpose than another. Scripture being unsystematic, and the faith which it propounds being scattered through its documents, and understood only when they are viewed as a whole, the Creeds aim at concentrating its general spirit, so as to give security to the Church, as far as may be, that its members take that definite view of that faith which alone is the true one. But, if this be case, how idle is it to suppose that to demand assent to a form of words which happens to be scriptural, is on that account sufficient to effect an unanimity in thought and action! If the Church would be vigorous and influential, it must be decided and plain-spoken in its doctrine, and must regard its faith rather as a character of mind than as a notion. To attempt comprehensions of opinion, amiable as the motive frequently is, is to mistake arrangements of words, which have no existence except on paper, for habits which are realities; and ingenious generalizations of discordant sentiments for that practical agreement which alone can lead to co-operation. We may indeed artificially classify light and darkness under one term or formula; but nature has her own fixed courses, and unites mankind by the sympathy of moral character, not by those forced resemblances which the imagination singles out at pleasure even in the most promiscuous collection of materials. However plausible may be the veil thus thrown over heterogeneous doctrines, the flimsy artifice is discomposed so soon as the principles beneath it are called upon to move and act. Nor are these attempted comprehensions innocent; for, it being the interest of our enemies to weaken the Church, they have always gained a point, when they have put upon us words for things, and persuaded us to fraternize with those who, differing from us in essentials, nevertheless happen, in the exclusive range of opinion, somewhere to intersect that path of faith, which centres in supreme and zealous devotion to the service of God.

Let it be granted, then, as indisputable, that there are no two opinions so contrary to each other, but some form of words may be found vague enough to comprehend them both. The Pantheist will admit that there is a God, and the Humanitarian that Christ is God, if they are suffered to say so without explanation. But if this be so, it becomes the duty, as well as the evident policy of the Church, to interrogate them, before admitting them to her fellowship. If the Church be the pillar and ground of the truth, and bound to contend for the preservation of the faith once delivered to it; if we are answerable as ministers of Christ for the formation of one, and one only, character in the heart of man; and if the Scriptures are given us, as a means indeed towards that end, but inadequate to the office of interpreting themselves, except to such as live under the same Divine Influence which inspired them, and which is expressly sent down upon us that we may interpret them, – then, it is evidently our duty piously and cautiously to collect the sense of Scripture, and solemnly to promulgate it in such a form as is best suited, as far as it goes, to exclude the pride and unbelief of the world. (*Ari*, 143–8)

*

ON THE INTRODUCTION OF RATIONALISTIC PRINCIPLES INTO REVEALED RELIGION

In the autumn of 1835 Newman wrote Tract 73, *later to be republished under the title "On the Introduction of Rationalistic Principles into Revealed Religion" as one of the essays collected in* Essays Critical and Historical (1870). *The following extract is taken from the first section, "The Rationalistic and the Catholic Tempers Contrasted".*

Rationalism is a certain abuse of Reason; that is, a use of it for purposes for which it never was intended, and is unfitted. To rationalize in matters of Revelation is to make our reason the standard and measure of the doctrines revealed; to stipulate that those doctrines should be such as to carry with them their own justification; to reject them, if they come in collision with our existing opinions or habits of thought, or are with difficulty harmonized with our existing stock of knowledge. And thus a rationalistic spirit is the antagonist of Faith; for Faith is, in its very nature, the acceptance of what our reason cannot reach, simply and absolutely upon testimony.

There is, of course, a multitude of cases in which we allowably and rightly accept statements as true, partly on reason, and partly on testimony. We supplement the information of others by our knowledge, by our own judgment of probabilities; and, if it be very strange or extravagant, we suspend our assent. This is undeniable; still, after all, there are truths which are incapable of reaching us except on testimony, and there is testimony, which by and in itself, has an imperative claim on our acceptance.

As regards Revealed Truth, it is not Rationalism to set about to ascertain, by the exercise of reason, what things are attainable by reason, and what are not; nor, in the absence of an express Revelation, to inquire into the truths of Religion, as they come to us by nature; nor to determine what proofs are necessary for the acceptance of a Revelation, if it be given; nor to reject a Revelation on the plea of insufficient proof; nor, after recognizing it as divine, to investigate the meaning of its declarations, and to interpret its language; nor to use its doctrines, as far as they can be fairly used, in inquiring into its divinity; nor to compare and connect them with our previous knowledge, with a view of making them parts of a whole; nor to bring them into dependence on each other, to trace their mutual relations, and to pursue them to their legitimate issues. This is not Rationalism; but it is Rationalism to accept the Revelation, and then to explain it away; to speak of it as the Word of God, and to treat it as the word of man; to refuse to let it speak for itself; to claim to be told the *why* and the *how* of God's dealings with us, as therein described, and to assign to Him a motive and a scope of our own; to stumble at the partial knowledge which He may give us of them; to put aside what is obscure, as if it had not been said at all; to accept one half of what has been told us, and not the other half; to assume that the contents of Revelation are also its proof; to frame some gratuitous hypothesis about them, and then to garble, gloss, and colour them, to trim, clip, pare away, and twist them, in order to bring them into conformity with the idea to which we have subjected them ...

... The Rationalist makes himself his own centre, not his Maker; he does not go to God, but he implies that God must come to him. And this, it is to be feared, is the spirit in which multitudes of us act at the present day. Instead of looking out of ourselves, and trying to catch glimpses of God's workings, from any quarter, – throwing ourselves forward upon Him and waiting on Him, we sit at home bringing everything to ourselves, enthroning ourselves in our own views, and refusing to believe anything that does not force itself upon us as true. Our private judgment is made everything to us – is contemplated, recognized, and consulted as the arbiter of all questions, and as independent of everything external to us. Nothing is considered to have an existence except so far forth as our minds discern it.

The notion of half views and partial knowledge, of guesses, surmises, hopes and fears, of truths faintly apprehended and not understood, of isolated facts in the great scheme of Providence, in a word, the idea of Mystery, is discarded.

Hence a distinction is drawn between what is called Objective and Subjective Truth, and Religion is said to consist in a reception of the latter. By Objective Truth is meant the Religious System considered as existing in itself, external to this or that particular mind: by Subjective, is meant that which each mind receives in particular, and considers to be such. To believe in Objective Truth is to throw ourselves forward upon that which we have but partially mastered or made subjective; to embrace, maintain, and use general propositions which are larger than our own capacity, of which we cannot see the bottom, which we cannot follow out into their multiform details; to come before and bow before the import of such propositions, as if we were contemplating what is real and independent of human judgment. Such a belief, implicit, and symbolized as it is in the use of creeds, seems to the Rationalist superstitious and unmeaning, and he consequently confines Faith to the province of Subjective Truth, or to the reception of doctrine, as, and so far as, it is met and apprehended by the mind, which will be differently, as he considers, in different persons, in the shape of orthodoxy in one, heterodoxy in another. That is, he professes to *believe* in that which he *opines*; and he avoids the obvious extravagance of such a avowal by maintaining that the moral trial involved in Faith does not lie in the submission of the reason to external realities partially disclosed, but in what he calls that candid pursuit of truth which ensures the eventual adoption of that opinion on the subject, which is best for us individually, which is most natural according to the constitution of our own minds, and, therefore, divinely intended for us. I repeat, he owns that Faith, viewed with reference to its objects, is never more than an opinion, and is pleasing to God, not as an active principle apprehending definite doctrines, but as a result and fruit, and therefore an evidence of past diligence, independent inquiry, dispassionateness, and the like. Rationalism takes the words of Scripture as signs of Ideas; Faith, of Things or Realities . . .

. . . Revelation, as a Manifestation, is a doctrine variously received by various minds, but nothing more to each than that which each mind comprehends it to be. Considered as a Mystery, it is a doctrine enunciated by inspiration, in human language, as the only possible medium of it, and suitably, according to the capacity of language; a doctrine *lying hid* in language, to be received in that language from the first by every mind, whatever be its separate power of understanding it; entered into more or less by this or that mind, as it may be; and admitting of being apprehended more and more perfectly according to the diligence of this mind and that. It is one and the same, independent and real, of depth unfathomable, and illimitable in its extent.

*

This is a fit place to make some remarks on the Scripture sense of the word Mystery. It may seem a contradiction in terms to call Revelation a Mystery; but is not the book of the Revelation of St. John as great a mystery from beginning to end as the most abstruse doctrine the mind ever imagined? yet it is even called a *Revelation*. How is this? The answer is simple. No revelation can be complete and systematic, from the weakness of the human intellect; *so far as* it is not such, it is mysterious. When nothing is revealed, nothing is known, and there is nothing to contemplate or marvel at; but when something is revealed, and only something, for all cannot be, there are forthwith difficulties and perplexities. A Revelation is religious doctrine viewed on its illuminated side; a Mystery is the selfsame doctrine viewed on the side unilluminated. Thus Religious Truth is neither light nor darkness, but both together; it is like the dim view of a country seen in the twilight, with forms half extricated from the darkness, with broken lines, and isolated masses. Revelation, in this way of considering it, is not a revealed *system*, but consists of a number of detached and incomplete truths belonging to a vast system unrevealed, of doctrines and injunctions mysteriously connected together; that is, connected by unknown media, and bearing upon unknown portions of the system. . . .

The practical inference to be drawn from this view is, first, that we should be very reverent in dealing with Revealed Truth; next, that we should avoid all rash theorizing and systematizing as relates to it, which is pretty much what looking into the Ark was under the Law: further, that we should be solicitous to hold it safely and entirely; moreover, that we should be zealous and pertinacious in guarding it; and lastly, which is implied in all these, that we should religiously adhere to the form of words and the ordinances under which it comes to us, through which it is revealed to us, and apart from which the Revelation does not exist, there being nothing else given us by which to ascertain or enter into it.

Striking indeed is the contrast presented to this view of the Gospel by the popular theology of the day! That theology is as follows: that the Atonement is the chief doctrine of the Gospel; again, that it is chiefly to be regarded, not as a wonder in heaven, and in its relation to the attributes of God and to the unseen world, but in its experienced effects on our minds, in the change it effects when it is believed. To this, as if to the point of sight in a picture, all the portions of the Gospel system are directed and made to converge; as if this doctrine were so fully understood, that it might fearlessly be used to regulate, adjust, correct, complete, everything else. Thus, the doctrine of the Incarnation is viewed as necessary and important to the Gospel, *because* it gives virtue to the Atonement; of the Trinity, *because* it includes the revelation, not only of the Redeemer, but also of the Sanctifier, by whose aid and influence the Gospel message is to be blessed to us. It follows that faith is nearly the whole of religious service, for through it the message or Manifestation is received; on the other hand, the scientific language of Catholicism, concerning the Trinity and Incarnation, is disparaged, as having no tendency to enforce the effect upon our minds of the doctrine of the Atonement, while the Sacraments are limited to the office of representing, and promising, and impressing on us the promise of divine influences, in no measure of conveying them. Thus the Dispensation, in its length, depth, and height, is practically identified with its Revelation, or rather its necessarily superficial Manifestation. Not that the reality of the Atonement, in itself, is formally denied, but it is cast in the background, except so far as it can be discovered to be influential, viz., to show God's hatred of sin, the love of Christ, and the like; and there is an evident tendency to consider it as a *mere* Manifestation of the love of Christ, to the denial of all real virtue in it as an expiation for sin; as if His death took place merely to show His love for us as a sign of God's infinite mercy, to calm and assure us, without any real connexion existing between it and God's forgiveness of our sins. And the Dispensation thus being hewn and chiselled into an intelligible human system, is represented, when thus mutilated, as affording a remarkable evidence of the truth of the Bible, an evidence level to the reason, and superseding the testimony of the Apostles. That is, according to the above observations, that Rationalism, or want of faith, which has in the first place invented a spurious gospel, next looks complacently on its own offspring, and pronounces it to be the very image of that notion of the Divine Providence, according to which it was originally modelled; a procedure, which, besides more serious objections, incurs the logical absurdity of arguing in a circle. (*Ess* i. 31–5, 41–2, 47–8)

2

THE "VIA MEDIA"*

THE PROPHETICAL OFFICE OF THE CHURCH

Lectures on the Prophetical Office of the Church viewed relatively to Romanism and Popular Protestantism were delivered in the Adam de Brome chapel in the University Church of St Mary the Virgin (of which Newman had become Vicar in 1828) between May and July 1836 and published on 11 March 1837. The following extract is taken from the tenth lecture, "On the Essentials of the Gospel".

LECTURE 10 ON THE ESSENTIALS OF THE GOSPEL

I say, then, that the Creed is a collection of definite articles set apart from the first, passing from hand to hand, rehearsed and confessed at Baptism, committed and received from Bishop to Bishop, forced upon the attention of each Christian, and thus demanding and securing due explanation of its meaning. It is received on what may fitly be called, if it must have a distinctive name, Episcopal Tradition. Besides it is delineated and recognized in Scripture itself, where it is called the Hypotyposis, or "outline of sound words;" and again, in the writings of the Fathers, as in some of the passages cited in the late Lecture. But independently of this written evidence in its favour, we may observe that a Tradition, thus formally and statedly enunciated and delivered from hand to hand, is of the nature of a written document, and has an evidence of its Apostolical origin the same in kind with that adducible for the Scriptures. For the same reason, though it is not pertinent here to insist on it, rites and ceremonies too are something more than mere oral Traditions, and, as being so, carry with them a considerable presumption in behalf of the things signified by them. And all this, let it be observed, is independent of the question of the Catholicity

*See also above, p. 16.

81

or Universality of the rites or doctrines which are thus formally sealed and handed down; a property which in this case attaches to both of them, and becomes an additional argument for their Apostolical origin.

Such then is Episcopal Tradition, – to be received according to the capacity of each individual mind. But besides this, there is what may be called Prophetical Tradition. Almighty God placed in His Church first Apostles, or Bishops, secondarily Prophets. Apostles rule and preach, Prophets expound. Prophets or Doctors are the interpreters of the revelation; they unfold and define its mysteries, they illuminate its documents, they harmonize its contents, they apply its promises. Their teaching is a vast system, not to be comprised in a few sentences, not to be embodied in one code or treatise, but consisting of a certain body of Truth, pervading the Church like an atmosphere, irregular in its shape from its very profusion and exuberance; at times separable only in idea from Episcopal Tradition, yet at times melting away into legend and fable; partly written, partly unwritten, partly the interpretation, partly the supplement of Scripture, partly preserved in intellectual expressions, partly latent in the spirit and temper of Christians; poured to and fro in closets and upon the housetops, in liturgies, in controversial works, in obscure fragments, in sermons, in popular prejudices, in local customs. This I call Prophetical Tradition, existing primarily in the bosom of the Church itself, and recorded in such measure as Providence has determined in the writings of eminent men. This is obviously of a very different kind from the Episcopal Tradition, yet in its first origin it is equally Apostolical, and, viewed as a whole, equally claims our zealous maintenance. "Keep that which is committed to thy charge," is St. Paul's injunction to Timothy, and for this reason, because from its vastness and indefiniteness it is especially exposed to corruption, if the Church fails in vigilance. This is that body of teaching which is offered to all Christians even at the present day, though in various forms and measures of truth, in different parts of Christendom, partly being a comment, partly an addition upon the articles of the Creed.

Now what has been said has sufficed to show, how it may easily happen that this Prophetical Tradition has been corrupted in its details, in spite of its general accuracy and its agreement with Episcopal; and if so, there will be lesser points of doctrine as well as greater points, whatever be their number and limit, from which a person may possibly dissent, as doubting their Apostolical origin, without incurring any anathema or public censure. And this is supposed on the Anglo-Catholic theory actually to be the case; that, though the Prophetical Tradition comes from God, and ought to have been religiously preserved, and was so in great measure and for a long time, yet that no such especial means were taken for its preservation as those which have secured to us the Creed, – that it was rather what St. Paul calls "the mind of the Spirit," the thought and principle which breathed in the Church, her accustomed and unconscious mode of viewing things, and the body of her received notions, than any definite and systematic collection of dogmas elaborated by the intellect. Partially, indeed, it was fixed and perpetuated in the shape of formal articles or doctrines, as the rise of errors or other causes gave occasion; and it is preserved to a considerable extent in the writings of the Fathers. For a time the whole Church agreed together in giving one and the same account of this Tradition; but in course of years, love waxing cold and schisms abounding, her various branches developed portions of it for themselves ... (*VM* i, 249–51)

3

JUSTIFICATION*

LECTURES ON THE DOCTRINE OF JUSTIFICATION

The first of the Lectures on the Doctrine of Justification *was delivered in the Adam de Brome chapel of the Church of St. Mary the Virgin on 13 April and the last on 1 June 1837. The lectures were published on 30 March 1838. The following extracts are taken from the fourth lecture on "Secondary Senses of the Term Justification", the sixth lecture on "The Gift of Righteousness", the seventh lecture on "The Characteristics of the Gift of Righteousness", the eleventh lecture on "The Nature of Justifying Faith", and the thirteenth lecture "On Preaching the Gospel".*

LECTURE IV SECONDARY SENSES OF THE TERM JUSTIFICATION

If justification be God's great act declaring us righteous, and thereby as its direct, necessary, and instantaneous result making us (in our degree) righteous, – if it be an act external to us, continued on into an act within us, – if it be a divine Voice issuing in a divine work, acceptance on the one part leading to acceptableness on the other, imputation to participation, – it requires very few words to explain how it comes to have been taken for what it involves; in other words, how justification has been said to be renewal, or to follow on or consist in renewal, or renewal said to be justification. And yet not a few words may be necessary to make familiar to our imaginations what is so obvious to the reason, – nay, to allay the feelings of distrust with which the very notion of such an attempt is commonly received at this day. Little indeed can anyhow be effected in the course of a single Lecture, yet suggestions on the subject may be of service to inquirers.

*See also above, p. 91.

I say, then, if the direct result of pronouncing righteous be actual righteousness, it is not at all unnatural or strange, that righteousness or renewal should be called our justification (as little as saying, as we do without scruple, that a man has no "life" in him, when we mean no "activity" or no "heat," – heat and activity being effects of life, – or in using "animation" first for life, then for liveliness); nor is it all justifiable, after the fashion of the day, to set down such a mode of speech to spiritual blindness, and to stigmatize it as perilous to its maintainers. My reasons are as follow: –

2.

1. Justification renews, therefore I say it may fitly be called renewal. Is not this an allowable variety of expression which is exemplified every day? For instance, to *tempt* is to solicit or assail with temptation, to invite towards evil; yet it not unfrequently means to overcome by temptation, or to seduce. To *persuade* means either to use persuasives or to succeed in persuading. To *cure* a patient, that is, to heal or restore to health, is properly nothing more than to take care of him. To gain a *battle* means to gain a victory, conquest being the intended object of engaging. A *commander* is one who is obeyed as well as commands. To *call* spirits from the deep is not merely to call, but so to call that they come, or to evoke. In such cases we anticipate the result of an action from its beginning, and contemplate it in its completeness. Certain implications or effects are necessary for the adequate notion of a thing, and in speaking of it we take their presence for granted; we realise the thing itself in our minds by affixing to it names which properly belong to its effects. To call spirits implies an effectual call; and to declare just is to make just.

It is a parallel mode of speaking, to say that justification *consists* in renewal, or that renewal *constitutes* justification. This is much the same as saying, which we are apt to do, that a certain remarkable event is a *Providence*. It is a result, a manifestation of Divine Providence. And so our works of obedience are said to be a justification or a declaring righteous, as being the result and token of that declaration. To be justified *by* or *through* works is nothing more or less than to be justified *in* works; and it may suitably be urged against the thoughtless, lukewarm, formal, and superstitious, how they can suppose themselves justified, seeing that God justifies in works, or that works are the mode, medium, or state of justification.

I have before now spoken of justification as a sort of sacrament; it is so, by a figure of speech, being an external word effecting an inward grace. Here, then, we shall have another illustration of the matter in hand, which is the more apposite because our Catechism become a party to it, allowing itself, as it so happens, in the same verbal inaccuracy, in explaining the nature of a sacrament, as is committed when justification and renewal are made equivalents of one another. A sacrament, it will be recollected, is there defined to be "an *outward visible sign* of an inward spiritual grace". But if so, the inward grace is *not* part of the sacrament, but a result distinct from it. Yet in the very next answer, upon the question, " *How many parts* are there *in* a sacrament?" we are told there are " *Two*; the outward visible sign, *and* the *inward spiritual grace* ", as if the inward *grace* were *not* distinct, but an internal result or essential *part* of the sacrament. Who does not see the real meaning in spite of this apparent inconsistency? viz. that the act of administering a sacrament so involves and secures the inward grace, that the grace comes under the meaning of the term, so that whether not it be *part* of the sacrament, is a mere question of words, the term in its elementary sense denoting the outward act, in its full meaning comprising the inward grace also. And in like manner we may say, without any inconsistency and with truth, first, that justification is *only* that acceptance on God's part, which is the earnest of renewal; next, that it consists of *two* parts, acceptance and renewal. Justification tends to sanctify; and to obstruct its sanctifying power, is as if we stopped a man's breath; it is the death of that from which it proceeds.

Again, we speak of being *baptized* with God's *grace*; and thus we may allowably say that we are *justified* or accepted by *obedience*. And we might of course with propriety urge that *baptism* is not a mere outward rite, but an *inward* power; and so may we say that *justification* is a *change of heart*.

3.

2. I have been arguing from the essential union between justification and renewal, that they are practically convertible terms; but there are still more urgent reasons why they should be so. God's justification does not merely work *some* changes or renewal in us; but it really makes us *just*. But how can we, children of Adam, be said *really and truly* to be righteous, in a sense distinct from the *imputation* of righteousness? This requires a word or two in explanation.

I observe, then, we become inwardly just or righteous in God's sight, upon our regeneration, in the same sense in which we are utterly reprobate and abominable by nature . . .

This, then, is the sense in which we are unrighteous or displeasing to God by nature; and in the same sense, on the other hand, we are actually righteous and pleasing to Him in a state of grace. Not that there is not abundant evil still remaining in us, but that justification coming to us in the power and "inspiration of the Spirit", so far dries up the fountain of bitterness and impurity, that we are forthwith released from God's wrath and damnation, and are enabled in our better deeds to please Him. It places us above the line in the same sense in which we were before below it. By nature we were not absolutely devilish, but had a curse within us which blighted and poisoned our most religious offerings; by grace we are gifted, not with perfection, but with a principle hallowing and sweetening all that we are, all that we do religiously, sustaining, hiding, and (in a sense) pleading for what remains of sin in us, "making intercession for us according to the will of God." As by nature sin was sovereign in us in spite of the remains of heaven, so now grace triumphs through righteousness in spite of the remains of sin.

4.

The justifying Word, then, conveys the Spirit, and the Spirit makes our works "pleasing" and "acceptable" to God, and acceptableness is righteousness; so that the justified are just, really just, in degree more or less, but really so far as this, – that their obedience has in it a gracious quality, which the obedience of unregenerate man had not. And here we see in what sense Christians are enabled to *fulfil* the Law, which they certainly are, in spite of modern divines, because St. Paul says so. He says expressly, that Christ came that "the *righteousness of the Law* might be *fulfilled in us*, who walk not after the flesh, but *after the Spirit*." He says, "*in us*," not only *externally to us*". And to make his statement still more certain, and to explain it, he adds, "The minding of the flesh," our natural state is "enmity against God; for *it* is *not subject to the Law of God*, neither indeed can be. So, then, they that are in the flesh, *cannot please God*." "*But ye*," he continues, *ye* are *not* in the flesh, but *in the Spirit*, if so be the Spirit of God dwell in you;" that is, Ye who have the Spirit *are* subject or obedient to the Law, and you *can* please God; in you the *righteousness* of the Law *is* fulfilled. Christians, then, fulfil the Law, in the sense that their obedience is pleasing to God; and "pleasing" is a very significant word when well weighed. Not that we are able to please Him simply and entirely (for "in many things we offend all;" and "if we say we have no sin, we deceive ourselves, and the truth is not in us'), but that the presence of the Spirit is a sanctifying virtue in our hearts, changing the character of our services, making our obedience new in kind, not merely fuller in degree, making it to live and grow, so that it is ever tending to perfect righteousness as its limit, and in this sense making it a satisfying obedience, rising up, answering to the *kind* of obedience which is due from **us**, – to the *nature* of the claims which our Creator, Redeemer, and Sanctifier has upon us.

And this, surely, is St. John's doctrine as well as St. Paul's, though brought forward by him in the way of warning, rather than encouragement. He declares solemnly in his general Epistle, that "He that *doeth righteousness* is righteous;" as if doing righteousness was that in which righteousness consists. And then, that there may be no mistake, he adds, "*even as He* is righteous." What very strong words! implying that our righteousness is a resemblance, and therefore a partial communication or infusion unto our hearts, of that super-human righteousness of Christ, which is our true justification. Again, presently, after saying that our possessing "love" gives us "boldness in the day of judgment," he adds, "because as *He is*, so are we in this world." That love, then, which He had in infinite perfection, and which, as being in him the fulfilling of the Law, is imputed to us for our justification, is also actually given us in measure, "shed abroad in our hearts by the Holy Ghost" as an earnest of what will be given without measure hereafter . . .

5.

3. There is yet a third sense which has naturally led to statements of our being justified by renewal of mind or by obedience, which I will briefly notice. We can do nothing good of ourselves; with God's grace we can do what is good. This is what I have been hitherto saying; but this is not all, – *with* His grace we are gifted not only with the capacity of being led into truth and holiness, but with the power of co-operating with Him. God's grace unfetters the will which by nature is in bondage, and thus restores to us the faculty of accepting or rejecting that grace itself. It enables us to obey, not as instruments merely, but as free agents, who, while they obey, are not constrained to obey, except that they choose to obey; and whose obedience is for that reason more pleasing to God, as proceeding more entirely from themselves, not by constraint," but "willingly" and "heartily." It does not follow from this, that there is any one good thought, word, or deed of ours, which proceeds from ourselves only, and which we present to God *as* ours; but the circumstance that in such acceptable offerings as we render to Him, there has been a co-operation on our part, has proved a reason, over and above those already mentioned, why justification has been said to consist in our services, not in God's imputation; those services forming a concurrent cause of that imputation would be void; as the grace of a sacrament is suspended when the recipient is not duly prepared. Hence, St. Peter urges us to "make our calling an election *sure;*" St. Paul, to " *work out* our own salvation with fear and trembling;" and St. John declares that "whatsoever we ask, we receive of Him, *because we keep His commandments*, and do those things *that are pleasing in His sight*."

For these reasons, then, though justification properly means an act external to us, it may be said to consist in evangelical obedience; first, because obedience is one with God's imputation by association; next, because that are one in fact, since He imputes in part within us the very thing which in its fulness

He imputes to us; and, lastly, because our concurrence in being justified is a necessary condition of His justifying.

6.

Further light will be thrown on what has been said by considering certain circumstances, which have tended still more to vary the language of theology on the subject.

1. Over and above the various senses attached to the word *justify*, the word *justification* varies in its grammatical force, and gives rise in consequence to no small apparent difference between parties who really agree together. I mean, it has two senses, an active and a passive; and though it is not always plain in which sense writers use it, yet on the whole, one class of divines use it actively, and another passively. The word may either mean *justifying*, or being *justified*; in the latter sense it is what man receives, in the former what God gives. This holds in the case of many other words; we speak, for instance, of a Bishop's confirmation and a child's confirmation; but the child is confirmed, the Bishop confirms. In like manner justification sometimes stands for an act on God's part, sometimes for an event or a state which comes upon man. Now it so happens that Protestant writers, for the most part, take the word to mean God's justifying us; whereas Roman writers seem to use it for our being or continuing justified. For instance, the Council of Trent defines it to be "not the mere remission of sins, but the *sanctification* and the *renovation* of the inner man by the voluntary acceptance of grace and gifts." And St. Thomas speaks of it as a *change, passage*, or *motion* of the soul from one state to another. Here the word is used in a passive sense. On the other hand, our own controversialists, of whatever cast of opinion, following the Protestants of the Continent, understand by justification the *act* on God's part, whether instantaneous or sustained, by which He justifies the sinner. Melanchthon used the word in both senses; – so do our Homilies, as the following passage will show. When, for instance, they declare that "justification is not the *office* of man, but *of God*," they adopt its active sense; yet, elsewhere, they speak of "this justification or *righteousness*, which we so receive of God's mercy and Christ's merits embraced by faith," as being "*taken, accepted*, and *allowed of God*

for our perfect and full justification," where the word denotes our *state* of acceptance, or that in which acceptance consists.

7.

Now this difference affects the language of the controversy in the following respect among others. Justification, I have said, is in its fulness a great appointment of God towards an individual, beginning in His Word spoken, and returning back to Him through him over whom it is spoken, laden with fruit. It is a Word having a work for its compliment. Such is the characteristic of God's doings, as manifested in Scripture, that what man does by working, God does by speaking. Man labours, and a work follows; God speaks, and a work follows. When man would raise a fabric, or achieve an object, he exerts himself by hands and strength, by thought and tongue, by ingenuity of contrivance, and multiplicity of resources, by a long and varied course of action, terminating in the work proposed. All the acts of the Divine Mind are of course an incomprehensible mystery to worms such as we are; but so much Scripture tells us, whatever it means, that God accomplished His work not by a process, but by "the word of His power." When man makes a thing, it is an effort on his part passing into a result; when God creates, it is by His fiat, by a word issuing in a work. He does not make, He says, "Let it be made." The Hebrew style accurately sets forth this token of Divine Majesty. The Psalmist says, not "He spake, and He did," but "He spake, and *it was done*." It was only a word on His part, but a substantial Word, with a work close upon it as its attendant shadow. In like manner its seems a true representation of the Scripture statements on the subject, to say, that He does not make us righteous, but He *calls* us righteous, and we are forthwith *made* righteous. But, if so, justification, which in its full meaning is the whole great appointment of God from beginning to end, may be viewed on its two sides, – active and passive, in its beginning and its completion, in what God does, and what man receives; and while in its passive sense man is made righteous, in its active, God calls or declares. That is, the word will rightly stand either for imputation or sanctification, according to the grammatical use of it. Thus divines, who in the main agree in what the great mercy of God is *as a whole*, may differ as to what should be called justification; for according as they view it as active or passive, God's giving or man's receiving, they will consider it God's accounting righteous or man's becoming righteous. One party, then, in the controversy consider it to be a mere acceptance, the other to be mainly renewal. The one consider it in its effects, the other in its primary idea. St. Austin, that is, *explains it*, and Protestants *define* it. The latter describe it theoretically, and the former practically. The Protestant sense is more close upon the word, the ancient use more close upon the thing. A man, for instance, who described bread as "the staff of life," need not disagree with another who defined it only chemically or logically, but he would be his inferior in philosophy and his superior in real knowledge.

If God's word and work be as closely united as action and result are in ourselves, surely as we use the word "work" in both senses, to mean both the doing and the thing done, so we may fairly speak of justification as if renewal, as well as mere acceptance. Serious men, dealing with realities, not with abstract conceptions, entering into the field of practical truth, not into the lists of controversy, not refuting an opponent, but teaching the poor, have ever found it impossible to confine justification to a mere declaring of that, which is also by the same grace effected. They have taken it to mean what they saw, felt, handled, as existing in fact in themselves and others. When they speak of justification, it is of a wonderful grace of God, not in the heavens, but nigh to them, even in their mouth and in their heart, which does not really exist at all unless brought into effect and manifested in renewal; and they let their idea of it run on into renewal as its just limit, there being no line of demarcation, no natural boundary in its course till it reached renewal. Till then, it was in their minds but a dead inchoate (as it is called); not complete, till it had sought and found, and assimilated to itself, the soul which was its subject. Unless it was thus ratified it passed away, as rays of light where there is nothing to reflect them, or a sound where there is a lack of air for it to vibrate upon.

Such is the contrast existing between the practical and the exact sense grammatically of the word *justification*; and it is remarkable that both the one and the other have been adopted by our standard writers, as has been already instanced from the Homilies. As controversialists they are Protestants, as pastoral teachers they are disciples of the Ancient Church. Who, for instance, is more clear than Bishop Bull in laying down that justification means *counting* righteous? yet who more strenuous in maintaining that it consists in *being* righteous? What he is, such are Hammond, Taylor, Wilson, and a multitude of others; who in this day are called inconsistent, as if holding two views, whereas those two views are rather proved to be one, because the same divines hold them.

8.

2. This difference, I say, in the grammatical sense attached to the word *justification*, even by those who mainly agree what it is to *justify*, is one additional cause of misunderstanding in the controversy. Another is the difference of aspect under which justification appears, according as this or that stage is taken in the whole period through which it continues ... Justification is imparted to us continually all through our lives. Now though it is substantially the same from the first to the last, yet the relative importance of its constituent parts varies with the length of its continuance. Its parts are differently developed as time goes on; and men may seem to differ as to what they understand by it, when they are but surveying it at a different date, and therefore in a different light. A very few words will show this.

The great benefit of justification, as all will allow, is this one thing, – the transference of the soul *from* the kingdom of darkness *into* the kingdom of Christ. We may, if we will, divide this event into parts, and say that it is *both* pardon *and* renovation, but such a division is merely mental, and does not affect the change itself, which is but one act. If a man is saved from drowning, you may, if you will, say he is *both* rescued from the water *and* brought into atmospheric air; this is a discrimination in words not in things. He cannot be brought out of the water which he cannot breathe, *except* by entering the air which he can breathe. In like manner, there is, in fact, no middle state between a state of *wrath* and a state of *holiness*. In justifying, God takes away what is past, *by* bringing in what is new. He snatches us out of the fire by lifting us in His everlasting hands, and enwrapping us in His own glory.

Such is justification as manifested in us continually all through our lives; but is it not plain that in its beginnings it will consist of scarcely anything but pardon? because all that we have hitherto done is sinful in its nature, and has to be pardoned; but to be renewed is a work of time, whereas as time goes on, and we become more holy, it will consist more in renewal, if not less in pardon, and at least there is no original sin, as when it was first granted, to be forgiven. It takes us then at Baptism out of original sin, and leads us all through life towards the purity of Angels. Naturally, then, when the word is used to denote the beginning of a justified state, it only, or chiefly, means acceptance; when the continuance, chiefly sanctification. Writers, then, of congenial sentiments, or the same writers on different occasions, will speak of it first as consisting in the remission of sins, with Calvin or Melanchthon, next, with the Roman Catholics, as consisting in renewal.

To conclude: all these things being considered it does seem like a want of faith not to hold, and a superstition not to profess, that in some sufficient sense Christ, as our righteousness, fulfils the Law *in us* as well as for us: that He justifies us, not only in word, but in power, bringing the ark with its mercy seat into the temple of our hearts; manifesting, setting up there His new kingdom, and the power and the glory of His Cross. (*Jfc.* 85–103)

LECTURE VI THE GIFT OF RIGHTEOUSNESS

When Faith is said to be the inward principle of acceptance, the question rises, what gives to faith its acceptableness? Why is faith more acceptable than unbelief? cannot we give any reason at all for it? or can we conceive unbelief being appointed as the token, instrument, state, or condition (it matters not here which word we use) of justification? Surely not; faith is acceptable as having a something in it, which unbelief has not; that something, what is it? It must be God's grace, if God's grace act *in* the soul, and not merely externally, as in the way of Providence. If it acts in us, and has a presence in us, when we have faith, then the having that grace or that presence, and not faith, which is its result, must be the real token, the real state of a justified man.

Again: if we say that justification consists in a supernatural quality imparted to the soul by God's grace, as Roman writers say, then, in like manner, the question arises, is this quality all that is in us of heaven? does not the grace itself, as an immediate divine power or presence, dwell in the hearts which are gifted with this renovating principle? It may or it may not; but if it does, then surely the possession of that grace is really our justification, and not renewal, or the principle of renewal.

And thus, by tracing farther back the lines of thought on which these apparently discordant views are placed, they are made to converge; they converge, that is, supposing there to be vouchsafed to us, an inward divine presence or grace, of which both faith and spiritual renovation are fruits. If such a presence be not vouchsafed, then certainly faith on the one hand, renovation on the other, are the ultimate elements to which our state of righteousness can be respectfully referred in the two theologies. But if it be vouchsafed, neither Protestant nor Romanist ought to refuse to admit, and in admitting to agree with each other, that the presence of the Holy Ghost shed abroad in our hearts, the Author both of faith and of renewal, this is really that which makes us righteous, and that our righteousness is the possession of that presence.

2. So much is gained from the views of the contending parties; next, I observe, in corroboration of the conjectured inference to which they have led us, that justification actually *is* ascribed in Scripture to the presence of the Holy Spirit, and that immediately, neither faith nor renewal intervening. For instance, St. Peter speaks of our being "elect through sanctification," or consecration "of the Spirit, *unto*," that is, in order to, "obedience and *sprinkling of the blood* of Jesus Christ," that is, the Holy Ghost is given us unto, or in order to, renovation and justification. Again: we are said by St. Peter to be "washed, sanctified, and *justified*, in the Name of the Lord Jesus, and by the *Spirit of our God*." The same Apostle says, "Ye have not received the spirit of bondage again to fear, but ye have received the *Spirit of adoption*, whereby we cry, Abba, Father." Again: "The law of the *Spirit of life* hath made me free from the law of sin and *death*." Again: Christ says, "It is the *Spirit* that giveth life,"[1] *life* being the peculiar attribute or state of "the *just*," as St. Paul, and the prophet Habakkuk before him, declare. These passages taken

together, to which others might be added from a former Lecture, show that justification is wrought by the power of the Spirit, or rather by His presence within us. And this being the real state of a justified man, faith and renewal are both present also, but as fruits of it; – faith, because it is said, "We through the Spirit wait for the hope of righteousness *by faith*;" and renewal, because in another passage, "*renewing* of the Holy Ghost" is made equivalent to "being justified by His grace."

Such is the doctrine of Scripture, which our Church plainly acknowledges, as is evident from the following passages in her formularies. In the 13th Article, for instance, which I have already cited, what in the title are called "works before justification," are in the body of the article called "works done before the *grace* of Christ, and the *inspiration of his Spirit*;" that is, justification may fitly be called an "inspiration of the Spirit of Christ," or a spiritual presence. Again in the Baptism Service, in which we pray God that the child to be baptized may "receive remission of his sins," which surely implies justification, "*by spiritual regeneration*," which is as surely the gift of the Spirit. The Homilies are in accordance; in which we are told, by way of comment upon St. Paul's words, "Who rose again for our *justification*," that Christ "rose again to send down *His Holy Spirit* to rule in our hearts, *to endow us with perfect righteousness*;" and that in this way David's words in the 85th Psalm are fulfilled, "Truth hath sprung out of the earth, and righteousness hath looked down from heaven," in that "from the earth is the Everlasting Verity, God's Son, risen to life, and *the true righteousness of the Holy Ghost*, looking out of heaven, and in most liberal largess dealt upon all the world." Justifying righteousness, then, consists in the coming and presence of the Holy Ghost within us.

5.

3. But further, Scripture expressly declares that righteousness is a definite inward gift while at the same time it teaches that it is not any mere quality of mind, whether faith or holiness; as I shall now proceed to show.

By a gift I mean a thing given. Now, there are four words used in Scripture to describe the special abiding gift of the Gospel, which either is, or at least includes justification, nay, which is expressly said to be justification, and they all signify a thing given, not a mere giving; – not a favour (as if we should say, "it is a great *mercy* we are saved," that is, an act, display, proof of mercy), but, as indeed the word gift means in English, a possession; as when you say a man has the gift of languages, it is a faculty in him; whereas you would not say that popularity was a gift, which is something external, but rather the talent of becoming popular, or influence, is the gift; nor would you say acceptance was a gift, but acceptableness.

For instance, in Rom. v. 17 we read, "They that receive the abundance of grace, and of the *gift* of righteousness, shall reign in life by One, Jesus Christ." The word *gift* here used certainly must mean a thing given; implying that the righteousness of justification, whatever it turns out to be, is a real and definite something in a person, implanted in him, like a talent or power, and not merely an act of the Divine Mind externally to him, as the forgiveness of sins may be.

But the preceding verses contain a still more convincing statement, on which indeed one might not be unwilling to rest the whole question. St. Paul says, "Not as the offence, so also is the *gift* ... the *gift* is of many offences *unto* justification." Here, observe, he distinctly declares that justification is the result of a *gift*. Now the word used for "gift" in the original, is the very word used elsewhere for extraordinary gifts, such as of healing, of tongues, and of miracles; that is, a definite power or virtue committed to us. Nowhere else does the word occur in Scripture without this meaning; indeed, it necessarily has it from its grammatical form. For instance, St. Paul says, he "longs to see" the Romans, "that he may impart unto them *some spiritual gift*;" again, that "the *gift* of God is eternal life." He enumerates as gifts, prophecy, ministry, teaching, exhortation, giving, ruling, and showing mercy. Speaking of continence, he says, "Every man has his proper *gift* from God." He says, there are "diversities of *gifts*, but the same Spirit." He exhorts Timothy "not to neglect the *gift* that was *in him*," but to stir up, to re-kindle, "the gift of God which was in him.; St. Peter too speaks of our "ministering" our "gifts as good stewards."[2]

If, then, by a gift is meant a certain faculty or talent, moral, intellectual, or other, justification is some such faculty. It is not a mere change of purpose or disposition in God towards us, or a liberty, privilege, or (as it may be called) citizenship, accorded to us, but a something lodged within us.

To the same effect is St. Paul's intimation, that righteousness is *ministered* or *dispensed* by the Spirit;[3] for surely the idea of dispensing, as well as the general office of the gracious Dispenser, lead us to conclude that the righteousness dispensed is a thing and not a name.

6.

To these passages we shall be right in adding a number of others which speak of the Gospel Gift, though not calling it justification. For they speak as if there was *one* great benefit given to us under the Gospel; and so great and essential is justification, that it must be either this or must be included in it.

For instance, our Lord says to the Samaritan woman, "If thou knewest the *gift* of God, and who it is that saith to thee, Give Me to drink, thou wouldst have asked of Him, and He would have given thee living water." The water was a real thing to be given and received.

Again: St. Peter says to the multitude, "Repent and be baptized every one of you in the name of Jesus Christ for the remission of sins, and ye shall receive the *gift* of the Holy Ghost;"[4] can we doubt that this is identical with the abundance of grace and of the *gift* of righteousness of which St. Paul speaks?

Again: the latter Apostle alludes elsewhere to "those who were once enlightened and have tasted of the heavenly *gift*."[5] Will it be said this means sanctification? then is sanctification represented as greater than justification; else why is not justification mentioned in a passage which is expressly speaking of a case in which a second justification is pronounced to be impossible? The contrast surely requires that justification should be mentioned; yet unless included in "the heavenly gift," it is passed over. We may add such a passage as the following: "The water that shall give him shall be *in him* a well of water springing up into everlasting life." And "He that believeth on Me, as the Scripture hath said, out of his belly shall flow rivers of living water." With such compare the words in the Prophet: "Then will I sprinkle clean water upon you, and ye shall be clean; from all your filthiness, and from all your idols, will I cleanse you."

(John 4: 14, 7: 38, Ezek. 36: 25) This means justifying purification, for renewal is not mentioned till the next verse: – "A new heart *also* will I give you, and a new spirit will I put within you." By water, I say, is typified justification, which accordingly is a something applied and communicated, not a change in the Divine Mind merely.

The same doctrine is implied in the Sacrament of Baptism, which certainly typifies the justifying gift. But if so, that gift is not an act merely on God's part, but a something, proximate and one, received and embraced by us.

Once more: whatever be the more precise meaning of the words, does not "the Bread of Life" which is to be "eaten" imply an *inward* gift, not merely an imputation? Yet who can deny that that gift carries with it the application of Christ's merits to the soul, that is, justification?

Moreover, the passages show that this gift, whatever it is, is not any moral excellence or grace, such as faith or a renewed state. For instance, to recur to the last instance, faith is but the *recipient* of the heavenly Bread, and therefore cannot be identical with it.

Thus an examination of the promises made to us in Scripture bears out the conclusion I had already drawn on other grounds, that the righteousness, by virtue of which we are called righteous, or are justified, – that in which justification results or consists, which conveys or applies the great gospel privileges, – that this justifying power though *within* us, as it must be, if it is to separate us from the world, yet is not properly speaking *of* us, not any quality or act of our minds, not faith, not renovation, not obedience, not anything cognizable by man, but a certain divine gift in which all these qualifications are included.

7.

4. Now to proceed a step further. I have said that, while justification is the application of Christ's *merits* to the individual, that application is the imparting of an inward gift; to this conclusion I have come chiefly by a consideration of the language of St. Paul. Now, turning to the gospel we shall find that such a gift is actually promised to us by our Lord; a gift which must of necessity be at once our justification and our sanctification, for

it is nothing short of the dwelling in us of God the Father and the Word Incarnate through the Holy Ghost. If this be so, we have found what we sought: *This* is to be justified, to receive the Divine Presence within us, and be made a Temple of the Holy Ghost.

God is everywhere as absolutely and entirely as if He were nowhere else; and it seems to be essential to the existence of every creature, rational and irrational, good and evil, in heaven and hell, that in some sense or other He should be present with it and be its life. Thus we are told concerning mankind, that "in Him we live, and move, and have our being." And He who lives in all creatures on earth in order to their mortal life, lives in Christians in a more divine way in order to their life immortal; and as we do not know how the creation exists and lives in Him as a Creator, and use words about it beyond our comprehension, so much more (were not comparison out of the question) are we ignorant of the mode or nature of that life of God in the soul, which is the wellspring of the Christian's sanctity, and the seed of everlasting happiness. If this notion of the literal indwelling of God within us, whether in the way of nature or of grace, be decried as a sort of mysticism, I ask in reply whether it is not a necessary truth that He is with and in us, if He is everywhere? And if He is everywhere and dwells in all, there is no antecedent objection against taking Scripture literally, no difficulty in supposing that the truth is as Scripture says, – that as He dwells in us in one mode in the way of nature, so He is in us in another in the way of grace;[6] that His infinite and incomprehensible Essence, which once existed by and in itself alone, and then at the creation so far communicated itself to His works as to sustain what He had brought into existence; and that according to the different measures of life necessary for their respective perfection, may in the Christian Church manifest itself in act and virtue in the hearts of Christians, as far surpassing what it is in unregenerate man, at its presence in man excels its presence in a brute or a vegetable. And those who without any antecedent difficulty still refuse to accept the literal interpretation of Scripture, should be reminded, that, since the promise expressly runs that we shall be made one *as* the Father and the Son are one, we are necessarily led either to think highly of the union of the Christian with God, or to disparage that of the Father and the Son; and that such schools of religion as maintain that the former is but figurative, will certainly be led at length to deny the real union of our Lord with His Father, and from avoiding mysticism, will fall into what is called Unitarianism.

With these thoughts let us turn to the review of the texts in which this wonderful promise is made to us.

Our Saviour, then, thus speaks of our communion with the Father and Son; – ''At that day ye shall know that I am in My Father, and ye in Me, and I in you.'' ''He that loveth Me, shall be loved of My Father; and I will love him, and will manifest Myself to him ... My Father will love him, and We will come unto him, and make Our abode with him.'' Again, He prays to His Father that His disciples ''all may be one, as Thou, Father, art in Me and I in Thee, that they also may be one in Us ... I in them and Thou in Me, that they may be made perfect in one.''[7]

Accordingly, St. John says, in his General Epistle, that ''if we love one another, God dwelleth in us, and His love is perfect in us ... He that dwelleth in love, dwelleth in God and God in him ... He that keepeth His commandments dwelleth in Him, and He in him.'' ''We are in Him that is true, even His Son Jesus Christ.'' ''Truly our fellowship is with the Father and with His Son Jesus Christ.''[8]

Further, this fellowship with the Son, and with the Father in the Son, is made through the Spirit. ''Hereby we know that we dwell in Him and He in us, because He hath given us of His Spirit.'' Hence St. Paul speaks of the ''Fellowship of the Holy Ghost;'' and that ''we are the temple of God, and that the Spirit of God dwelleth in us;'' and that ''our body is the temple of the Holy Ghost which is in us, which we have of God, and we are not on our own.''[9] Agreeably to which our Saviour's words, who, when He promised the indwelling of Father and Son in His followers, said also, ''I will pray the Father, and He shall give you another Comforter that He may abide with you for ever, even the Spirit of Truth ... He dwelleth in you, and shall be in you.'' And then He adds: ''I will not leave you comfortless, I will come to you.''

Moreover, this indwelling had been promised as the *distinguishing* grace of the Gospel. St. Paul declares both the prophecy and its fulfilment, when he says "Ye are the temple of the Living God; as God hath said, I will dwell in them, and walk in them; and I will be their God, and they shall be My people." Again, in our Saviour's words, "He that believeth on Me, as the Scripture hath said, out of his belly shall flow rivers of living water; but this spake He of the Spirit, which they that believe on Him should receive; for the Holy Ghost was not yet given, because that Jesus was not yet glorified."[10] Accordingly, in some of the texts just quoted, He who dwells in Christians is called "He that is *True*," and the Comforter is "the Spirit of *Truth*," grace and *truth* being the characteristic of the New Covenant.

And further let it be remarked that the Divine Presence vouchsafed to us, besides being that of the Holy Trinity, is specially said to be the presence of Christ; which would seem to imply that the "Word made flesh" is in some mysterious manner bestowed upon us. Thus He says: "If any man hear my voice, and open the door, I will come in to him, and will sup with him, and he with Me."[11] This allusion to a feast is conveyed in still more sacred and wonderful language in the following passage, to which I have already referred: "I am the living Bread which came down from heaven; if any man eat of this Bread, he shall live for ever, and the Bread that I will give is My flesh, which I will give for the life of the world." . . . "He that eateth My flesh and drinketh My blood, dwelleth in Me and I in him." Again: "We are members of His body, from His flesh and from His bones."[12]

8.

Such, as far as the words of Scripture go, is the great gift of the Gospel which Christ has purchased for all believers; – not many words are necessary to connect it with justification. I observe then –

1. First, this indwellng accurately answers, as I have already said, to what the righteousness which justifies has already been shown to consist in; an inward gift conveying the virtue of Christ's Atoning Blood. The coincidence of one and the other in such a definition proves their identity; if to justify be to impart a certain inward token of our personal redemption, and if the

presence of God within us is such a token, our justification must consist in God's coming to us and dwelling in us. It were the same to maintain, though knowing that God lives in us in the way of nature, that our mortal life does not consist in that dwelling, as to allow that He dwells in us Christians in a supernatural and singular way, yet deny that our new life of privilege and blessing depends on that Mystical Presence, – to belive that we are temples of God, yet are not justified thereby. On the other hand, since this great gift is the possession of all Christians from the time they become Christians, justification, whatever be the measures of increase which it admits, as certainly presupposes the gift, as the gift involves justification. In a word, what is it to have His presence within us, but to be His consecrated Temple? what to be His Temple, but to be set apart from a state of nature, from sin and Satan, guilt and peril? what to be thus set apart, but to be declared and treated as righteous? and what is this but to be justified?

2. Next, it may be remarked that whatever blessings in detail we ascribe to justification, are ascribed in Scripture to this sacred indwelling. For instance, is justification *remission of sins*? the Gift of the Spirit conveys it, as is evident from the Scripture doctrine about Baptism: "One Baptism for the remission of sins." Is justification *adoption* into the family of God? in like manner the Spirit is expressly called the Spirit of adoption, "the Spirit whereby we cry, Abba, Father." Is justification *reconciliation* with God? St. Paul says, "Jesus Christ is in you, unless ye be reprobates." Is justification *life*? the same Apostle says, "Christ liveth in me." Is justification given to *faith*? it is his prayer "That *Christ* may dwell in" Christian "hearts by faith." Does justification lead to holy *obedience*? Our Lord assures us that he that abideth in Him and He in him, the same bringeth forth much fruit." Is it through justification that we rejoice in *hope of the glory* of God? In like manner "Christ in us" is said to be "the hope of glory." Christ then is our Righteousness by dwelling in us by the Spirit: He justifies us by entering into us, He continues to justify us by remaining in us. *This* is really and truly our justification, not faith, not holiness, not (much less) a mere imputation; but through God's mercy, the very Presence of Christ.

3. It appears, moreover, that this inward presence is some-

times described as God's presence or indwelling; sometimes that of Father and Son; sometimes of the Holy Ghost; sometimes of Christ the Incarnate Mediator; sometimes "of God through the Spirit;" sometimes of Christ, of His Body and Blood, of His Body in "flesh and bones," and this through the Spirit. Different degrees or characteristics of the gift are perhaps denoted by these various terms, though to discriminate them is far beyond our powers. What is common to all Christians, as distinguished from good men under other Dispensations, is that, however the latter were justified in God's inscrutable resources, Christians are justified by the communication of an inward, most sacred, and most mysterious gift. From the very time of Baptism they are temples of the Holy Ghost. This, I say, is what is common to all; yet it is certain too, that over and above what all have, a still further communication of God's glory is promised to the obedient, and that so considerable as sometimes to be spoken of as the special communication, as if there were none previously. "He that loveth Me," says our Lord, "shall be loved of My Father, and I will love him, and will manifest Myself to him;" and "Blessed are the pure in heart, for they shall see God.'

9.

4. Further, we here see in what sense it is true that justification admits of increase, and in what not. The fact that we are the temple of God does not admit of more or less; such words have no meaning when applied to it. Righteousness then, considered as the state of being God's temple, cannot be increased; but, considered as the divine glory which that state implies, it can be increased, as the pillar of the cloud which guided the Israelites could become more or less bright. Justification being acceptableness with God, all beings who are justified differ from all who are not, in their very condition, in a certain property, which the one body has and the other has not. In this sense, indeed, it is as absurd to speak of our being more justified, as of life, or colour, or any other abstract idea increasing. But when we compare the various orders of just and acceptable beings with one another, we see that though they all are in God's favour, some may be more "pleasant," "acceptable," "righteous," than others, and may have more of the light of God's countenance

shed on them; as a glorified Saint is more acceptable than one still in the flesh. In this sense then justification does admit of increase and of degrees; and whether we say justification depends on faith or on obedience, in the same degree faith or obedience grows, so does justification. And again (to allude to a point not yet touched on), if justification is conveyed peculiarly through the Sacraments, then as Holy Communion conveys a more awful presence of God than Holy Baptism, so must it be the instrument of a higher justification. On the other hand, those who are declining in their obedience, as they are quenching the light within them, so are they diminishing their justification.

5. And this view of the subject enables us to understand how infants may be regenerate, though they give no indication of being so. For as God dwelt secretly in His material Temple, ever hallowing it, yet only in season giving sensible evidences of what was there, so may He be present with their souls, rescuing them from Satan, and imparting new powers, manifesting new objects, and suggesting new thoughts and desires, without their being conscious, or others witnesses, of His work.

6. Moreover, if justification be the inward application of the Atonement, we are furnished at once with a sufficient definition of a Sacrament for the use of our Church. The Roman Catholic Church considers that there are seven; we do not strictly determine the number. We define the word generally to be an "outward sign of an inward grace." without saying to how many ordinances this applies. However, what we do determine is, that Christ has ordained two Special Sacraments, as *generally necessary to salvation*. This, then, is the characteristic mark of those two, separating them from all other whatever; and what is this but saying in other words that they are the only *justifying* rites, or instruments of communicating the Atonement, which *is* the one thing necessary to us? Ordination, for instance, gives *power* yet without making the soul *acceptable* to God; Confirmation gives light and strength, yet it is the mere completion of Baptism; and Absolution may be viewed as a negative ordinance removing the barrier which sin has raised between us and that grace which by inheritance is ours. But the two Sacraments "of the gospel," as they may be emphatically styled, are the instruments of inward life, according to our Lord's declaration, that Baptism is a new *birth*, and that in the Eucharist we eat the *living* Bread.

10.

7. Lastly, We now may see what the connection really is between justification and renewal. They are both included in that one great gift of God, the indwelling of Christ in the Christian soul. That indwelling is *ipso facto* our justification and sanctification, as its necessary results. It is the Divine Presence that justifies us, not faith, as say the Protestant schools, not renewal, as say the Roman. The word justification is the substantive living Word of God, entering the soul, illuminating and cleansing it, as fire brightens and purifies material substances. He who justifies also sanctifies, because it is He. The first blessing runs into the second as its necessary limit; and the second being rejected, carries away with the first. And the one cannot be separated from the other except in idea, unless the sun's rays can be separated from the sun, or the power of the purifying from fire or water. I shall resume the subject in the next Lecture. (*Jfc.* 136–54)

LECTURE VII THE CHARACTERISTICS OF THE GIFT OF RIGHTEOUSNESS

... It is the fashion of the day to sever these two from one another, which God has joined, the seal and the impression, justification and renewal. You hear men speak of glorying in the Cross of Christ, who are utter strangers to the notion of the Cross as actually applied to them in water and blood, in holiness and mortification. They think the Cross can be theirs *without* being applied, – without its coming near them, – while they keep at a distance from it, and only gaze at it. They think individuals are justified immediately by the great Atonement, – justified by Christ's death and not, as St. Paul says, by means of His Resurrection, – justified by what they consider *looking* at His death. Because the Brazen Serpent in the wilderness healed by being looked at, they consider that Christ's Sacrifice saves by the mind's contemplating it. This is what they call casting themselves upon Christ, – coming before Him simply and without self-trust, and being saved by faith. Surely we ought so to *come* to Christ; surely we must believe; surely we must look; but the question is, in what form and manner He *gives* Himself to us; and it will be found that, when he enters into

us, glorious as He is Himself, pain and self-denial are His attendants. Gazing on the Brazen Serpent did not heal; but God's invisible communication of the gift of health to those who gazed.
So also justification is wholly the work of God; it comes from
God to us; it is a power exerted on our souls by Him, as the healing
of the Israelites was a power exerted on their bodies. The gift
must be brought *near* to us; it is not like the Brazen Serpent, a
mere external, material, local sign; it is a spiritual gift, and, as
being such, admits of being applied to us individually. Christ's
Cross does not justify by being looked at, but by being applied;
not by a merely beheld by faith, but by being actually set up within
us, and that not by our act, but by God's invisible grace. Men
sit, and gaze, and speak of the great Atonement, and think this
is appropriating it; not more truly than kneeling to the material
cross itself is appropriating it. Men say that faith is an apprehending and applying; faith cannot really apply the Atonement; man
cannot make the Saviour of the world his own; the Cross must
be brought home to us, not in word, but in power, and this is
the work of the Spirit. This is justification; but when imparted
to the soul, it draws blood, it heals, it purifies, it glorifies . . .

As then the Cross, in which St. Paul glorified, was not the
material cross on which Christ suffered, – so neither is it simply
the Sacrifice on the cross, but it is the Sacrifice coming in power
to him who has faith in it, and converting body and soul into
a sacrifice. It is the Cross, realised, present, living in him, sealing
him, separating him from the world, sanctifying him, afflicting
him. Thus the great Apostle clasped it to his heart, though it
pierced it through like a sword; held it fast in his hands, though
it cut them; reared it aloft, preached it, exulted in it. And thus
we in our turn are allowed to hold it, commemorating and renewing individually, by the ministry of the Holy Ghost, the death
and resurrection of our Lord. (*Jfc.* 174–5, 177–8)

LECTURE XI THE NATURE OF JUSTIFYING FAITH

Why do they say it only works *by* love and results *in* obedience,
if they maintain that it *is* trust? why must trust be part of its
essence, yet love and obedience external to it? why must trust
be any more than its necessary exhibition, if obedience is to be
considered as nothing more? why should it cease to be justifying

faith if called love or obedience, yet not if it be called trust? Yet such is the way of viewing it, to which multitudes have accustomed themselves. They escape from the strict definition, then pitch their tent in the very middle of their route, dread to go forward, and fire up at the very notion of going back, and have recourse to cries of alarm, protestations, and threats, if any the most gentle persuasion or most intelligible reasonings be used to turn them one way or the other.

This then is the false position, if I may so speak, which the schools in question have taken up. Their idea of faith is a mere theory, neither true in philosophy nor in fact; and hence it follows that their whole theology is shadowy and unreal. I do not say that there is no such thing as a trusting in Christ's mercy for salvation, and a comfort resulting from it. This would be resisting what we may witness daily, and what, under circumstances, it is our duty to exercise. Bad and good feel it. What *is* so unreal, is to say that it is necessarily a holy feeling, that it can be felt by none but the earnest, that a mere trust, without anything else, without obedience, love, self-denial, consistent conduct, conscientiousness, that this mere trust in Christ's mercy, existing in a mind which has as yet no other religious feeling, will necessarily renew the soul and leads to good works. This is the mere baseless and extravagant theory I speak of. Men may be conscious they trust; they may be conscious they gain comfort from trusting; they cannot be conscious that such a trust is of a practical character; they cannot be conscious that it changes the heart. The event alone determines this. That it raises present emotions they may be conscious; that it is such as permanently to impress their inner man they cannot know, except they be prophets; for that is a thing future. It may, or it may not; and it is pernicious to say it must. However, to enter into its practical results is beside my present subject.

Viewed in its theological aspect, in which it is now before us, the Protestant account will be found to give a character of vagueness and equivocation to the whole system built upon it. What indeed can be expected but arbitrary distinctions and unreal subtleties in the conformation of a theology, which has a flaw in its leading principle, which starts with maintaining that faith is, what nothing ever was or can be, an abstraction in actual existence, – an object or thing which contains in it in fact only what the name contains, – an aspect, side, quality, and property standing by itself, – and, as if this were not enough, which lays down, when we go on to inquire *what* faith is, that it is mere *trust*, and yet necessarily *spiritual*? Hence, not unnaturally, it is a source of never-ending disputes between persons who seem to agree together, yet go away and act differently, and still wonder why they differ. I describe faith, and another describes it, and perhaps we even use the same terms yet agree in nothing else. Why is this? because I aim at contemplating things as they are, and must be, in their embodied form; and he, on the contrary, has a notion that he may seize a certain portion of the idea conveyed by the word faith, more than assent, less than obedience, and may give it a substantive existence, and carry it on to results such as he pleases to assign to it.

The one view then differs from the other as the likeness of a man differs from the original. The picture resembles him but it is not he. It is not a reality, it is all surface. It has no depth, no substance; touch it, and you will find it is not what it pretends to be. When I assign an office to faith, I am not speaking of an abstraction or creation of the mind, but of something existing. I wish to deal with things, not with words. I do not look to be put off with a name or a shadow. I would treat of faith as it is actually found in the soul; and I say it is as little an isolated grace, as a man is a picture. It has a depth, a breadth, and a thickness; it has an inward life which is something over and above itself; it has a heart, and blood, and pulses, and nerves, though not upon the surface. All these indeed are not *spoken* of, when we make mention of faith; nor are they painted on the canvas; but they are implied in the word, because they exist in the thing. What has been observed above, of the distinction between the meaning of the word and of the thing, *righteousness*, applies here. Love and fear, and heavenly-mindedness, and obedience, and firmness, and zeal, and humility, are as certainly one with justifying faith, considered as a thing existing, as bones, muscles, and vital organs, are necessary to that outward frame of man which meets the eye, though they do not meet it. Love and fear and obedience are not really posterior to justifying faith for even a moment of time, unless bones or muscles are formed after the countenance and complexion. It is unmeaning to speak of living faith, as being independent of newness of mind, as of solidity as divisible from body, or tallness from stature, or colour from the landscape. As well might it be said that an arm or a foot can exist out of the body, and that man is born with only certain portions, head and heart, and that the rest accrues after-wards, as that faith comes first and gives birth to other graces. This illustration holds with only one limitation; that faith, though connatural with other graces, has a power of reacting upon them, by placing more constraining objects before them. as motives to their more vigorous exercise.

This then is what is meant by the doctrine that faith is not justifying unless formed or animated by love; isolated or bare faith being impossible in a Christian, or in any one else, and existing only in our conceptions, and not being a grace or virtue when so conceived. That such is the doctrine of Scripture has been variously shown in the discussion of the subjects which have come before us. Here I will but cite two celebrated passages from St. James and St. Paul. St. Paul says, "Though I have *all faith*, so that I could remove mountains, and have *not love*, I am nothing." And St. James, after warning his brethren against "holding the *faith*" of Christ "in respect of persons," that is, in an *unloving* spirit, as the context shows, proceeds to say, that it is "*perfected* by works," and that "without works" it is "dead," as a body without the soul. That is, as the presence of the soul changes the nature of the dust of the earth, and makes it flesh and blood, giving it a life which otherwise it could not have, so love is the modelling and harmonizing principle on which justifying faith depends, and in which it exists and acts.

I conclude, then, by stating what *is*, as I conceive, the special fruit or work of faith under the Gospel, and its influence upon the Christian; in doing which I shall assume, what this is not the place to prove, that it is an original means of knowledge, not resolving into sense, or the faculty of reasoning, confirmed indeed by experience, as they are, but founded in a supernatur-ally implanted instinct; an instinct developed by religious obedience, and leading the mind to the world of Christ and of His Apostles as its refuge.

The Gospel, then, as contrasted with all religious systems which have gone before and come after, even those in which God has spoken, is specially the system of faith and "the law of faith," and its obedience is the "obedience of faith," and justification is "by faith," and it is a "power of God unto salvation to every one that believeth." For at the time of its first preaching the Jews went by sight and the Gentiles by reason; both might believe, but on a belief resolvable into sight or reason, – neither went simply by faith. The Greeks sought after "wisdom," some original and recondite philosophy, which might serve as an "evidence" or ground of proof for "things not seen." The Jews, on the other hand, "required a sign," some sensible display of God's power, a thing of sight and touch, which might be "the substance," the earnest and security "of things hoped for." They wanted some carnal and immediate good, as "the praise of men;" for this they did their alms, fasted and prayed, not looking on to witnesses unseen, but for an earthly reward; or, if they wrought for God, it was in a a grudging calculating way, as if to make their services go as far as possible, resting in them as ends, and suspicious of God as of a hard or unjust Master. Such was the state of the world, when it pleased Almighty God, in furtherance of His plan of mercy, to throw men's minds upon the next world, without any other direct medium of evidence than the word of man claiming to be His; to change the face of the world by what the world called "the foolishness of preaching" and the unreasoning zeal and obstinacy of faith, using a principle in truth's behalf which in the world's evil history has ever been the spring of great events and strange achievements. Faith, which in the natural man has manifested itself in the fearful energy of superstition and fanaticism, is in the Gospel grafted on the love of God, and made to mould the heart of man into His image.

The Apostles then proceeded thus: – they did not rest their cause on argument; they did not rely on eloquence, wisdom, or reputation; nay, nor did they make miracles necessary to the enforcement of their claims. They did not resolve faith into sight or reason; they contrasted it with both, and bade their hearers believe, sometimes in spite, sometimes in default, sometimes in aid, of sight and reason. They exhorted them to make trial of the Gospel, since they would find their account in so doing. And of their hearers "some believed the things which were spoken, some believed not." Those believed whose hearts were "opened," who were "ordained to eternal life;" those did not whose hearts were hardened. This was the awful exhibition of which the Apostles and their fellow workers were witnesses; for faith, as a principle of knowledge, cannot be exactly analyzed or made intelligible to man, but is the secret, inexplicable, spontaneous movement of the mind (however arising) towards the external word, – a movement not to the exclusion of sight and reason, for the miracles appeal to both, nor of experience, for all who venture for Christ receive daily returns of good in confirmation of their choice, but independent of sight or reason before, or of experience after. The apostles appealed to men's hearts, and, according to their hearts, so they answered them. They appealed to their secret belief in a superintending providence, to their hopes and fears thence resulting; and they professed to reveal to them the nature, personality, attributes, will, and works of Him "whom their hearers ignorantly worshipped." They came as commissioned from Him, and declared that mankind was a guilty and outcast race, – that sin was a misery, – that the world was a snare, – that life was a shadow, – that God was everlasting, – that His Law was holy and true, and its sanctions certain and terrible; – that He also was all-merciful, – that He had appointed a Mediator between Him and them, who had removed all obstacles, and was desirous to restore them, and that He had sent themselves to explain how. They said that that Mediator had come and gone; but had left behind Him what was to be His representative till the end of all things, His mystical Body, the Church, in joining which lay the salvation of the world. So they preached, and so they prevailed; using indeed persuasives of every kind as they were given them, but resting at bottom on a principle higher than the senses or the reason. They used many arguments, but as outward forms of something beyond argument. Thus they appealed to the miracles they wrought, as sufficient signs of their power, and assuredly divine, in spite of those which other systems could show or pretended. They expostulated with the better sort on the ground of their instinctive longings and dim visions of something greater than the world. They awed and overcame the passionate by means of what remained of heaven in them, and of the involuntary homage which such men pay to the more realised tokens of heaven in others. They asked the more generous-minded whether it was not worth while to risk something on the chance of augmenting and perfecting those precious elements of good which their hearts still held; and they could not hide what they cared not to "glory in," their own disinterested sufferings, their high deeds, and their sanctity of life. They won over the affectionate and gentle by the beauty of holiness, and the embodied mercies of Christ as seen in the ministrations and ordinances of His Church. Thus they spread their nets for disciples, and caught thousands at a cast; thus they roused and inflamed their hearers into enthusiasm, till "the Kingdom of Heaven suffered violence, and the violent took it by force." And when these has entered it, many of them, doubtless, would wax cold in love, and fall away; for many had entered only on impulse; many, with Simon Magus, on wonder or curiosity; many from a mere argumentative belief, which leads as readily into hearsay as into the Truth. But still, those who had the seed of God within them, would become neither offences in the Church, nor apostates, nor heretics; but would find day by day, as love increased, increasing experience that what they had ventured boldly amid conflicting evidence, of sight against sight, and reason against reason, with many things against it, and more things for it, they had ventured well. The examples of meekness, cheerfulness, contentment, silent endurance, private self-denial, fortitude, brotherly love, perseverance in well-doing, which would from time to time meet them in their new Kingdom, – the sublimity and harmony of the Church's doctrine, – the touching and subduing beauty of her services and appointments, – their consciousness of her virtue, divinely imparted, upon themselves, in subduing, purifying, changing them, – the bountifulness of her alms-giving, – her power, weak as she was and despised, over the statesmen and philosophers of the world, – her consistent and steady aggression upon it, moving forward in spite of it on all sides at once, like the wheels in the Prophet's vision, and this contrast with the ephemeral and variable outbreaks of sectarianism, – the unanimity and intimacy existing between her widely-separated branches, – the mutual sympathy and correspondence of men of hostile nations and foreign languages, – the simplicity of her ascetics, the gravity of her Bishops, the awful glory shed around her Martyrs, and the mysterious and recurring traces of miraculous agency here and there, once and again, according as the Spirit willed, – these and the like persuasives acted on them day by day, turning the whisper of their hearts into an habitual conviction, and establishing in the reason what had begun in the will. And thus has the Church been upheld ever since by an appeal to the People, – to the necessities of human nature, the anxieties of conscience, and the instincts of purity; forcing upon Kings a sufferance or protection which they fain would dispense with, and upon Philosophy a grudging submission and a reserved and limited recognition.

Such was the triumph of Faith, spreading like a leaven through the thoughts, words, and works of men, till the whole was leavened. It did not affect the substance of religion; it left unaltered both its external developments and its inward character; but it gave strength and direction to its lineaments. The sacrifice of prayer and praise, and the service of an obedient heart and life, remained as essential as before; but it has infused a principle of growth. It has converted grovelling essays into high aspirings, – partial glimpses into calm contemplation, – niggard payments into generous self-devotion. It enjoyed the law of love for retaliation; it put pain above enjoyment; it supplanted polygamy by the celibate; it honoured poverty before affluence, the communion of Saints before the civil power, the next world before this. It made the Christians independent of all men and all things, except of Christ; and provided for a deeper humility, while it supplied an overflow of peace and joy. (*Jfc.* 272–3)

LECTURE XIII ON PREACHING THE GOSPEL

Moreover, it may fairly be questioned whether religion does not necessarily imply the belief in such sensible tokens of God's favour, as the Sacraments are accounted by the Church. Religion is of a personal nature, and implies the acknowledgment of a particular Providence, of a God speaking not merely to the world at large, but to this person or that, to me and not to another. The Sacred Volume is a common possession, and speaks to one man as much and as little as to his neighbour. Our nature requires something special; and if we refuse what has been actually given, we shall be sure to adopt what has not been given. We shall set up calves at Dan and Bethal, if we give up the true Temple and the Apostle Ministry. This we see fulfilled before our eyes in many ways; those who will not receive Baptism as the token of God's election, have recourse to certain supposed experiences of it in their hearts. This is the idolatry of a refined age, in which the superstitions of barbarous times displease, in consequence of their grossness. Men congratulate themselves on their emancipation from forms and their enlightened worship, when they are but in the straight course to a worse captivity, and are exchanging dependence on the creature for dependence on self.

And thus we are led to the consideration of the opposite side of the question before us, that is, whether at this day it is not rather the accusing party itself than the Church that is accused, to which the charge of Judaism properly attaches. At first sight a suggestion of this kind will look like a refinement, or as only a sharp retort in controversy, and not to be seriously dwelt on. But I wish it dwelt on most seriously, and if rejected, rejected after being dwelt on. I observe, then, that what the Jews felt concerning their Law, is exactly what many upholders of the tenet of "faith only," feel concerning what they consider faith; that they substitute faith for Christ; that they so regard it, that instead of being the way to Him, it is in the way; that they make it a something to rest in; nay, that they alter the meaning of the word, as the Jews altered the meaning of the word Law; in short, that, under the pretence of light and liberty, they have brought into the Gospel the narrow, minute, technical, nay, I will say carnal and hollow system of the Pharisees. Let me explain what I mean.

I would say this then: – that a system of doctrine has risen up during the last three centuries, in which faith or spiritual-mindedness is contemplated and rested on as the end of religion instead of Christ. I do not mean to day that Christ is not mentioned as the Author of all good, but that stress is laid rather on the believing than on the Object of belief, on the comfort and persuasiveness of the doctrine rather than on the doctrine itself. And in this way religion is made to consist in contemplating ourselves instead of Christ; not simply in looking to Christ, but in ascertaining that we look to Christ, not in His Divinity and Atonement, but in our conversion and our faith in those truths.

Of course nothing is more natural or suitable than for a Christian to describe and dwell on the difference between one who believes and one who does not believe. The fault here spoken of is the giving to our "experiences" a more prominent place in our thoughts than to the nature, attributes, and work of Him from whom they profess to come, – the insisting on them as a special point for the consideration of all who desire to be recognized as converted and elect. When men are to be exhorted to newness of life, the true Object to be put before them, as I conceive, is "Jesus Christ, the same yesterday, to-day, and for ever;" the true Gospel preaching is to enlarge, as they can bear it, on the Person, natures, attributes, offices, and work of Him who once regenerated them, and is now ready to pardon; to dwell upon His recorded words and deeds on earth; to declare reverently and adoringly His mysterious greatness as the Only-begotten Son, One with the Father, yet distinct from Him; of Him, yet not apart from Him; eternal, yet begotten, a Son, yet as if a servant; and to combine and to contrast His attributes and relations to us as God and man, as our Mediator, Saviour, Sanctifier, and Judge. The true preaching of the Gospel is to preach Christ. But the fashion of the day has been, instead of this, to preach conversion; to attempt to convert by insisting on conversion; to exhort men to undergo a change; to tell them to be sure they look at Christ, instead of simply holding up Christ to them; to tell them to have faith, rather than supply its Object; to lead them to stir up and work up their minds, instead of impressing on them the thought of Him who can savingly work in them; to bid them take care that their faith is justifying, not dead, formal, self-righteous, and merely moral, whereas the image of Christ fully delineated of itself destroys deadness, formality, and self-righteousness; to rely on words, vehemence, eloquence, and the like, rather than to aim at conveying the one great evangelical idea whether in words or not. And thus faith and (what is called) spiritual-mindedness are dwelt on as *ends*, and obstruct the view of Christ, just as the Law was perverted by the Jews ... Poor miserable captives, to whom such doctrine is preached as the Gospel! What! is *this* the liberty wherewith Christ has made us free, and wherein we stand, the home of our own thoughts, the prison of our own sensations, the province of self, a monotonous confession of what we are by nature, not what Christ is in us, and a resting at best not on His love towards us, but in our faith towards Him! This is nothing but a specious idolatry; a man thus minded does not simply think of God when he prays to Him, but is observing whether he feels properly or not; does not believe and obey, but considers it enough to be a conscious that he is what he calls warm and spiritual; does not contemplate the grace of the Blessed Eucharist; the Body and Blood of His Saviour Christ, except – O shameful and fearful error! – except as a quality of his own mind. . .

And now if we proceed to inquire where the real difference lies between this view, which our Church does hold, and that which pretends to be hers, it will be found to be this, which it is worth while insisting on; – that the Church considers the doctrine of justification by faith only to be a *principle*, and the religion of the day takes it as *a rule of conduct*. Principles are great truths or laws which embody in them the character of a system, enable us to estimate it, and indirectly guide us in practice. For instance, "all is of grace," is a great principle of the Gospel. So are the following: – "we conquer by suffering," – "the saints of God are hidden," – "obedience is of the spirit not of the letter," – "the blood of the Martyrs is the seed of the Church," – "to gain happiness we must not seek it." It is a characteristic of such statements of principles to be short, pointed, strong, and often somewhat paradoxical in appearance. Such, for example, is the political maxim, which has a clear and true meaning, but in form is startling, "The King can do no wrong;" or in physics, that "nature abhors a vacuum." They are laws or exhibitions of general truths; and are not directly practical. I mean, a man will be sure to get into difficulty or error if he attempts to use them as guides in matters of conduct and duty. They mean nothing, or something wide of the truth, taken as literal directions. They are like the Sun in the heavens, too high, too distant, to light your lamp by, though indirectly and secondarily useful even for that.

Proverbs, again, are of the same nature; we recognize their truth in the course of life, but we do not walk by them. They come after us, not go before. They confirm, they do not explore for us. They are reflections upon human conduct, not guides for it. Thus "Honesty is the best policy," suggests the natural reward of honesty, not the way to be honest.

Such are principles: – rules, on the other hand, are adapted for immediate practise, they aim at utility, and are directed and moulded according to the end proposed, not by correctness or reasoning or analysis. We follow blindly; content, so that we arrive where we propose, whether we know or not. We take them literally and without reasoning, and act upon them. Thus, if I ask my way, I shall be told, perhaps, to go first right forward, then to take a bend, then to watch for a hill or a river. There is no room for philosophy here; it were out of place; all is practical.

Now justification by faith only is a principle, not a rule of conduct; and the popular mistake is to view it as a rule. This is when men go wrong. They think that the long and the short of religion is to have faith; that is the whole, faith independent of every other duty; a something which can exist in the mind by itself, and from which all other holy exercises follow; – faith, and then forthwith they will be justified; which will as surely mislead them as the great principle that "the Saints are hidden" would mislead such as took it for a rule, and thought by hiding themselves from the eye of the world to become Saints. They who *are* justified, certainly are justified by *faith*; but having faith is not more truly the *way* to be justified, than being hidden is the way to be a Saint.

The doctrine of justifying faith is a summary of the whole process of salvation from first to last; a sort of philosophical analysis of the Gospel, a contemplation of it as a whole, rather than a practical direction. If it must be taken as a practical direction, and in a certain sense it may, then we must word it, not, "justification through faith," but, "justification by Christ." Thus, interpreted, the rule it gives is, " *go* to Christ;" but taken in the letter, it seems to say merely, "Get *faith*; become spiritual; see that you are not mere moralists, mere formalists, see that you feel. If you do not feel, Christ will profit you nothing: you must have a spiritual taste; you must see yourself to be a sinner; you must accept, apprehend, appropriate the gift; you must understand and acknowledge that Christ is the 'pearl of great price;' you must be conscious of a change wrought in you, for the most part going through the successive stages of darkness, trouble, error, light, and comfort." Thus the poor and sorrowful soul, instead of being led at once to the source of all good, is taught to make much of the conflict of truth and falsehood within itself as the pledge of God's love, and to picture to itself faith, as a sort of passive quality which sits amid the ruins of human nature, and keeps up what may be called a silent protest, or indulges a pensive meditation over its misery. And, indeed, faith thus regarded cannot do more; for while it acts, not to lead the soul to Christ, but to detain it from Him, how can the soul but remain a prisoner, in that legal or natural state described by the Apostle in the seventh of Romans? – a passage of Scripture which the upholders of this doctrine confess, nay boast that they feel to be peculiarly their own. Such is their first error, and a second obviously follows. True faith is what may be called colourless, like air or water; it is but the medium through which the soul sees Christ; and the soul as little really rests upon it and contemplates it, as the eye can see the air. When, then, men are bent on holding it (as it were) in their hands, curiously inspecting, analysing, and so aiming at it, they are obliged to colour and thicken it, that it may be seen and touched. That is, they substitute for it something or other, a feeling, notion, sentiment, conviction, or act of reason, which they may hang over, and doat upon. They rather aim at experiences (as they are called) within them, than at Him that is without them. They are led to enlarge upon the signs of conversion, the variations of their feelings, their aspirations and longings, and to tell all this to others; – to tell others how they fear, and hope, and sin, and rejoice, and renounce themselves, and rest in Christ only; how conscious they are that their best deeds are but "filthy rags," and all is of grace, till in fact they have little time left them to guard against what they are condemning, and to exercise what they think they are so full of. Now men in a battle are brief-spoken; they realize their situation and are intent upon it. And men who are acted upon by news good or bad, or sights beautiful or fearful, admire, rejoice, weep, or are pained, but are moved spontaneously, not with a direct consciousness of their emotion. Men of elevated minds are not their own historians and panegyrists. So it is with faith and other Christian graces. Bystanders see our minds; but our minds, if healthy, see but the objects which possess them. As God's grace elicits our faith, so His holiness stirs our fear, and His glory kindles our love. Others may say of us "here is faith," and "there is conscientiousness," and "there is love;" but we can only say, "this is God's grace," and "that is His holiness," and "that is His glory."

And this being the difference between true faith and self-contemplation, no wonder that where the thought of self obscures the thought of God, prayer and praise languish, and only preaching flourishes. Divine worship is simply contemplating our Maker, Redeemer, Sanctifier, and Judge; but discoursing, conversing, making speeches, arguing, reading, and writing about religion, tend to make us forget Him in ourselves. The Ancients worshipped; they went out of their own minds into the Infinite Temple which was around them. They saw Christ in the Gospel, in the Creed, in the Sacraments and other Rites; in the visible structure and ornaments of His House, in the Altar, and in the Cross; and, not content with giving the service of their eyes, they gave Him their voices, their bodies, and their time, gave up their rest by night and their leisure by day, all that could evidence the offering of their hearts to Him. Theirs was not a service once a week, or some one day, now and then, painfully, as if ambitiously and lavishly given to thanksgiving or humiliation; not some extraordinary address to the throne of grace, offered by one for many, when friends met, with much point and impressiveness, and as much like an exhortation, and as little like a prayer, as might be; but every day and every portion of the day was begun and sanctified with devotion. Consider those Seven Services of the Holy Church Catholic in her best ages, which, without encroaching upon her children's duties towards this world, secured them in their duties to the world unseen. Unwavering, unflagging, not argued by fits and starts, not heralding forth their feelings, but resolutely, simply, perseveringly, day after day, Sunday and week-day, fast-day and festival, week by week, season by season, year by year, in youth and in age, through a life, thirty years, forty years, fifty years, in prelude of the everlasting chant before the Throne, – so they went on, ''continuing *instant* in prayer,'' after the pattern of Psalmists and Apostles, in the day with David, in the night with Paul and Silas, winter and summer, in heat and in cold, in peace and in danger, in a prison or in a cathedral, in the dark, in the day-break, at sun-rising, in the forenoon, at noon, in the afternoon, at eventide, and on going to rest, still they had Christ before them; His thought in their mind, His emblem in their eye, His name in their mouth, His service in their posture, magnifying Him, and calling on all that lives to magnify Him, joining with Angels in heaven and Saints in Paradise to bless and praise

Him for ever and ever. O great and noble system, not of the Jews who rested in their rights and privileges, not of those Christians who are taken up with their own feelings, and who describe what they should exhibit, but of the true Saints of God, the undefiled and virgin souls who follow the Lamb withersoever He goeth! Such is the difference between those whom Christ praises and those whom He condemns or warns. The Pharisee recounted the signs of God's mercy upon and in Him; the Publican simply looked to God. The young Ruler boasted of his correct life, but the penitent woman anointed Jesus' feet and kissed them. Nay, holy Martha herself spoke of her "much service;" while Mary waited on Him for the "one thing needful." The one thought of Christ. To look to Christ is to be justified by faith; to think of being justified by faith is to look from Christ and to fall from grace. He who worships Christ and works for Him, is acting out that doctrine which another does but enunciate; his worship and his works are acts of faith, and avail to his salvation, because he does not do them *as* availing.

But I must end a train of thought, which, left to itself would run on into a whole work. And in doing so I make one remark, which is perhaps the great moral of the history of Protestantism. Luther found in the Church great moral corruptions countenanced by its highest authorities; he felt them; but instead of meeting them with divine weapons, he used one of his own. He adopted a doctrine original, specious, fascinating, persuasive, powerful against Rome, and wonderfully adapted, as if prophetically, to the genius of the times which were to follow. He found Christians in bondage to their works and observances; he released them by his doctrine of faith; and he left them in bondage to their feelings. He weaned them from seeking assurance of salvation in standing ordinances, at the cost of teaching them that a personal consciousness of it was promised to every one who believed. For outward sign of grace he substituted inward; for reverence towards the Church contemplation of self. And thus, whereas he himself held the proper efficacy of the Sacraments, he has led others to disbelieve it; whereas he preached against reliance on self, he introduced it in a more subtle shape; whereas he professed to make the written word all in all, he sacrificed it in its length and breadth to the doctrine which he had wrested from a few texts.

This is what comes of fighting God's battles in our own way, of extending truths beyond their measure, of anxiety after a teaching more compact, clear, and spiritual, than the Creed of the Apostles. Thus the Pharisees were more careful of their Law than God who gave it; thus Saul saved the cattle he was bid destroy, ''to sacrifice to the Lord;'' thus Judas was concerned at the waste of the ointment, which might have been given to the poor. In these cases bad men professed to be more zealous for God's honour, more devotional, or more charitable, than the servants of God; and in a parallel way Protestants would be more spiritual. Let us be sure things are going wrong with us, when we see doctrines more clearly, and carry them out more boldly, than they are taught us in Revelation. (*Jfc.* 323-6, 330, 333-41)

4

DEVELOPMENT OF DOCTRINE*

THE THEORY OF DEVELOPMENTS IN RELIGIOUS DOCTRINE

"The Theory of Developments in Religious Doctrine" was preached on 2 February 1943. It took an hour and a half to deliver. Newman had been working for twelve years on a theory of development. He was not very surprised that it immediately aroused controversy: if the principle of doctrinal development was valid in the kind of way Newman suggested, then it would be hard to resist the claims of Roman Catholicism. The sermon was published in the same month it was delivered as the last of Newman's collected volume of Oxford University Sermons. *The author thought it was his best, if not his most perfect, book. But he was astonished to hear in March that the book was already going into a second edition: none of his other volumes of sermons had been sold out within a year of publication, and many of the sermons in the present volume were very abstruse: it looked as if the book was selling so well partly at least because of all the personal publicity surrounding the famous Tractarian leader who was widely rumoured to be about to defect to the Roman Church.*

SERMON XV
THE THEORY OF DEVELOPMENTS IN RELIGIOUS DOCTRINE
(Preached on the Purification, 1813)
Luke 2:19
"But Mary kept all these things and pondered them in her heart".

Little is told us in the Scripture concerning the Blessed Virgin, but there is one grace of which the Evangelists make her the pattern, in a few simple sentences, – of Faith. Zacharias questioned the Angel's message, but "Mary said, Behold the handmaid of the Lord; Be it unto me according to thy word." Accordingly Elisabeth, speaking with an apparent allusion to

*See also above, p. 29.

123

the contrast thus exhibited between her own highly-favoured husband, righteous Zacharias, and the still more highly-favoured Mary, said, on receiving her salutation, "Blessed art thou among women, and blessed is the fruit of thy womb; Blessed is she that believed, for there shall be a performance of those things which were told her from the Lord."

2. But Mary's faith did not end in a mere acquiescence in Divine providences and revelations: as the text informs us, she "pondered" them. When the shepherds came, and told of the vision of Angels which they had seen at the time of the Nativity, and how one of them announced that the Infant in her arms was "the Saviour, which is Christ the Lord", while others did but wonder, "Mary kept all these things, and pondered them in her heart." Again, when her Son Saviour had come to the age of twelve years, and had left her for awhile for His Father's service, and had been found, to her surprise, in the Temple, amid the doctors, both hearing them and asking them questions, and had, on her addressing Him, vouchsafed to justify His conduct, we are told, "His mother kept all these sayings in her heart." And accordingly, at the marriage-feast in Cana, her faith anticipated His first miracle, and she said to the servants, "Whatsoever He said unto you do it.

3. Thus St. Mary is our pattern of Faith, both in the reception and in the study of Divine Truth. She does not think it enough to accept, she dwells upon it; not enough to possess, she uses it; not enough to assent, she develops it; not enough to submit the Reason, she reasons upon it; not indeed reasoning first, and believing afterwards, with Zacharias, yet first believing without reasoning, next from love and reverence, reasoning after believing. And thus she symbolizes to us, not only the faith of the unlearned, but of the doctors of the Church also, who have to investigate, and weigh, and define, as well as to profess the Gospel; to draw the line between truth and heresy; to anticipate or remedy the various aberrations of wrong reason; to combat pride and recklessness with their own arms; and thus to triumph over the sophist and the innovator.

4. If, then, on a Day dedicated to such high contemplations as the Feast which we are now celebrating, it is allowable to occupy the thoughts with a subject not of a devotional or practical nature, it will be some relief of the omission to select one in

which St. Mary at least will be our example, – the use of Reason in investigating the doctrines of Faith; a subject, indeed, far fitter for a volume than for the most extended notice which can here be given to it; but one which cannot be passed over altogether in silence, in any attempt at determining the relation of Faith to Reason.

5. The overthrown of the wisdom of the world was one of the earliest, as well as the noblest of the triumphs of the Church; after the pattern of her Divine Master, who took His place among the doctors before He preached His new Kingdom, or opposed Himself to the world's power. St. Paul, the learned Pharisee, was the first fruits of that gifted company, in whom the pride of science is seen prostrated before the foolishness of preaching. From his day to this the Cross has enlisted under its banner all those great endowments of mind, which in former times had been expended on vanities, or dissipated in doubt and specula- tion. Nor was it long before the schools of heathenism took the alarm, and manifested an unavailing jealousy of the new doc- trine, which was robbing them of their most hopeful disciples. They had hitherto taken for granted that the natural home of the Intellect was the Garden of the Porch; and it reversed their very first principles to be called on to confess, what yet they could not deny, that a Superstition, as they considered it, was attracting to itself all the energy, the keenness, the originality, and the eloquence of the age. But these aggressions upon heathenism were only the beginning of the Church's conquests; in the course of time the whole mind of the world, as I may say, was absorbed into the philosophy of the Cross, as the element in which it lived, and the form upon which it was moulded. And how many centuries did this endure, and what vast ruins still remain of its dominion! In the capitals of Christen- dom the high cathedral and the perpetual choir still witness to the victory of Faith over the world's power. To see its triumph over the world's wisdom, we must enter those solemn cemeteries in which are stored the relics and the monuments of ancient Faith – our libraries. Look along their shelves, and every name you read there is, in one sense or other, a trophy set up in record of the victories of Faith. How many long lives, what high aims, what single-minded devotion, what intense contemplation, what fervent prayer, what deep erudition, what untiring diligence,

what toilsome conflicts has it taken to establish its supremacy! This has been the object which has given meaning to the life of Saints, and which is the subject-matter of their history. For this they have given up the comforts of earth and the charities of home, and surrendered themselves to an austere rule, nay, even to confessorship and persecution, if so be they could make some small offering, or do some casual service, or provide some additional safeguard towards the great work which was in progress. This has been the origin of controversies, long and various, yes, and the occasion of much infirmity, the test of much hidden perverseness, and the subject of much bitterness and tumult. The world has been moved in consequence of it, populations excited, leagues and alliances formed, kingdoms lost and won: and even zeal, when excessive, evinced a sense of its preciousness; nay, even rebellions in some sort did homage to it, as insurgents imply the actual sovereignty of the power which they are assailing. Meanwhile the work went on, and at length a large fabric of divinity was reared, irregular in its structure, and diverse in its style, as beseemed the slow growth of centuries; nay, anomalous in its details, from the peculiarities of individuals, or the interference of strangers, but still, on the whole, the development of an idea, and like itself, and unlike anything else, its most widely-separated parts having relation with each other, and betokening a common origin.

6. Let us quit this survey of the general system, and descend to the history of the formation of any Catholic dogma. What a remarkable sight it is, as almost all unprejudiced persons will admit, to trace the course of the controversy, from its first disorders to its exact and determinate issue. Full of deep interest, to see how the great idea takes hold of a thousand minds by its living force, and will not be ruled or stinted, but is "like a burning fire," as the Prophet speaks, "shut up" within them, till they are "weary of forbearing, and cannot stay," and grows in them, and at length is born through them, perhaps in a long course of years, and even successive generations; so that the doctrine may rather be said to use the minds of Christians, than to be used by them. Wonderful it is to see with what effort, hesitation, suspense, interruption, – with how many swayings to the right and to the left – with how many reverse, yet with what certainty of advance, with what precision in its march,

and with what ultimate completeness, it has been evolved; till the whole truth "self-balanced on its centre hung," part answering to part, one, absolute, integral, indissoluble, while the world lasts! Wonderful, to see how heresy has but thrown that idea into fresh forms, and drawn out from it farther developments, with an exuberance which exceeded all questioning, and a harmony which baffled all criticism, like Him, its Divine Author, who, when put on trial by the Evil One, was but fortified by the assault, and is ever justified in His sayings, and overcomes when He is judged.

7. And this world of thought is the expansion of a few words, uttered, as if casually, by the fishermen of Galilee. Here is another topic which belongs more especially to that part of the subject to which I propose to confine myself. Reason has not only submitted, it has ministered to Faith; it has illustrated its documents; it has raised illiterate peasants into philosophers and divines; it has elicited a meaning from their words which their immediate hearers little suspected. Stranger surely is it that St. John should be a theologian, than that St. Peter should be a prince. This is a phenomenon proper to the Gospel, and a note of divinity. Its half sentences, its overflowings of language, admit of development[13]; they have a life in them which shows itself in progress; a truth, which has the token of consistency; a reality, which is fruitful in resources; a depth, which extends into mystery: for they are representations of what is actual, and has a definite location and necessary bearings and a meaning in the great system of things, and a harmony in what it is, and a compatibility in what it involves. What forms of Paganism can furnish a parallel? What philosopher has left his words to posterity as a talent which could be put to usury, as a mine which could be wrought? Here, too, is the badge of heresy; its dogmas are unfruitful; it has no theology; so far forth as it is heresy, it has none. Deduct its remnant of Catholic theology, and what remains? Polemics, explanations, protests. It turns to Biblical Criticism, or to the Evidences of Religion, for want of a province. Its *formulae* end in themselves, without development, because they are words; they are barren, because they are dead. If they had life, they would increase and multiply; or, if they do live and bear fruit, it is but as "sin, when it is finished, bringeth forth death." It develops into dissolution; but it creates nothing,

it tends to no system, its resultant dogma is but the denial of all dogmas, any theology, under the Gospel. No wonder it denies what it cannot attain.

8. Heresy denies to the Church what is wanting in itself. Here, then, we are brought to the subject to which I wish to give attention. It need not surely formally be proved that this disparagement of doctrinal statements, and in particular of those relating to the Holy Trinity and Incarnation, is especially prevalent in our times. There is a suspicion widely abroad, – felt, too, perhaps, by many who are unwilling to confess it, – that the development of ideas and formation of dogmas is a mere abuse of Reason, which, when it attempted such sacred subjects, went beyond its powers, and could do nothing more than multiply words without meaning, and deductions which come to nothing. The conclusion follows, that such an attempt does but lead to mischievous controversy, from that discordance of doctrinal opinions, which is its immediate consequence; that there is, in truth, no necessary or proper connexion between inward religious belief and scientific expositions; and that charity, as well as good sense, is best consulted by reducing creeds to the number of private opinions, which, if individuals will hold for themselves, at least they have no right to impose upon others.

9. It is my purpose, then, in what follows, to investigate the connexion between Faith and Dogmatic Confession, as far as relates to the sacred doctrines which were just now mentioned, and to show the office of the Reason in reference to it; in doing so, I shall make as little allusion as may be to erroneous views on the subject, which have been mentioned only for the sake of perspicuity; following rather the course which the discussion may take, and pursuing those issues on which it naturally opens. Nor am I here in any way concerned with the question, who is the legitimate framer and judge of these dogmatic inferences under the Gospel, or if there be any. Whether the Church is infallible, or the individual, or the first ages, or none of these, is not the point here, but the theory of developments itself.

10. Theological dogmas are propositions expressive of the judgment which the mind forms, or the impressions which it receives, of Revealed Truth. Revelation sets before it certain supernatural facts and actions, beings and principles; these make a certain impression or image upon it; and this impression spontaneously,

or even necessarily, becomes the subject of reflection on the part of the mind itself, which proceeds to investigate it, and to draw it forth in successive and distinct sentences. Thus the Catholic doctrine of Original Sin, or of Sin after Baptism, or of the Eucharist, or of Justification, is but the expression of the inward belief of Catholics on these several points, formed upon an analysis of that belief.[14] Such, too, are the high doctrines with which I am especially concerned.

11. Now, here I observe, first of all, that naturally as the inward idea of divine truth, such as has been described, passes into explicit form by the activity of our reflective powers, still such an actual delineation is not essential to its genuineness and perfection. A peasant may have such a true impression, yet be unable to give any intelligible account of it, as will easily be understood. But what is remarkable at first sight is this, that there is good reason for saying that the impression made upon the mind need not even be recognized by the parties possessing it. It is no proof that persons are not possessed, because they are not conscious, of an idea. Nothing is of more frequent occurrence, whether in things sensible or intellectual, than the existence of such unperceived impressions. What do we mean when we say, that certain persons do not know themselves, but that they are ruled by views, feelings, prejudices, objects which they do not recognize? How common is it to be exhilarated or depressed, we do not recollect why, though we are aware that something has been told us, or has happened, good or bad, which accounts for our feeling, could we recall it! What is memory itself, but a vast magazine of such dormant, but present and excitable ideas? Or consider, when persons would trace the history of their own opinions in past years, how baffled they are in the attempt to fix the date of this or that conviction, their system of thought having been all the while in continual, gradual, tranquil expansion; so that it were as easy to follow the growth of the fruit of the earth, "first the blade, then the car, after that the full corn in the car," as to chronicle changes, which involved no abrupt revolution, or reaction, or fickleness of mind, but have been the birth of an idea, the development, in explicit form, of what was already latent within it. Or, again, critical disquisitions are often written about the idea which this or that poet might have in his mind in certain of his compositions

and characters; and we call such analysis the philosophy of poetry, not implying thereby of necessity that the author wrote upon a theory in his actual delineation, or knew what he was doing; but that, in matter of fact, he was possessed, ruled, guided by an unconscious idea. Moreover, it is a question whether that strange and painful feeling of unreality, which religious men experience from time to time, when nothing seems true, or good, or right, or profitable, when Faith seems a name, and duty a mockery, and all endeavours to do right, absurd and hopeless, and all things forlorn and dreary, as if religion were wiped out from the world, may not be the direct effect of the temporary obscuration of some master vision, which unconsciously supplies the mind with spiritual life and peace.

12. Or, to take another class of instances which are to the point so far as this, that at least they are real impressions, even though they be not influential. How common is what is called vacant vision, when objects meet the eye, without any effect of the judgment to measure or locate them; and that absence of mind, which recollects minutes afterwards the occurrence of some sound, the striking of the hour, or the question of a companion, which passes unheeded at the time it took place! How, again, happens it in dreams, that we suddenly pass from one state of feeling, or one assemblage of circumstances to another, without any surprise at the incongruity, except that, while we are impressed first in this way, then in that, we take no active cognizance of the impression? And this, perhaps, is the life of inferior animals, a sort of continuous dream, impressions without reflections; such, too, seems to be the first life of infants; nay, in heaven itself, such may be the high existence of some exalted orders of blessed spirits, as the Seraphim, who are said to be, not Knowledge, but all Love.

13. Now, it is important to insist on this circumstance, because it suggests the reality and permanence of inward knowledge, as distinct from explicit confession. The absence, or partial absence, or incompleteness of dogmatic statements is no proof of the absence of impressions or implicit judgments, in the mind of the Church. Even centuries might pass without the formal expression of a truth, which had been all along the secret life of millions of faithful souls. Thus, not till the thirteenth century was there any direct and distinct avowal, on the part of the

Church, of the numerical Unity of the Divine Nature, which the language of some of the principal Greek fathers, *prima facie*, though not really, denies. Again, the doctrine of the Double Procession was no Catholic dogma in the first ages, though it was more or less clearly stated by individual Fathers; yet, if it is now to be received, as surely it must be, as part of the Creed, it was really held everywhere from the beginning, and therefore, in a measure, held as a mere religious impression, and perhaps an unconscious one.

14. But, further, if the ideas may be latent in the Christian mind, by which it is animated and formed, it is less wonderful that they should be difficult to elicit and define; and of this difficulty we have abundant proof in the history whether of the Church, or of individuals. Surely it is not at all wonderful, that, when individuals attempt to analyze their own belief, they should find the task arduous in the extreme, if not altogether beyond them; or, again, a work of many years; or, again, that they should shrink from the true developments, if offered to them, as foreign to their thoughts. This may be illustrated in a variety of ways.

15. It will often happen, perhaps from the nature of things, that it is impossible to master and express an idea in a short space of time. As to individuals, sometimes they find they cannot do so at all; at length, perhaps, they recognize, in some writer they meet, with the very account of their own thoughts, which they desiderate; and then they say, that "here is what they have felt all along, and wanted to say, but could not," or "what they have ever maintained, only better expressed." Again, how many men are burdened with an idea, which haunts them through a great part of their lives, and of which only at length, with much trouble, do they dispossess themselves? I suppose most of us have felt at times the irritation, and that for a long period, of thoughts and views which we felt, and felt to be true, only dimly showing themselves, or flitting before us; which at length we understand must not be forced, but must have their way, and would, if it were so ordered, come to light in their own time. The life of some men, and those not the least eminent among divines and philosophers, has centred in the development of one idea; nay, perhaps has been too short for the process. Again, how frequently it happens, that, on first hearing a doc-

trine propounded, a man hesitates, first acknowledges, then disowns it; then says that he has always held it, but finds fault with the mode in which it is presented to him, accusing it of paradox or over-refinement; that is, he cannot at the moment analyze his own opinions, and does not know whether he holds the doctrine or not, from the difficulty of mastering his thoughts.

16. Another characteristic, as I have said, of dogmatic statements, is the difficulty of recognizing them, even when attained, as the true representation of our meaning. This happens for many reasons; sometimes, from the faint hold we have of the impression itself, whether its nature be good or bad, so that we shrink from principles in substance, which we acknowledge in influence. Many a man, for instance, is acting on utilitarian principles, who is shocked at them in set treatises, and disowns them. Again, in sacred subjects, the very circumstance that a dogma professes to be a direct contemplation, and, if so be, a definition of what is infinite and eternal, is painful to serious minds. Moreover, from the hypothesis, it is the representation of an idea in a medium not native to it, not as originally conceived, but, as it were, in projection; no wonder, then, that, though there be an intimate correspondence, part by part, between the impression and the dogma, yet there should be an harshness in the outline of the latter; as, for instance, a want of harmonious proportion; and yet this is unavoidable, from the infirmities of our intellectual powers.

17. Again, another similar peculiarity in developments in general, is the great remoteness of the separate results of a common idea, or rather at first sight the absence of any connexion. Thus it often happens that party spirit is imputed to persons, merely because they agree with one another in certain points of opinion and conduct, which are thought too minute, distant, and various, in the large field of religious doctrine and discipline, to proceed from any but an external influence and a positive rule; whereas an insight into the wonderfully expansive power and penetrating virtue of theological or philosophical ideas would have shown, that what is apparently arbitrary in rival or in kindred schools of thought, is after all rigidly determined by the original hypothesis. The remark has been made, for instance, that rarely have persons maintained the sleep of the soul before the Resurrection, without falling into more grievous

errors; again, those who deny the Lutheran doctrine of Justification, commonly have tendencies towards a ceremonial religion; again, it is a serious fact that Protestantism has at various times unexpectedly developed into an allowance or vindication of polygamy; and heretics in general, however opposed in tenets, are found to have an inexplicable sympathy for each other, and never wake up from their ordinary torpor, but to exchange courtesies and meditate coalitions. One other remark is in point here, and relates to the length to which statements run, though, before we attempted them, we fancied our idea could be expressed in one or two sentences. Explanations grow under our hands, in spite of our effort at compression. Such, too, is the contrast between conversation and epistolary correspondence. We speak our meaning with little trouble; our voice, manner, and half words completing it for us; but in writing, when details must be drawn out, and misapprehensions anticipated, we seem never to be rid of the responsibility of our task. This being the case, it is surprising that the Creeds are so short, not surprising that they need a comment.

18. The difficulty, then, and hazard of developing doctrines implicitly received, must be fully allowed; and this is often made a ground for inferring that they have no proper developments at all; that there is no natural connexion between certain dogmas and certain impressions; and that theological science is a matter of time, and place, and accident, though inward belief is ever and every where one and the same. But surely the instinct of every Christian revolts from such a position; for the very first impulse of his faith is to try to express itself about the "great sight" which is vouchsafed to it; and this seems to argue that a science there is, whether the mind is equal to its discovery or no. And, indeed, what science is open to every chance inquirer? which is not recondite in its principles? which requires not special gifts of mind for its just formation? All subject-matters admit of true theories and false, and the false are no prejudice to the true. Why should this class of ideas be different from all other? Principles of philosophy, physics, ethics, politics, taste, admit both of implicit reception and explicit statement; why should not the ideas, which are the secret life of the Christian, be recognized also as fixed and definite in themselves, and as capable of scientific analysis? Why should not there be that real

connexion between science and its subject-matter in religion, which exists in other departments of thought? No one would deny that the philosophy of Zeno or Pythagoras was the exponent of a certain mode of viewing things; or would affirm that Platonist and Epicurean acted on one and the same idea of nature, life, and duty, and meant the same thing, though they verbally differed, merely because a Plato or an Epicurus was needed to detect the abstruse elements of thought, out of which each philosophy was eventually constructed. A man surely may be a Peripatetic or an Academic in his feelings, views, aims, and acts, who never heard the name. Granting, then, extreme cases, when individuals who would analyze their views of religion are thrown entirely upon their own reason, and find that reason unequal to the task, this will be no argument against a general, natural, and ordinary correspondence between the dogma and the inward idea. Surely, if Almighty God is ever one and the same, and is revealed to us as one and the same, the true inward impression of Him, made on the recipient of the revelation, must be one and the same; and, since human nature proceeds upon fixed laws, the statement of the impression must be one and the same, so that we may as well say that there are two Gods as two Creeds. And considering the strong feelings and energetic acts and severe sufferings which age after age have been involved in the maintenance of the Catholic dogmas, it is surely a very shallow philosophy to account such maintenance a mere contest about words, and a very abject philosophy to attribute it to mere party spirit, or to personal rivalry, or to ambition, or to covetousness.

19. Reasonable, however, as is this view of doctrinal developments in general, it cannot be denied that those which relate to the Objects of Faith, of which I am particularly speaking, have a character of their own, and must be considered separately. Let us, then, consider how the case stands, as regards the sacred doctrines of the Trinity and the Incarnation.

20. The Apostle said to the Athenians, "Whom ye ignorantly worship, Him declare I unto you;"and the mind which is habituated to the thought of God, of Christ, of the Holy Spirit, naturally turns, as I have said, with a devout curiosity to the contemplation of the Object of its adoration, and begins to form statements concerning Him before it knows whither, or how

far, it will be carried. One proposition necessarily leads to another, and a second to a third; then some limitation is required; and the combination of these opposites occasions some fresh evolutions from the original idea, which indeed can never be said to be entirely exhausted. This process is its development, and results in a series, or rather body of dogmatic statements, till what was at first an impression on the Imagination has become a system or creed in the Reason.

21. Now such impressions are obviously individual and complete above other theological ideas, *because* they are the impressions of Objects. Ideas and their developments are commonly not identical, the development being but the carrying out of the idea into its consequences. Thus the doctrine of Penance may be called a development of the doctrine of Baptism, yet still is a distinct doctrine; whereas the developments in the doctrines of the Holy Trinity and the Incarnation are mere portions of the original impression, and modes of representing it. As God is one, so the impression which He gives us of Himself is one; it is not a thing of parts; it is not a system; nor is it any thing imperfect, and needing a counterpart. It is the vision of an object. When we pray, we pray, not to an assemblage of notions, or to a creed, but to One Individual Being; and when we speak of Him we speak of a Person, not of a Law or a Manifestation. This being the case, all our attempts to delineate our impression of Him go to bring out one idea, not two or three or four; not a philosophy, but an individual idea in its separate aspects.

22. This may be fitly compared to the impressions made on us through the senses. Material objects are whole, and individual; and the impressions which they make on the mind, by means of the senses, are of a corresponding nature, complex and manifold in their relations and bearings, but considered in themselves integral and one. And in like manner the ideas which we are granted of Divine Objects under the Gospel, from the nature of the case and because they are ideas, answers to the Originals so far as this, that they are whole, indivisible, substantial, and may be called real, as being images of what is real. Objects which are conveyed to us through the senses, stand out in our minds, as I may say, with dimensions and aspects and influences various, and all of these consistent with one another, and many of them beyond our memory or even knowl-

edge, while we contemplate the objects themselves; thus forcing on us a persuasion of their reality from the spontaneous congruity and coincidence of these accompaniments, as if they could not be creations of our minds, but were the images of external and independent beings. This of course will take place in the case of the sacred ideas which are the objects of our faith. Religious men, according to their manner, have an idea or vision of the Blessed Trinity in Unity, of the Son Incarnate and of His Presence, not as a number of qualities, attributes, and actions, not as the subject of a number of propositions, but as one, and individual, and independent of words, as an impression conveyed through the senses.

23. Particular propositions, then, which are used to express portions of the great idea vouchsafed to us, can never really be confused with the idea itself, which all such propositions taken together can but reach, and cannot exceed. As definitions are not intended to go beyond their subject, but to be adequate to it, so the dogmatic statements of the Divine Nature used in our confessions, however multiplied, cannot say more than is implied in the original idea, considered in its completeness, without the risk of heresy. Creeds and dogmas live in the one idea which they are designed to express, and which alone is substantive; and are necessary only because the human mind cannot reflect upon that idea, except piecemeal, cannot use it in its oneness and entireness, nor without resolving it into a series of aspects and relations. And in matter of fact these expressions are never equivalent to it; we are able, indeed, to define the creations of our own minds, for they are what we make them and nothing else; but it were as easy to create what is real as to define it; and thus the Catholic dogmas are, after all, but symbols of a Divine fact, which, far from being compassed by those very propositions, would not be exhausted, nor fathomed, by a thousand.

24. Now of such sacred ideas and their attendant expressions, I observe:–

(1.) First, that an impression of this intimate kind seems to be what Scripture means by "knowledge". "This is life eternal", says our Saviour, "that they might know Thee the only True God and Jesus Christ whom Thou hast sent." In like manner St. Paul speaks of willingly losing all things, "for the excellency of the knowledge of Christ Jesus,'' and St. Peter of ''the knowledge of Him who hath called us to glory and virtue[15].'' Knowledge is the possession of those living ideas of sacred things, from which alone change of heart or conduct can proceed. This awful vision is what Scripture seems to designate by the phrases ''Christ in us,'' ''Christ dwelling in us by faith,'' ''Christ formed in us,''and ''Christ manifesting Himself unto us''. And though it is faint and doubtful in some minds, and distinct in others, as some remote object in the twilight or in the day, this arises from the circumstances of the particular mind, and does not interfere with the perfection of the gift itself.

25. (2.) This leads me next, however, to observe, that these religious impressions differ from those of material objects, in the mode in which they are made. The senses are direct, immediate, and ordinary informants, and act spontaneously without any will or effort on our part; but no such faculties have been given us, as far as we know, for realizing the Objects of Faith. It is true that inspiration may be a gift of this kind to those who have been favoured with it; nor would it be safe to deny to the illumination grace of Baptism a power, at least of putting the mind into a capacity for receiving impressions; but the former of these is not ordinary, and both are supernatural. The secondary and intelligible means by which we receive the impression of Divine Verities, are, for instance, the habitual and devout perusal of Scripture, which gradually acts upon the mind; again, the gradual influence of intercourse with those who are in themselves in possession of the sacred ideas; again, the study of Dogmatic Theology, which is our present subject; again, a continual round of devotion; or again, sometimes, in minds both fitly disposed and apprehensive, the almost instantaneous operation of a keen faith. This obvious distinction follows between sensible and religious ideas, that we put the latter into language in order to fix, teach, and transmit them, but not the former. No one defines a material object by way of conveying to us what we know so much better by the senses, but we form creeds as a chief mode of perpetuating the impression.

26. (3.) Further, I observe, that though the Christian mind reasons out a series of dogmatic statements, one from another, this it has ever done, and always must do, not from those statements taken in themselves, as logical propositions, but as being

itself enlightened and (as if) inhabited by that sacred impression which is prior to them, which acts as a regulating principle, ever present, upon the reasoning, and without which no one has any warrant to reason at all. Such sentences as "the Word was God," or "the Only-begotten Son who is in the bosom of the Father," or "the Word was made flesh," or "the Holy Ghost which proceedeth from the Father," are not a mere letter which we may handle by the rules of art at our own will, but august tokens of most simple, ineffable, adorable facts, embraced, enshrined according to its measure in the believing mind. For though the development of an idea is a deduction of proposition from proposition, these propositions are ever formed in and round the idea itself (so to speak), and are in fact one and all only aspects of it. Moreover, this will account both for the mode of arguing from particular texts or single words of Scripture, practised by the early Fathers, and for their fearless decision in practising it; for the great Object of Faith on which they lived both enabled them to appropriate to itself particular passages of Scripture, and became a safeguard against heretical deductions from them. Also, it will account for the charge of weak reasoning, commonly brought against those Fathers; for never do we seem so illogical to others as when we are arguing under the continual influence of impressions to which they are insensible.

27. (4.) Again, it must of course be remembered, as I have just implied, (though as being an historical matter it hardly concerns us here), that Revelation itself has provided in Scriptures the main outlines and also large details of the dogmatic system. Inspiration has superseded the exercise of human Reason in great measure, and left it but the comparatively easy task of finishing the sacred work. The question, indeed, at first sight occurs, why such inspired statements are not enough without further developments; but in truth, when Reason has once been put on the investigation, it cannot stop till it has finished it; one dogma creates another, by the same right by which it was itself created; the Scripture statements are sanctions as well as informants in the inquiry; they begin and they do not exhaust.

28. (5.) Scripture, I say, begins a series of developments which it does not finish; that is to say, in other words, it is a mistake to look for every separate proposition of the Catholic doctrine

in Scripture. This is plain from what has gone before. For instance, the Athanasian Creed professes to lay down the right faith, which we must hold on its most sacred subjects, in order to be saved. This must mean that there is one view concerning the Holy Trinity, or concerning the Incarnation, which is true, and distinct from all others; one definite, consistent, entire view, which cannot be mistaken, not contained in any certain number of propositions, but held as a view by the believing mind, and not held, but denied by Arians, Sabellians, Tritheists, Nestorians, Monophysites, Socinians, and other heretics. That idea is not enlarged, if propositions are added, nor impaired if they are withdrawn: if they are added, this is with a view of conveying that one integral view, not of amplifying it. That view does not depend on such propositions: it does not consist in them; they are but specimens and indications of it. And they may be multiplied without limit. They are necessary, but not needful to it, being but portions or aspects of that previous impression which has at length come under the cognizance of Reason and the terminology of science. The question, then, is not whether this or that proposition of the Catholic doctrine is in *terminis* in Scripture, unless we would be slaves to the letter, but whether that one view of the Mystery, of which all such are the exponents, be not there; a view which would be some other view, and not itself, if any one of such propositions, if any one of a number of similar propositions, were not true. Those propositions imply each other, as being parts of one whole; so that to deny one is to deny all, and to invalidate one is to deface and destroy the view itself. One thing alone has to be impressed on us by Scripture, the Catholic idea, and in it they all are included. To object, then, to the number of propositions, upon which an anathema is placed, is altogether to mistake their use; for their multiplication is not intended to enforce many things, but to express one, – to form within us that one impression concerning Almighty God, as the ruling principle of our minds, and that, whether we can fully recognize our own possession of it or no. And surely it is no paradox to say that such ideas may exert a most powerful influence, at least in their various aspects, on our moral character, and on the whole man: as no one would deny in the case of belief or disbelief of a Supreme Being.

29. (6.) And here we see the ordinary mistake of doctrinal

innovators, viz. to go away with this or that proposition of the Creed, instead of embracing that one idea which all of them together are meant to convey; it being almost a definition of heresy, that it fastens on some one statement as if the whole truth, to the denial of all others, and as the basis of a new faith; erring rather in what it rejects, than in what it maintains: though, in truth, if the mind deliberately rejects any portion of the doctrine, this is a proof that it does not really hold even that very statement for the sake of which it rejects the others. Realizing is the very life of true developments; it is peculiar to the Church, and the justification of her definitions.

30. Enough has now been said on the distinction, yet connexion, between the implicit knowledge and the explicit confession of the Divine Objects of Faith, as they are revealed to us under the Gospel. An objection, however, remains, which cannot be satisfactorily treated in a few words. And what is worse than prolixity, the discussion may bear with it some appearance of unnecessary or even wanton refinement; unless, indeed, it is thrown into the form of controversy, a worse evil. Let it suffice to say, that my wish is, not to discover difficulties in any subject, but to solve them.

31. It may be asked, then, whether the mistake of words and names for things is not incurred by orthodox as well as heretics, in dogmatizing at all about the ''secret things which belong unto the Lord our God,'' inasmuch as the idea of a supernatural object must itself be supernatural, and since no such ideas are claimed by ordinary Christians, no knowledge of Divine Verities is possible to them. How should any thing of this world convey ideas which are beyond and above this world? How can teaching and intercourse, how can human words, how can earthly images, convey to the mind an idea of the Invisible? They cannot rise above themselves. They can suggest no idea but what is resolvable into ideas natural and earthly. The words ''Person,'' ''Substance,'' ''Consubstantial,'' ''Generation,'' ''Procession,'' ''Incarnation,'' ''Taking of the manhood into God,'' and the like, have either a very abject and human meaning, or none at all. In other words, there is no such inward view of these doctrines, distinct from the dogmatic language used to express them, as was just now supposed. The metaphors by which they are signified are not mere symbols of ideas which exist indepen-

dently of them, but their meaning is coincident and identical with the ideas. When, indeed, we have knowledge of a thing from other sources, then the metaphors we may apply to it are but accidental appendages to that knowledge; whereas our ideas of Divine things are just co-extensive with the figures by which we express them, neither more nor less, and without them are not; and when we draw inferences from those figures, we are not illustrating one existing idea, but drawing mere logical inferences. We speak, indeed, of material objects freely, because our senses reveal them to us apart from our words; but as to these ideas about heavenly things, we learn them from words, yet (it seems) we are to say what we, without words, conceive of them, as if words could convey what they do not contain. It follows that our anathemas, our controversies, our struggles, our sufferings, are merely about the poor ideas conveyed to us in certain figures of speech.

32. Some obvious remarks suggest themselves in answer to this representation. First, it is difficult to determine what divine grace may not do for us, if not in immediately implanting now ideas, yet in refining and elevating those which we gain through natural informants. If, we all acknowledge, grace renews our moral feelings, yet through outward means, if it opens upon us new ideas about virtue and goodness and heroism and heavenly peace, it does not appear why, in a certain sense, it may not impart ideas concerning the nature of God. Again, the various terms and figures which are used in the doctrine of the Holy Trinity or of the Incarnation, surely may by their combination create ideas which will be altogether new, though they are still of an earthly character. And further, when it is said that such figures convey no knowledge of the Divine Nature itself, beyond those figures, whatever they are, it should be considered whether our senses can be proved to suggest any real idea of matter. All that we know, strictly speaking, is the existence of the impressions our senses make on us; and yet we scruple not to speak as if they conveyed to us the knowledge of material substances. Let, then, the Catholic dogmas, as such, be freely admitted to convey no true idea of Almighty God, but only an earthly one, gained from earthly figures, provided it be allowed, on the other hand, that the senses do not convey to us any true idea of matter, but only an idea commensurate with sensible impressions.

33. Nor is there any reason why this should not be fully granted. Still there may be a certain correspondence between the idea, though earthly, and its heavenly archetype, such that that idea belongs to the archetype, in a sense in which no other earthly idea belongs to it, as being the nearest approach to it which our present state allows. Indeed Scripture itself intimates the earthly nature of our present ideas of Sacred Objects, when it speaks of our now "seeing in a glass *darkly ἐν αἰνίγματι*, but then face to face;" and it has ever been the doctrine of divines that the Beatific Vision, or true sight of Almighty God, is reserved for the world to come. Meanwhile we are allowed such an approximation to the truth as earthly images and figures may supply to us.

34. It must not be supposed that this is the only case in which we are obliged to receive information needful to us, through the medium of our existing ideas, and consequently with but a vague apprehension of its subject-matter. Children, who are made our pattern in Scripture, are taught, by an accommodation, on the part of their teachers, to their immature facilities and their scanty vocabulary. To answer their questions in the language which we should use towards grown men, would be simply to mislead them, if they could construe it at all. We must dispense and "divide"the word of truth, if we would not have it changed, as far as they are concerned, into a word of falsehood; for what is short of truth in the letter may be to them the most perfect truth, that is, the nearest approach to truth, compatible with their condition. The case is the same as regards those who have any natural defect or deprivation which cuts them off from the circle of ideas common to mankind in general. To speak to a blind man of light and colours, in terms proper to those phenomena, would be to mock him; we must use other media of information accommodated to his circumstances, according to the well-known instance in which his own account of scarlet was to liken it to the sound of a trumpet. And so again, as regards savages, or the ignorant, or weak, or narrow-minded, our representations and arguments must take a certain form, if they are to gain admission into their minds at all, and to reach them. Again, what impediments do the diversities of language place in the way of communicating ideas! Language is a sort of analysis of thought; and, since ideas are infinite, and infinitely combined,

and infinitely modified, whereas language is a method definite and limited, and confined to an arbitrary selection of a certain number of these innumerable materials, it were idle to expect that the courses of thought marked out in one language should, except in their great outlines and main centres, correspond to those of another. Multitudes of ideas expressed in the one do not even enter into the other, and can only be conveyed by some economy or accommodation, by circumlocutions, phrases, limiting words, figures, or some bold and happy expedient. And sometimes, from the continual demand, foreign words become naturalized. Again, the difficulty is extreme, as all persons know, of leading certain individuals (to use a familiar phrase) to understand one another; their habits of thought turning apparently on points of mutual repulsion. Now this is always in a measure traceable to moral diversities between the parties; still, in many cases, it arises mainly from difference in the principle on which they have divided and subdivided that world of ideas, which comes before them both. They seem ever to be dodging each other, and need a common measure or economy to mediate between them.

35. Fables, again, are economies or accommodations, being truths and principles cast into that form in which they will be most vividly recognized; as in the well-known instance attributed to Menenius Agrippa. Again, mythical representations, at least in their better form, may be considered facts or narratives, untrue, but like the truth, intended to bring out the action of some principle, point of character, and the like. For instance, the tradition that St. Ignatius was the child whom our Lord took in His arms, may be unfounded; but it realizes to us his special relation to Christ and His Apostles, with a keenness peculiar to itself. The same remark may be made upon certain narratives of martyrdoms, or of the details of such narratives, or of certain alleged miracles, or heroic acts, or speeches, all which are the spontaneous produce of religious feeling under imperfect knowledge. If the alleged facts did not occur, they ought to have occurred (if I may so speak); they are such as might have occurred, and would have occurred, under circumstances; and they belong to the parties to whom they are attributed, potentially, if not actually; or the like of them did occur; or occurred to others similarly circumstanced, though not to those very per-

sons. Many a theory or view of things, on which an institution is founded, or a party held together, is of the same kind. Many an argument, used by zealous and earnest men, has this economical character, being not the very ground on which they act, (for they continue in the same course, though it be refuted), yet, in a certain sense, a representation of it, a proximate description of their feelings in the shape of argument, on which they can rest, to which they can recur when perplexed, and appeal when questioned. Now, in this reference to accommodation or economy in human affairs, I do not meddle with the question of casuistry, viz. which of such artifices, as they may be called, are innocent, or where the line is to be drawn. That some are immoral, common sense tells us; but it is enough for my purpose, if some are necessary, as the same common sense will allow; and then the very necessity of the use will account for the abuse and perversion.

36. Even between man and man, then, constituted as men are, alike, various distinct instruments, keys, or *calculi* of thought obtain, on which their ideas and arguments shape themselves respectively, and which we must use, if we would reach them. The cogitative method, as it may be called, of one man is notoriously very different from that of another; of the lawyer from that of the soldier, of the rich from that of the poor. The territory of thought is portioned out in a hundred different ways. Abstractions, generalizations, definitions, propositions, all are framed on distinct standards; and if this is found in matters of this world between man and man, surely much more must it exist between the ideas of men, and the thoughts, ways, and works of God.

37. One of the obvious instances of this contrariety it seen in the classifications we make of the subjects of the animal or vegetable kingdoms. Here a very intelligible order has been observed by the Creator Himself; still one of which we have not, after all, the key. We are obliged to frame one of our own; and when we apply it, we find that it will not exactly answer the Divine idea of arrangement, as it discovers itself to us; there being phenomena which we cannot locate, or which, upon our system of division, are anomalies in the general harmony of the Creation.

38. Mathematical science will afford us a more extended illustration of this distinction between supernatural and eternal laws, and our attempts to represent them, that is, our economics. Vari-

ous methods or *calculi* have been adopted to embody these immutable principles and dispositions of which the science treats, which are really independent of any, yet cannot be contemplated or pursued without one or other of them. The first of these instruments of investigation employs the medium of extension; the second, that of number; the third, that of motion; the fourth proceeds on a more subtle hypothesis, that of increase. These methods are very distinct from each other, at least the geometrical and the differential; yet they are, one and all, analyses, more or less perfect, of those same necessary truths, for which we have not a name, of which we have no idea, except in the terms of such economical representations. They are all developments of one and the same range of ideas; they are all instruments of discovery as to those ideas. They stand for real things, and we can reason with them, though they be but symbols, as if they were the things themselves, for which they stand. Yet none of them carries out the lines of truth to their limits; first, one stops in the analysis, then another; like some calculating tables which answer for a thousand times, and miss in the thousand and first. While they answer, we can use them just as if they were the realities which they represent, and without thinking of those realities; but at length our instrument of discovery issues in some great impossibility or contradiction, or what we call in religion, a mystery. It has run its length; and by its failure shows that all along it has been but an expedient for practical purposes, not a true analysis or adequate image of those recondite laws which are investigated by means of it. It has never fathomed their depth, because it now fails to measure their course. At the same time, no one, because it cannot do every thing, would refuse to use it within the range in which it will act: no one would say that it was a system of empty symbols, though it be but a shadow of the unseen. Though we use it with caution, still we use it, as being the nearest approximation to the truth which our condition admits.

39. Let us take another instance, of an outward and earthly form, or economy, under which great wonders unknown seem to be typified; I mean musical sounds, as they are exhibited most perfectly in instrumental harmony. There are seven notes in the scale; make them fourteen; yet what a slender outfit for so vast an enterprise! What science brings so much out of so little? Out

of what poor elements does some great master in it create his new world! Shall we say that all this exuberant inventiveness is a mere ingenuity or trick of art, like some game or fashion of the day, without reality, without meaning? We may do so; and then, perhaps, we shall also account the science of theology to be a matter of words; yet as there is a divinity in the theology of the Church, which those who feel cannot communicate, so is there also in the wonderful creation of sublimity and beauty of which I am speaking. To many men the very names which the science employs are utterly incomprehensible. To speak of an idea or a subject seems to be fanciful or trifling, to speak of the views which it opens upon us to be childish extravagance; yet is it possible that inexhaustible evolution and disposition of notes, so rich yet so simple, so intricate yet so regulated, so various yet so majestic, should be a mere sound, which is gone and perishes? Can it be that those mysterious stirrings of heart, and keen emotions, and strange yearnings after we know not what, and awful impressions from we know not whence, should be wrought in us by what is unsubstantial, and comes and goes, and begins and ends in itself? It is not so; it cannot be. No; they have escaped from some higher sphere; they are the outpourings of eternal harmony in the medium of created sound; they are echoes from our Home; they are the voice of Angels, or the Magnificat of Saints, or the living laws of Divine Governance, or the Divine Attributes; something are they besides themselves, which we cannot compass, which we cannot utter – though mortal man, and he perhaps not otherwise distinguished above his fellows, has the gift of eliciting them.

40. So much on the subject of musical sound; but what if the whole series of impressions, made on us through the senses, be, as I have already hinted, but a Divine economy suited to our need, and the token of realities distinct from themselves, and such as might be revealed to us, nay, more perfectly, by other senses, different from our existing ones as they from each other? What if the properties of matter, as we conceive of them, are merely relative to us, so that facts and events, which seem impossible when predicted concerning it in terms of those impressions, are impossible only in those terms, not in themselves, – impossible only because of the imperfection of the idea, which, in consequence of those impressions, we have conceived

of material substances? If so, it would follow that the laws of physics, as we consider them, are themselves but generalizations of economical exhibitions, inferences from figure and shadow, and not more real than the phenomena from which they are drawn. Scripture, for instance, says that the sun moves and the earth is stationary; and science, that the earth moves, and the sun is comparatively at rest. How can we determine which of these opposite statements is the very truth, till we know what motion is? If our idea of motion be but an accidental result of our present senses, neither proposition is true, and both are true; neither true philosophically, both true for certain practical purposes in the system in which they are respectively found; and physical science will have no better meaning when it says that the earth moves, than plane astronomy when it says that the earth is still.

41. And should any one fear lost thoughts such as these should tend to a dreary and hopeless scepticism, let him take into account the Being and Providence of God, the Merciful and True; and he will at once be relieved of his anxiety. All is dreary till we believe, what our hearts tell us, that we are subjects of His Governance; nothing is dreary, all inspires hope and trust, directly we understand that we are under His hand, and that whatever comes to us is from Him, as a method of discipline and guidance. What is it to us whether the knowledge He gives us be greater or less, if it be He who gives it? What is it to us whether it be exact or vague, if He bids us trust it? What have we to care whether we are or are not given to divide substance from shadow, if He is training us heavenward by means of either? Why should we vex ourselves to find whether our deductions are philosophical or no, provided they are religious? If our senses supply the media by which we are put on trial, by which we are all brought together, and hold intercourse with each other, and are disciplined and are taught, and enabled to benefit others, it is enough. We have an instinct within us, impelling us, we have external necessity forcing us, to trust our senses, and we may leave the question of their substantial truth for another world, "till the day break, and the shadows flee away." And what is true of reliance on our senses, is true of all the information which it has pleased God to vouchsafe to us, whether in nature or in grace.

42. Instances, then, such as these, will be found both to sober and to encourage us in our theological studies, – to impress us with a profound sense of our ignorance of Divine Verities, when we know most; yet to hinder us from relinquishing their contemplation, though we know so little. On the one hand, it would appear that even the most subtle questions of the schools may have a real meaning, as the most intricate *formulae* in analytics; and since we cannot tell how far our instrument of thought reaches in the process of investigation, and at what point it fails us, no questions may safely be despised. "Whether God was any where before creation?" "whether He knows all creatures in Himself?" "whether the blessed see all things possible and future in Him?" "whether relation is the form of the Divine Persons?" "in what sense the Holy Spirit is Divine Love?" these, and a multitude of others, far more minute and remote, are all sacred from their subject.

43. On the other hand, it must be recollected that not even the Catholic reasonings and conclusions, as contained in Confessions, and most thoroughly received by us, are worthy of the Divine Verities which they represent, but are the truth only in as full a measure as our minds can admit it; the truth as far as they go, and under the conditions of thought which human feebleness imposes. It is true that God is without beginning, if eternity may worthily be considered to imply succession; in every place, if He who is a Spirit can have relations with space. It is right to speak of His Being and Attributes, if He be not rather superessential; it is true to say that He is wise or powerful, if we may consider Him as other than the most simple Unity. He is truly Three, if He is truly One; He is truly One, if the idea of Him falls under earthly number. He has a triple Personality, in the sense in which the Infinite can be understood to have Personality at all. If we know any thing of Him, – if we may speak of Him in any way, – if we emerge from Atheism or Pantheism into religious faith, – if we would have any saving hope, any life of truth and holiness within us, – this only do we know, with this only confession, we must begin and end our worship – that the Father is the One God, the Son the One God, and the Holy Ghost the One God; and that the Father is not the Son, the Son not the Holy Ghost, and the Holy Ghost not the Father.

44. The fault, then, which we must guard against in receiving such Divine intimations, is the ambition of being wiser than what is written; of employing the Reason, not in carrying out what is told us, but in impugning it; not in support, but in prejudice of Faith. Brilliant as are such exhibitions of its powers, they bear no fruit. Reason can but ascertain the profound difficulties of our condition, it cannot remove them; it has no work, it makes no beginning, it does but continually fall back, till it is content to be a little child, and to follow where Faith guides it.

45. What remains, then, but to make our prayer to the Gracious and Merciful God, the Father of Lights, that in all our exercises of Reason, His gift, we may thus use it, – as He would have us, in the obedience of Faith, with a view to His glory, with an aim at His Truth, in dutiful submission to His will, for the comfort of His elect, for the edification of Holy Jerusalem, His Church, and in recollection of His own solemn warning, ''Every idle word that men shall speak, they shall give account thereof in the day of judgment; for by thy words thou shalt be justified, and by thy words thou shalt be condemned.''

AN ESSAY ON THE DEVELOPMENT OF CHRISTIAN DOCTRINE

Newman decided in December 1844 to write the book which he had been turning over in his mind since March of the same year. It would be a good way of testing his growing conviction that he must join the Roman Catholic Church. He began writing at the beginning of 1845. No book he had yet written cost him so much toil and trouble, as he wrote and rewrote. He had still not finished in September when he decided not to wait any longer but to seek admission to the Roman Catholic Church. The unfinished book was sent to the printer in late September and was published before the end of the year. The first edition was soon sold out and a second edition was published in 1846. In 1878 Newman published a new edition; nothing of substance was altered, but the contents were largely re-arranged and the text revised. This is the text used for the following extracts which are taken from the introduction and chapters I (''On the Development of Ideas''), II (''On the Antecedent Argument in behalf of Developments in Christian Doctrine''), and V ('Genuine Developments contrasted with Corruptions'').

AN ESSAY ON THE DEVELOPMENT OF CHRISTIAN DOCTRINE

INTRODUCTION

The following Essay is directed towards a solution of the difficulty which has been stated, – the difficulty, as far as it exists, which lies in the way of our using in controversy the testimony of our most natural informant concerning the doctrine and worship of Christianity, viz, the history of eighteen hundred years. The view on which it is written has at all times, perhaps, been implicitly adopted by theologians, and I believe, has recently been illustrated by several distinguished writers of the continent, such as De Maistre and Möhler: viz. that the increase and expansion of the Christian Creed and Ritual, and the variations which have attended the process in the case of individual writers and Churches, are the necessary attendants on any philosophy or polity which takes possession of the intellect and heart, and has had any wide or extended dominion; that, from the nature of the human mind, time is necessary for the full comprehension and perfection of great ideas; and most wonderful truths, though communicated to the world once for all by inspired teachers, could not be comprehended all at once by the recipients, but, as being received and transmitted by minds not inspired and through media which were human, have required only the longer time and deeper thought for their full elucidation. This may be called the *Theory of Development of Doctrine*; and, before proceeding to treat of it, one remark may be in place.

It is undoubtedly an hypothesis to account for a difficulty; but such too are the various explanations given by astronomers from Ptolemy to Newton of the apparent motions of the heavenly bodies, and it is as unphilosophical on that account to object to the one as to object to the other. Nor is it more reasonable to express surprise, that at this time of day a theory is necessary, granting for argument's sake that the theory is novel, than to have directed a similar wonder in disparagement of the theory of gravitation, or the Plutonian theory in geology. Doubtless, the theory of doctrinal Developments are expedients, and so is the dictum of Vincentius; so is the art of grammar or the use of the quadrant; it is an expedient to enable us to solve what has now become a necessary and an anxious problem. For three hundred years the documents and the facts of Christianity have been exposed to a jealous scrutiny; works have been judged spurious which once were received without a question; facts have been discarded or modified which were once first principles in argument; new facts and new principles have been brought to light; philosophical views and polemical discussions of various tendencies have been maintained with more or less success. Not only has the relative situation of controversies and theologies altered, but infidelity itself is in a different, – I am obliged to say in a more hopeful position, – as regards Christianity. The facts of Revealed Religion, though in their substance unaltered, present a less compact and orderly front to the attacks of its enemies now than formerly and allow of the introduction of new inquiries and theories concerning its sources and its rise. The state of things is not as it was, when an appeal lay to the supposed works of the Areopagite, or to the primitive Decretals, or to St. Dionysius's answers to Paul, or to the Cœna Domini of St. Cyprian. The assailants of dogmatic truth have got the start of its adherents of whatever Creed; philosophy is completing what criticism has begun; and apprehensions are not unreasonably excited lest we should have a new world to conquer before we have weapons for the warfare. Already infidelity has its views and conjectures, on which it arranges the facts of ecclesiastical history; and it is sure to consider the absence of any antagonist theory as an evidence of the reality of its own. That the hypothesis, here to be adopted, accounts not only for the Athanasian Creed, but for the Creed of Pope Pius, is no fault of those who adopt it. No one has power over the issues of his principles; we cannot manage our argument, and have as much of it as we please and no more. An argument is needed, unless Christianity is to abandon the province of argument; and those who find fault with the explanation here offered of its historical phenomena will find it their duty to provide one for themselves.

And as no special aim at Roman Catholic doctrine need be supposed to have given a direction to the inquiry, so neither can a reception of that doctrine be immediately based on its results. It would be the work of a life to apply the Theory of Developments so carefully to the writings of the Fathers, and to the history of controversies and councils, as thereby to vindicate the reasonableness of every decision of Rome; much less can such an undertaking be imagined by one who, in the middle of his days, is beginning life again. Thus much, however, might be gained even from an Essay like the present, an explanation of so many of the reputed corruptions, doctrinal and practical of Rome, as might serve as a fair ground for trusting her in parallel cases where the investigation had not been pursued.

(*Dev.* 29–30)

CHAPTER I
ON THE DEVELOPMENT OF IDEAS

SECTION I
ON THE PROCESS OF DEVELOPMENT IN IDEAS

It is the characteristic of our minds to be ever engaged in passing judgment on the things which come before us. No sooner do we apprehend than we judge: we allow nothing to stand by itself: we compare, contrast, abstract, generalize, connect, adjust, classify: and we view all our knowledge in the associations with which these processes have invested it.

Of the judgments thus made, which become aspects in our minds of the things which meet us, some are mere opinions which come and go, or which remain with us only till an accident displaces them, whatever be the influence which they exercise meanwhile. Others are firmly fixed in our minds, with or without good reason, and have a hold upon us, whether they relate to matters of fact, or to principles of conduct, or are views of life and the world, or are prejudices, imaginations, or convictions. Many of them attach to one and the same object, which is thus variously viewed, not only by various minds, but by the same. They sometimes lie in such near relation, that each implies the others; some are only not inconsistent with each other, in that they have a common origin: some, as being actually incompatible with each other, are, one or other, falsely associated in our minds with their object, and in any case they may be nothing more than ideas, which we mistake for things.

Thus Judaism is an idea which once was objective, and Gnosticism is an idea which was never so. Both of them have various aspects: those of Judaism were such as monotheism, a certain ethical discipline, a ministration of divine vengeance, a preparation for Christianity: those of the Gnostic idea are such as the doctrine of two principles, that of emanation, the intrinsic malignity of matter, the inculpability of sensual indulgence, or the guilt of every pleasure of sense, of which last two one or other must be in the Gnostic a false aspect and subjective only.

2.

The idea which represents an object or supposed object is commensurate with the sum total of its possible aspects, however they may vary in the separate consciousness of individuals; and in proportion to the variety of aspects under which it presents itself to various minds is its force and depth, and the argument for its reality. Ordinarily an idea is not brought home to the intellect as objective except through this variety; like bodily substances, which are not apprehended except under the clothing of their properties and results, and which admit to being walked round, and surveyed on opposite sides, and in different perspectives, and in contrary lights, in evidence of their reality. And, as views of a material object may be taken from points so remote or so opposed, that they seem at first sight incompatible, and especially as their shadows will be disproportionate, or even monstrous, and yet all these anomalies will disappear and all these contrarieties be adjusted, on ascertaining the point of vision or the surface of projection in each case; so also all the aspects of an idea are capable of coalition, and of a resolution into the object to which it belongs; and the *prima facie* dissimilitude of its aspects becomes, when explained, an argument for its substantiveness and integrity, and their multiplicity for its originality and power.

3.

There is no one aspect deep enough to exhaust the contents of a real idea, no one term or proposition which will serve to define it; though of course one representation of it is more just and exact than another, and though when an idea is very complex, it is allowable, for the sake of convenience, to consider its distinct aspects as if separate ideas. Thus, with all our intimate knowledge of animal life and of the structure of particular animals, we have not arrived at a true definition of any one of them, but are forced to enumerate properties and accidents by way of description. Nor can we inclose in a formula that intellectual fact, or system of thought, which we call the Platonic philosophy, or that historical phenomenon of doctrine and conduct, which we call the heresy of Montanus or of Manes. Again, if Protestantism were said to lie in its theory of private judgment, and Lutheranism in its doctrine of justification, this indeed would be an approximation to the truth; but it is plain that to argue or to act as if the one or the other aspect were a sufficient account of those forms of religion severally, would be a serious mistake. Sometimes an attempt is made to determine the "leading idea," as it has been called, of Christianity, an ambitious essay as employed on a supernatural work, when, even as regards the visible creation and the inventions of man, such a task is beyond us. Thus its one idea has been said by some to be the restoration of our fallen race, by others philanthropy, by others the tidings of immortality, or the spirituality of true religious service, or the salvation of the elect, or mental liberty, or the union of the soul with God. If, indeed, it is only thereby meant to use one or other of these as a central idea for convenience, in order to group others around it, no fault can be found with such a proceeding: and in this sense I should myself call the Incarnation the central aspect of Christianity, out of which the three main aspects of its teaching take their rise, the sacramental, the hierarchical, and the ascetic. But one aspect of Revelation must not be allowed to exclude or to obscure another; and Christianity is dogmatical, devotional, practical all at once; it is esoteric and exoteric; it is indulgent and strict; it is light and dark; it is love, and it is fear.

4.

When an idea, whether real or not, is of a nature to arrest and possess the mind, it may be said to have life, that is, to live in the mind which is its recipient. Thus mathematical ideas, real as they are, can hardly properly be called living, at least ordinarily. But, when some great enuciation, whether true or false, about human nature, or present good, or government, or duty, or religion, is carried forward into the public throng of men and draws attention, then it is not merely received passively in this or that form into many minds, but it becomes an active principle within them, leading them to an ever-new contemplation of itself, to an application of it in various directions, and a propagation of it on every side. Such is the doctrine of the divine right of kings, or of the rights of man, or of the anti-social bearings of a priesthood, or utilitarianism, or free trade, or the duty of benevolent enterprises, or the philosophy of Zeno or Epicurus, doctrines which are of a nature to attract and influence, and have so far a *prima facie* reality, that they may be looked at on many sides and strike various minds very variously. Let one such idea get possession of the popular mind, or the mind of any portion of the community, and it is not difficult to understand what will be the result. At first men will not fully realize what it is that moves them, and will express and explain themselves inadequately. There will be a general agitation of thought, and an action of mind upon mind. There will be a time of confusion, when conceptions and misconceptions are in conflict, and it is uncertain whether anything is to come of the idea at all, or which view of it is to get the start of the others. New lights will be brought to bear upon the original statements of the doctrine put forward; judgments and aspects will accumulate. After a while some definite teaching emerges; and, as time proceeds, one view will be modified or expanded by another, and then combined with a third; till the idea to which these various aspects belong, will be to each mind separately what at first it was only to all together. It will be surveyed too in its relation to other doctrines or facts, to other natural laws or established customs, to the varying circumstances of times and places, to other religions, politics, philosophies, as the case may be. How it stands affected towards other systems, how it affects them, how far it may be made to combine with them, how far it tolerates them when it interferes with them, will be gradually wrought out. It will be interrogated and criticized by enemies, and defended by well-wishers. The multitude of opinions formed concerning it in these respects and many others will be collected, compared, sorted, sifted, selected, rejected, gradually attached to it, separated from it, in the minds of individuals and of the community. It will, in proportion to its native vigour and subtlety, introduce itself into the framework and details of social life, changing public opinion, and strengthening or undermining the foundations of established order. Thus in time it will have grown into an ethical code, or into a system of government, or into a theology, or into a ritual. according to its capabilities: and this body of thought, thus laboriously gained, will after all be little more than the proper representative of one idea, being in substance what that idea meant from the first, its complete image as seen in a combination of diversified aspects, with the suggestions and corrections of many minds, and the illustration of many experiences.

5.

This process, whether it be longer or shorter in point of time, by which the aspects of an idea are brought into consistency and form, I call its development, being the germination and maturation of some truth or apparent truth on a large mental field. On the other hand this process will not be a development, unless the assemblage of aspects, which constitute its ultimate shape, really belongs to the idea from which they start. A republic, for instance, is not a development from a pure monarchy, though it may follow upon it; whereas the Greek "tyrant" may be considered as included in the idea of a democracy. Moreover a development will have this characteristic, that, its action being in the busy scene of human life, it cannot progress at all without cutting across, and thereby destroying or modifying and incorporating with itself existing modes of thinking and operating. The development then of an idea is not like an investigation worked out on paper, in which each successive advance is a pure evolution from a foregoing, but it is carried on through and by means of communities of men and their leaders and guides; and it employs their minds as its instruments, and depends upon them, while it uses them. And so, as regards existing opinions, principles, measures, and institutions of the community which it has invaded; it develops by establishing relations between itself and them; it employs itself, in giving them a new meaning and direction, in creating what may be called a jurisdiction over them, in throwing off whatever in them it cannot assimilate. It grows when it incorporates, and its identity is found, not in isolation, but in continuity and sovereignty.

This it is that imparts to the history both of states and of religions, its specially turbulent and polemical character. Such is the explanation of the wranglings, whether of schools or of parliaments. It is the warfare of ideas under their various aspects striving for the mastery, each of them enterprising, engrossing, imperious, more or less incompatible with the rest, and rallying followers or rousing foes, according as it acts upon the faith, the prejudices, or the interest of parties or classes.

6.

Moreover, an idea not only modifies, but is modified, or, or at least influenced, by the state of things in which it is carried out, and is dependent in various ways on the circumstances which surround it. Its development proceeds quickly or slowly, as it may be; the order of succession in its separate stages is variable; it shows differently in a small sphere of action and in an extended; it may be interrupted, retarded, mutilated, distorted, by external violence; it may be enfeebled by the effort of ridding itself of domestic foes; it may be impeded and swayed or even absorbed by counter energetic ideas; it may be coloured by the received tone of thought into which it comes, or depraved by the intrusion of foreign principles, or at length shattered by the development of some original fault within it.

7.

But whatever be the risk of corruption from intercourse with the world around, such a risk must be encountered if a great idea is duly to be understood, and much more if it is to be fully exhibited. It is elicited and expanded by trial, and battles into perfection and supremacy. Nor does it escape the collision of opinion even in its earlier years, nor does it remain truer to itself, and with a better claim to be considered one and the same, though externally protected from vicissitude and change. It is indeed sometimes said that the stream is clearest near the spring. Whatever use may fairly be made of this image, it does not apply to the history of a philosophy or belief, which on the contrary is more equable, and purer, and stronger, when its bed has become deep, and broad, and full. It necessarily rises out of an existing state of things, and for a time savours of the soil. Its vital element needs disengaging from what is foreign and temporary, and is employed in efforts after freedom which become more vigorous and hopeful as its years increase. Its beginnings are no measure of its capabilities, nor of its scope. At first no one knows what it is, or what it is worth. It remains perhaps for a time quiescent; it tries, as it were, its limbs, and proves the ground under it, and feels its way. From time to time it makes essays which fail, and are in consequence abandoned. It seems in suspense which way to go; it wavers, and at length strikes out in one definite direction. In time it enters upon strange territory; points of controversy alter their bearing; parties rise and fall around it; dangers and hopes appear in new relations; and old principles reappear under new forms. It changes with them in order to remain the same. In a higher world it is otherwise, but here below to live is to change, and to be perfect is to have changed often.

SECTION II
ON THE KINDS OF DEVELOPMENT IN IDEAS

To attempt an accurate analysis or complete enumeration of the processes of thought, whether speculative or practical, which come under the notion of development, exceeds the pretensions of an Essay like the present; but, without some general view of the various mental exercises which go by the name we shall have no security against confusion in our reasoning and necessary exposure to criticism.

1. First, then, it must be borne in mind that the word is commonly used, and is used here, in three senses indiscriminately, from defect of our language; on the one hand for the process of development, on the other for the result; and again either generally for a development, true or not true, (that is, faithful or unfaithful to the idea from which it started,) or exclusively for a development deserving the name. A false or unfaithful development is more properly to be called a corruption.

2. Next, it is plain that *mathematical* developments, that is, the system of truths drawn out from mathematical definitions or equations, do not fall under our present subject, though alto-

gether analogous to it. There can be no corruption in such developments, because they are conducted on strict demonstration; and the conclusions in which they terminate, being necessary, cannot be declensions from the original idea.

3. Nor, of course, do *physical* developments, as the growth of animal or vegetable nature, come into consideration here; excepting that, together with mathematical, they may be taken as illustrations of the general subject to which we have to direct our attention.

4. Nor have we to consider *material* developments, which, though effected by human contrivance, are still physical; as the development, as it is called, of the national resources. . . .

5. When society and its various classes and interests are the subject-matter of the ideas which are in operation, the development may be called *political*; as we see it in the growth of States or the changes of a Constitution. . . .

6. In other developments the intellectual character is so prominent that they may even be called *logical*, as in the Anglican doctrine of the Royal Supremacy, which has been created in the courts of law, not in the cabinet or in the field. Hence it is carried out with a consistency and minute application which the history of constitutions cannot exhibit. It does not only exist in statutes, or in articles, or in oaths, it is realized in details. . . .

7. Another class of developments may be called *historical*; being the gradual formation of opinion concerning persons, facts, and events. Judgments, which were at one time confined to a few, at length spread through a community, and attain general reception by the accumulation and concurrence of testimony. Thus some authoritative accounts die away; others gain a footing, and are ultimately received as truths. . . .

8. *Ethical* developments are not properly matter for argument and controversy, but are natural and personal, substituting what is congruous, desirable, pious, appropriate, generous, for strictly logical inference. . . .

9. It remains to allude to what, unless the word were often so vaguely and variously used, I should be led to call *metaphysical* developments; I mean such as are a mere analysis of the idea contemplated, and terminate in its exact and complete delineation. . . .

So much on the development of ideas in various subject matters; it may be necessary to add that, in many cases, *development* simply stands for *exhibition*, as in some of the instances adduced above. Thus both Calvinism and Unitarianism may be called developments, that is, exhibitions, of the principle of Private Judgment, though they have nothing in common, viewed as doctrines.

As to Christianity, supposing the truths of which it consists to admit of development, that development will be one or other of the last five kinds. Taking the Incarnation as its central doctrine, the Episcopate, as taught by St. Ignatius, will be an instance of political development, the *Theotokos* of logical, the determination of the date of our Lord's birth of historical, the Holy Eucharist of moral, and the Athanasian Creed of metaphysical.

(*Dev.* 33–42, 45–7, 52–40)

CHAPTER II
ON THE ANTECEDENT ARGUMENT IN BEHALF OF DEVELOPMENTS IN CHRISTIAN DOCTRINE

SECTION I
DEVELOPMENTS OF DOCTRINE TO BE EXPECTED

1. If Christianity is a fact, and impresses an idea of itself on our minds and is a subject-matter of exercises of the reason, that idea will in course of time expand into a multitude of ideas, and aspects of ideas, connected and harmonious with one another, and in themselves determinate and immutable, as is the objective fact itself which is thus represented. It is a characteristic of our minds, that they cannot take an object in, which is submitted to them simply and integrally. We conceive by means of definition; whole objects do not create in the intellect whole ideas, but are, to use a mathematical phrase, thrown into series, into a number of statements, strengthening, interpreting, correcting each other, and with more or less exactness approximating, as they accumulate, to a perfect image. There is no other way of learning or of teaching. We cannot teach except by aspects or views, which are not identical with the thing itself which we are teaching. Two persons may each convey the same truth to a third, yet by methods and through representations altogether different. The same person will treat the same argument differently in an essay or speech, according to the accident of

the day of writing, or of the audience, yet it will be substantially the same.

And the more claim an idea has to be considered living, the more various will be its aspects; and the more social and political is its nature, the more complicated and subtle will be its issues, and the longer and more eventful will be its course. And in the number of these special ideas, which from their very depth and richness cannot be fully understood at once, but are more and more clearly expressed and taught the longer they last, – having aspects many and bearings many, mutually connected and growing one out of another, and all parts of a whole, with a sympathy and correspondence keeping pace with the over-changing necessities of the world, multiform, prolific, and ever resourceful, – among these great doctrines surely we Christians shall not refuse a foremost place to Christianity. Such previously to the determination of the facts, must be our anticipation concerning it from a contemplation of its initial achievements.

2.

It may be objected that its inspired documents at once determine the limits of its mission without further trouble; but ideas are in the writer and reader of the revelation, not the inspired text itself: and the question is whether those ideas which the letter conveys from writer to reader, reach the reader at once in their completeness and accuracy on his first perception of them, or whether they open out in his intellect and grow to perfection in the course of time. Nor could it surely be maintained without extravagance that the letter of the New Testament, or of any assignable number of books, comprises a delineation of all possible forms which a divine message will assume when submitted to a multitude of minds.

Nor is the case altered by supposing that inspiration provided in behalf of the first recipients of the Revelation, what the Divine Fiat effected for herbs and plants in the beginning, which were created in maturity. Still, the time at length came, when its recipients ceased to be inspired; and on these recipients the revealed truths would fall, as in other cases, at first vaguely and generally, though in spirit and in truth, and would afterwards be completed by developments.

Nor can it fairly be made a difficulty that thus to treat of Christianity is to level it in some sort to sects and doctrines of the world, and to imput to it the imperfections which characterize the productions of man. Certainly it is a sort of degradation of a divine work to consider it under an earthly form; but it is no irreverence, since our Lord Himself, its Author and Guardian, bore one also. Christianity differs from other religions and philosophies, in what is superadded to earth from heaven; not in kind, but in origin; not in its nature, but in its personal characteristics; being informed and quickened by what is more than intellect, by a divine spirit. It is externally what the Apostle calls an "earthen vessel," being the religion of men. And considered as such, it grows "in wisdom and stature;" but the powers which it wields, and the words which proceed out of its mouth, attest its miraculous nativity.

Unless then some special ground of exception can be assigned, it is as evident that Christianity, as a doctrine and worship, will develope in the minds of recipients, as that it conforms in other respects, in its external propagation or its political framework, to the general methods by which the course of things is carried forward.

3.

2. Again, if Christianity be an universal religion, suited not simply to one locality or period, but to all times and places, it cannot but vary in its relations and dealings towards the world around it, that is, it will develope. Principles require a very various application according as persons and circumstances vary, and must be thrown into new shapes according to the form of society which they are to influence. Hence, all bodies of Christians, orthodox or not, develope the doctrines of Scripture. Few but will grant that Luther's view of justification had never been stated in words before his time; that his phraseology and his positions were novel, whether called for by circumstances or not. It is equally certain that the doctrine of justification defined at Trent was, in some sense, new also. The refutation and remedy of errors cannot precede their rise; and thus the fact of false developments or corruptions involves the correspondent manifestation of true ones. Moreover, all parties appeal to Scripture,

that is, argue from Scripture; but argument implies deduction, that is, development. Here there is no difference between early times and late, between a Pope *ex cathedrá* and an individual Protestant, except that their authority is not on a par. On either side the claim of authority is the same, and the process of development.

Accordingly, the common complaint of Protestants against the Church of Rome is, not simply that she has added to the primitive or the Scriptural doctrine, (for this they do themselves,) but that she contradicts it, and moreover imposes her additions as fundamental truths under sanction of an anathema. For themselves they deduce by quite as subtle a method, and act upon doctrines as implicit and on reasons as little analyzed in time past, as Catholic schoolmen. What prominence has the Royal Supremacy in the New Testament, or the lawfulness of bearing arms, or the duty of public worship, or the substitution of the first day of the week for the seventh, or infant baptism, to say nothing of the fundamental principle that the Bible and Bible only is the religion of Protestants? These doctrines and usages, true or not, which is not the question here, are surely not gained by the direct use and immediate application of Scripture, nor by a mere exercise of argument upon words and sentences placed before the eyes, but by the unconscious growth of ideas suggested by the letter and habitual to the mind.

4.

3. And, indeed, when we turn to the consideration of particular doctrines on which Scripture lays the greatest stress, we shall see that it is absolutely impossible for them to remain in the mere letter of Scripture, if they are to be more than mere words, and to convey a definite idea to the recipient. When it is declared that "the Word became flesh,"three wide questions open upon us on the very announcement. What is meant by "the Word," what by "flesh," what by "became"? The answers to these involve a process of investigation, and are developments. Moreover, when they have been made, they will suggest a series of secondary questions; and thus at length a multitude of propositions is the result, which gather round the inspired sentence

of which they come, giving it externally the form of a doctrine, and creating or deepening the idea of it in the mind.

It is true that, so far as such statements of Scripture are mysteries, they are relatively to us but words, and cannot be developed. But as a mystery implies in part what is incomprehensible or at least unknown, so does it in part imply what is not so; it implies a partial manifestation, or a representation by economy. Because then it is in a measure understood, it can so far be developed, though each result in the process will partake of the dimness and confusion of the original impression.

5.

4. This moreover should be considered, – that great questions exist in the subject-matter of which Scripture treats, which Scripture does not solve; questions too so real, so practical, that they must be answered, and, unless we suppose a new revelation, answered by means of the revelation which we have, that is, by development. Such is the question of the Canon of Scripture and its inspiration; that is, whether Christianity depends upon a written document as Judaism; – if so, on what writings and how many; – whether that document is self-interpreting, or requires a comment, and whether any authoritative comment or commentator is provided; – whether the revelation and the document are commensurate, or the one outruns the other; – all these questions surely find no solution on the surface of Scripture, nor indeed under the surface in the case of most men, however long and diligent might be their study of it. Nor were these difficulties settled by authority, as far as we know, at the commencement of the religion; yet surely it is quite conceivable that an Apostle might have dissipated them all in a few words, had Divine Wisdom thought fit. But in matter of fact the decision has been left to time, to the slow process of thought, to the influence of mind upon mind, the issues of controversy, and the growth of opinion.

6.

To take another instance just now referred to:- if there was a point on which a rule was desirable from the first, it was concerning the religious duties under which Christian parents lay as regards their children. It would be natural indeed in any Christian father, in the absence of a rule, to bring his children for baptism; such in this instance would be the practical development of his faith in Christ and love for his offspring; still a development it is, – necessarily required, yet as far as we know, not provided for his need by direct precept in the Revelation as originally given.

Another very large field of thought, full of practical considerations, yet, as far as our knowledge goes, but only partially occupied by any Apostolical judgment, is that which the question of the effects of Baptism opens upon us. That they who came in repentance and faith to that Holy Sacrament received remission of sins, is undoubtedly the doctrine of the Apostles; but is there any means of a second remission for sins committed after it? St. Paul's Epistles, where we might expect an answer to our inquiry, contain no explicit statement on the subject; what they do plainly say does not diminish the difficulty; – viz., first, that baptism is intended for the pardon of sins before it, not in prospect; next, that those who have received the gift of Baptism in fact live in a state of holiness, not of sin. How do statements such as these meet the actual state of the Church as we see it at this day?

Considering that it was expressly predicted that the Kingdom of Heaven, like the fisher's net, should gather of every kind, and that the tares should grow with the wheat until the harvest, a graver and more practical question cannot be imagined than that which it has pleased the Divine Author of the Revelation to leave undecided, unless indeed there be means given in that Revelation of its own growth or development. ... Since then Scripture needs completion, the question is brought to this issue, whether defect or inchoateness in its doctrines be or be not an antecedent probability in favour of a development of them.

7.

There is another subject, though not so immediately practical, on which Scripture does not, strictly speaking, keep silence, but says so little as to require, and so much as to suggest, information beyond its letter, – the intermediate state between death and the Resurrection. Considering the long interval which separates Christ's first and second coming, the millions of faithful souls who are waiting it out, and the intimate concern which every Christian has in the determination of its character, it might have been expected that Scripture would have spoken explicitly concerning it, whereas in fact its notices are but brief and obscure. We might indeed have argued that this silence of Scripture was intentional, with a view of discouraging speculations upon the subject, except for the circumstance that, as in the question of our post-baptismal state, its teaching seems to proceed upon an hypothesis inapplicable to the state of the Church after the time when it was delivered. As Scripture contemplates Christians, not as backsliders, but as saints, so does it apparently represent the Day of Judgment as immediate, and the interval of expectation as evanescent. It leaves on our minds the general impression that Christ was returning on earth at once, "the time short," worldly engagement superseded by "the present distress," persecutors urgent, Christians, as a body, sinless and expectant, without home, without plan for the future, looking up to heaven. But outward circumstances have changed, and with the change, a different application of the revealed word has of necessity been demanded, that is, a development. When the nations were converted and offences abounded, then the Church came out to view, on the one hand as a temporal establishment, on the other as a remedial system, and passages of Scripture aided and directed the development which before were of inferior account. Hence the doctrine of Penance as the complement of Baptism and of Purgatory as the explanation of the Intermediate State. So reasonable is this expansion of the original creed, that, when some ten years since the true doctrine of Baptism was expounded among us without any mention of Penance, our teacher was accused by many of us of Novatianism; while, on the other hand, heterodox divines have before now advocated the doctrine of the sleep of the soul because they said it was the only successful preventive of belief in Purgatory.

8.

Thus developments of Christianity are proved to have been in the contemplation of its Divine Author, by an argument parallel to that by which we infer intelligence in the system of the physical world. In whatever sense the need and its supply are a proof of design in the visible creation, in the same do the gaps, if the word may be used, which occur in the structure of the original creed of the Church, make it probable that those developments, which grow out of the truths which lie around it, were intended to fill them up. ....

9.

5. The method of revelation observed in Scripture abundantly confirms this anticipation. For instance, Prophecy, if it had so happened, need not have afforded a specimen of development; separate predictions might have been made to accumulate as time went on, prospects might have opened, definite knowledge might have been given, by communications independent of each other, as St. John's Gospel or the Epistles of St. Paul are unconnected with the first three Gospels, though the doctrine of each Apostle is a development of their matter. But the prophetic Revelation is, in matter of fact, not of this nature, but a process of development; the earlier prophecies are pregnant texts out of which the succeeding announcements grow; they are types. It is not that one truth is told, then another; but the whole truth or large portions of it are told at once, yet only in their rudiments, or in miniature, and they are expanded and finished in their parts, as the course of revelation proceeds. The Seed of the woman was to bruise the serpent's head; the sceptre was not to depart from Judah till Shiloh came, to whom was to be the gathering of the people. He was to be Wonderful, Counsellor, the Prince of Peace. The question of the Ethiopian rises in the reader's mind, "Of whom speaketh the Prophet this?" Every word requires a comment. Accordingly, it is no uncommon theory with unbelievers, that the Messianic idea, as they call it, was gradually developed in the minds of the Jews by a continuous and traditional habit of contemplating it, and grew into its full proportions by a mere human process; and so far seems certain, without trenching on the doctrine of inspiration, that the books of Wisdom and Ecclesiasticus are developments of the writings of the Prophets, expressed or elicited by means of

167

current ideas in the Greek philosophy, and ultimately adopted and ratified by the Apostle in his Epistle to the Hebrews.

10.

But the whole Bible, not its prophetical portions only, is written on the principle of development. As the Revelation proceeds, it is ever new, yet ever old. St. John, who completes it, declares that he writes no ''new commandment unto his brethren'', but an old commandment which they ''had from the beginning.'' And then he adds, ''A new commandment I write unto you''. The same test of development is suggested in our Lord's words on the Mount, as has already been noticed, ''Think not that I am come to destroy the Law and the Prophets; I am not come to destroy, but to fulfil''. He does not reverse, but perfect, what has gone before. Thus with respect to the evangelical view of the rite of sacrifice, first the rite is enjoined by Moses; next Samuel says, ''to obey is better than sacrifice;'' then Hosea, I will have mercy and not sacrifice;'' Isaiah, ''incense is an abomination unto me;'' then Malachi, describing the times of the Gospel, speaks of the ''pure offering'' of wheatflour; and our Lord completes the development, when He speaks of worshipping ''in spirit and in truth.'' If there is anything here left to explain, it will be found in the usage of the Christian Church immediately afterwards, which shows that sacrifice was not removed, but truth and spirit added.

Nay, the *effata* of our Lord and His Apostles are of a typical structure, parallel to the prophetic announcements above mentioned, and predictions as well as injunctions of doctrine. If then the prophetic sentences have had that development which has really been given them, first by succeeding revelations, and then by the event, it is probable antecedently that those doctrinal, political, ritual, and ethical sentences, which have the same structure, should admit the same expansion. Such are, ''This is My Body,'' or ''Thou art Peter, and upon this Rock I will build My Church,'' or ''The meek shall inherit the earth,'' or ''Suffer little children to come unto Me,'' or ''The pure in heart shall see God.'' . . .

11.

Moreover, while it is certain that developments of Revelation proceeded all through the Old Dispensation down to the very end of our Lord's ministry, on the other hand, if we turn our attention to the beginnings of Apostolical teaching after His ascension, we shall find ourselves unable to fix an historical point at which the growth of doctrine ceased, and the rule of faith was once for all settled. Not on the day of Pentecost, for St. Peter had still to learn at Joppa that he was to baptize Cornelius; not at Joppa and Cæsarea, for St. Paul had to write his Epistles; not on the death of the last Apostle, for St. Ignatius had to establish the doctrine of Episcopacy; not then, nor for centuries after, for the Canon of the New Testament was still undetermined. Not in the Creed, which is no collection of definitions, but a summary of certain *credenda*, an incomplete summary, and, like the Lord's Prayer or the Decalogue, a mere sample of divine truths, especially of the more elementary. No one doctrine can be named which starts complete at first, and gains nothing afterwards from the investigations of faith and the attacks of heresy. The Church went forth from the old world in haste, as the Israelites from Egypt "with their dough before it was leavened, their kneading troughs being bound up in their clothes upon their shoulders."

12.

Further, the political developments contained in the historical parts of Scripture are as striking as the prophetical and the doctrinal. Can any history wear a more human appearance than that of the rise and growth of the chosen people to whom I have just referred? What had been determined in the counsels of the Lord of heaven and earth from the beginning, what was immutable, what was announced to Moses in the burning bush, is afterwards represented as the growth of an idea under successive emergencies. . . .

13.

6. It is in point to notice also the structure and style of Scripture, a structure so unsystematic and various, and a style so figurative

and indirect, that no one would presume at first sight to say what is in it and what is not. It cannot, as it were, be mapped, or its contents catalogued; but after all our diligence, to the end of our lives and to the end of the Church, it must be an unexplored and unsubdued land, with heights and valleys, forests and streams, on the right and left of our path and close about us, full of concealed wonders and choice treasures. Of no doctrine whatever, which does not actually contradict what has been delivered, can it be peremptorily asserted that it is not in Scripture; of no reader, whatever be his study of it, can it be said that he has mastered every doctrine which it contains. . . .

14.

It may be added that, in matter of fact, all the definitions or received judgements of the early and medieval Church rest upon definite, even though sometimes obscure sentences of Scripture. Thus Purgatory may appeal to the "saving by fire," and "entering through much tribulation into the kingdom of God;" the communication of the merits of the Saints to our "receiving a prophet's reward" for "receiving a prophet in the name of a prophet," and "a righteous man's reward" for "receiving a righteous man in the name of a righteous man;" the Real Presence to "This is My Body;" Absolution to "Whosoever sins ye remit, they are remitted;" Extreme Unction to "Anointing him with oil in the Name of the Lord;" Voluntary poverty to "Sell all that thou hast;" obedience to "He was in subjection to His parents.". . .

15.

7. Lastly, while Scripture nowhere recognizes itself or asserts the inspiration of those passages which are most essential, it distinctly anticipates the development of Christianity, both as a polity and as a doctrine. In one of our Lord's parables "the Kingdom of Heaven" is even compared to "a grain of mustard-seed, which a man took and hid in his field; which indeed is the least of all seeds, but when it is grown it is the greatest among herbs, and becometh a tree," and, as St. Mark words it, "shooteth out great branches, so that the birds of the air

come and lodge in the branches thereof." And again, in the same chapter of St. Mark, "So is the kingdom of God, as if a man should cast seed into the ground, and should sleep, and rise night and day, and the seed should spring and grow up, he knoweth not how; for the earth bringeth forth fruit of herself." Here an internal element of life, whether principle or doctrine, is spoken of rather than any mere external manifestation; and it is observable that the spontaneous, as well as the gradual, character of the growth is intimated. This description of the process corresponds to what has been above observed respecting development, viz. that it is not an effect of wishing and resolving, or of forced enthusiasm, or of any mechanism of reasoning, or of any mere subtlety of intellect; but comes of its own innate power of expansion within the mind in its season, though with the use of reflection and argument and original thought, more or less as it may happen, with a dependence on the ethical growth of the mind itself, and with a reflex influence upon it. Again, the Parable of the Leaven describes the development of doctrine in another respect, in its active, engrossing, and interpenetrating power.

SECTION II
AN INFALLIBLE DEVELOPING AUTHORITY TO BE EXPECTED

It has now been made probable that developments of Christianity were but natural, as time went on, and were to be expected; and that these natural and true developments, as being natural and true, were of course contemplated and taken into account by its Author, who in designing the work designed its legitimate results. These, whatever they turn out to be, may be called absolutely "the developments" of Christianity. That, beyond reasonable doubt, there are such is surely a great step gained in the inquiry; it is a momentous fact. The next question is, *What* are they? and to a theologian, who could take a general view, and also possessed an intimate and minute knowledge, of its history, they would doubtless on the whole be easily distinguishable by their own characters, and require no foreign aid to point them out, no external authority to ratify them. But it is difficult to say who is exactly in this position. Considering that Christians, from the nature of the case, live under the bias of the doctrines, and in the very midst of the facts, and during the process of the controversies, which are to be the subject of criticism, since they are exposed to the prejudices of birth, education, place, personal attachment, engagements, and party, it can hardly be maintained that in matter of fact a true development carries with it always its own certainty even to the learned, or that history or present, is secure from the possibility of a variety of interpretations. . . .

2.

This need of an authoritative sanction is increased by considering . . ., that Christianity, though represented in prophecy as a kingdom, came into the world as an idea rather than an institution, and has had to wrap itself in clothing and fit itself with armour of its own providing, and to form the instruments and methods of its prosperity and warfare. If the developments, which have above been called *moral*, are to take place to any great extent, and without them it is difficult to see how Christianity can exist at all, if only its relations towards civil government have been ascertained, or the qualifications for the profession of it have to be defined, surely an authority is necessary to impart decision to what is vague, and confidence to what is empirical, to ratify the successive steps of so elaborate a process, and to secure the validity of inferences which are to be made the premises of more remote investigations.

Tests, it is true, for ascertaining the correctness of developments in general may be drawn out, as I show in the sequel; but they are insufficient for the guidance of individuals in the case of so large and complicated a problem as Christianity, though they may aid our inquiries and support our conclusions in particular points. They are of a scientific and controversial, not of a practical character, and are instruments rather than warrants of right decisions. Moreover, they rather serve as answers to objections brought against the actual decisions of authority, than are proofs of the correctness of those decisions. While, then, on the one hand, it is probable that some means will be granted for ascertaining the legitimate and true developments of Revelation, it appears, on the other, that these means must of necessity be external to the developments themselves.

3.

Reasons shall be given in this Section for concluding that, in proportion to the probability of true developments of doctrine and practice in the Divine Scheme, so is the probability also of the appointment in that scheme of an external authority to decide upon them, thereby separating them from the mass of mere human speculation, extravagance, corruption, and error, in and out of which they grow. This is the doctrine of the infallibility of the Church; for by infallibility I suppose is meant the power of deciding whether this, that, and any number of theological or ethical statements are true.

4.

1. Let the state of the case be carefully considered. If the Christian doctrine, as originally taught, admits of true and important developments, as was argued in the foregoing Section, this is a strong antecedent argument in favour of a provision in the Dispensation for putting a seal of authority upon those developments. The probability of their being known to be true varies with that of their truth. The two ideas indeed are quite distinct, I grant, of revealing and of guaranteeing a truth, and they are often distinct in fact. There are various revelations all over the earth which do not carry with them the evidence of their divinity. Such are the inward suggestions and secret illuminations granted to so many individuals; such are the traditionary doctrines which are found among the heathen. ... There is nothing impossible in the notion of a revelation occurring without evidence that it is a revelation; just as human sciences are a divine gift, yet are reached by our ordinary powers and have no claim on our faith. But Christianity is not of this nature: it is a revelation which comes to us as a revelation, as a whole, objectively, and with a profession of infallibility; and the only question to be determined relates to the matter of the revelation. If then there are certain great truths, or duties, or observances, naturally and legitimately resulting from the doctrines originally professed, it is but reasonable to include these true results in the idea of the revelation itself, to consider them parts of it, and if the revelation be not only true, but guaranteed as true, to anticipate that they

too will come under the privilege of that guarantee. Christianity, unlike other revelations of God's will, except the Jewish, of which it is a continuation, is an objective religion, or a revelation with credentials; it is natural, I say, to view it wholly as such and not partly *sui generis*, partly like others. Such as it begins, such let it be considered to continue; granting that certain large developments of it are true, they must surely be accredited as true.

5.

2. An objection, however, is often made to the doctrine of infallibility *in limine*, which is too important not to be taken into consideration. It is urged that, as all religious knowledge rests on moral evidence, not on demonstration, our belief in the Church's infallibility must be of this character; but what can be more absurd than a probable infallibility, or a certainty resting on doubt – I believe, because I am sure; and I am sure because I suppose. Granting then that the gift of infallibility be adapted, when believed, to unite all intellects in one common confession, the fact that it is given is as difficult of proof as the developments which it is to prove, and nugatory therefore, and in consequence improbable in a Divine Scheme. . . .

6.

This argument, however, except when used, as is intended in this passage, against such persons as would remove all imperfection in the proof of Religion, is certainly a fallacious one. For since, as all allow, the Apostles were infallible, it tells against their infallibility, or the infallibility of Scripture, as truly as against the infallibility of the Church; for no one will say that the Apostles were made infallible for nothing, yet we are only morally certain that they were infallible. Further, if we have but probable grounds for the Church's infallibility, we have but the like for the impossibility of certain things, the necessity of others, the truth, the certainty of others; and therefore the words *infallibility, necessity, truth, and certainty* ought all of them to be banished from the language. But why is it more inconsistent to speak of an uncertain infallibility than of a doubtful truth or a contingent necessity, phrases which present ideas clear and undeniable? In sooth we are playing with words when we use arguments of this sort. When we say that a person is infallible, we mean no more than that what he says is always true, always to be believed, always to be done. The term is resolvable into these phrases as its equivalents; either then the phrases are inadmissible, or the idea of infallibility must be allowed. A probable infallibility is a probable gift of never erring; a reception of the doctrine of a probable infallibility is faith and obedience towards a person founded on the probability of his never erring in his declarations or commands. What is inconsistent in this idea? Whatever then be the particular means of determining infallibility, the abstract objection may be put aside. . . .

. . . Revelation has introduced a new law of divine governance over and above those laws which appear in the natural course of the world; and in consequence we are able to argue for the existence of a standing authority in matters of faith on the analogy of Nature, and from the fact of Christianity. Preservation is involved in the idea of creation. As the Creator rested on the seventh day from the work which He had made, yet He "worketh hitherto;" so He gave the Creed once for all in the beginning, yet blesses its growth still, and provides for its increase. His word "shall not return unto Him void, but accomplish" His pleasure. As creation argues continual governance, so are Apostles harbingers of Popes.

7.

5. Moreover, it must be borne in mind that, as the essence of all religion is authority and obedience, so the distinction between natural religion and revealed lies in this, that the one has a subjective authority, and the other an objective. Revelation consists in the manifestation of the Invisible Divine Power, or in the substitution of the voice of a Lawgiver for the voice of conscience. The supremacy of conscience is the essence of natural religion; the supremacy of Apostle, or Pope, or Church, or Bishop, is the essence of revealed; and when such external authority is taken away, the mind falls back again of necessity upon that inwards guide which it possessed even before Revelation was vouchsafed. Thus, what conscience is in the system of nature,

such is the voice of Scripture, or of the Church, or of the Holy See, as we may determine it, in the system of Revelation. . . .

8.

6. The common sense of mankind does but support a conclusion thus forced upon us by analogical considerations. It feels that the very idea of revelation implies a present informant and guide, and that an infallible one; not a mere abstract declaration of Truths unknown before to man, or a record of history, or the result of an antiquarian research, but a message and a lesson speaking to this man and that. This is shown by the popular notion which has prevailed among us since the Reformation, that the Bible itself is such a guide; and which succeeded in overthrowing the supremacy of Church and Pope, for the very reason that it was a rival authority, not resisting merely, but supplanting it. In proportion, then, as we find, in matter of fact, that the inspired Volume is nor adapted or intended to subserve that purpose, are we forced to revert to that living and present Guide, who, at the era of our rejection of her, had been so long recognized as the dispenser of Scripture, according to times and circumstances, and the arbiter of all true doctrine and holy practice to her children. We feel a need, and she alone of all things under heaven supplies it. We are told that God has spoken. Where? In a book? We have tried it and it disappoints; it disappoints us, that most holy and blessed gift, not from fault of its own, but because it is used for a purpose for which it was not given. The Ethiopian's reply, when St. Philip asked him if he understood what he was reading, is the voice of nature: "How can I, unless some man shall guide me?" The Church undertakes that office; she does what none else can do, and this is the secret of her power. The most obvious answer, then, to the question, why we yield to the authority of the Church in the questions and developments of faith, is, that some authority there must be if there is a revelation given, and other authority there is none but she. A revelation is not give, if there be no authority to decide what it is that is given. In the words of St. Peter to her Divine Master and Lord, "To whom shall we go?" Nor must it be forgotten in confirmation, that Scripture expressly calls the Church "the pillar and ground of the Truth,"

and promises her as by covenant that "the Spirit of the Lord that is upon her, and His words which He has put in her mouth shall not depart out of her mouth, not out of the mouth of her seed, nor out of the mouth of her seed's seed, from henceforth and for ever."[16]

9.

7. And if the very claim to infallible arbitration in religious disputes is of so weighty importance and interest in all ages of the world, much more is it welcome at a time like the present, when the human intellect is so busy, and thought so fertile, and opinion so manifold. The absolute need of a spiritual supremacy is at present the strongest of arguments in favour of the fact of its supply. Surely, either an objective revelation has not been given, or it has been provided with means for impressing its objectiveness on the world. If Christianity be a social religion, as it certainly is, and if it be based on certain ideas acknowledged as divine, or a creed, (which shall here be assumed,) and if these ideas have various aspects, and make distinct impressions on different minds, and issue in consequence in a multiplicity of developments, true, or false, or mixed, as has been shown, what power will suffice to meet and to do justice to these conflicting conditions, but a supreme authority ruling and reconciling individual judgments by a divine right and a recognized wisdom? In barbarous times the will is reached through the senses; but in an age in which reason, as it is called, is the standard of truth and right, it is abundantly evident to any one, who mixes ever so little with the world, that, if things are left to themselves, every individual will have his own view of them, and take his own course; that two or three will agree to-day to part company to-morrow; that Scripture will be read in contrary ways, and history, according to the apologue, will have to different comers its silver shield and its golden; that philosophy, taste, prejudice, passion, party, caprice, will find no common measure, unless there be some supreme power to control the mind and to compel agreement.

There can be no combination on the basis of truth without an organ of truth. As cultivation brings out the colours of flowers, and domestication changes the character of animals, so does education of necessity develope differences of opinion; and while it is impossible to lay down first principles in which all will unite, it is utterly unreasonable to expect that this man should yield to that, or all to one. I do not say there are no eternal truths, ... which all acknowledge in private, but that there are none sufficiently commanding to be the basis of public union and action. The only general persuasive in matters of conduct is authority; that is, (when truth is in question,) a judgment which we feel to be superior to our own. If Christianity is both social and dogmatic, and intended for all ages, it must humanly speaking have an infallible expounder. Else you will secure unity of form at the loss of unity of doctrine, or unity of doctrine at the loss of unity of form; you will have to choose between a comprehension of opinions and a resolution into parties, between latitudinarian and sectarian error. You may be tolerant or intolerant of contrarieties of thought, but contrarieties you will have. By the Church of England a hollow uniformity is preferred to an infallible chair; and by the sects of England, an interminable division. Germany and Geneva began with persecution, and have ended in scepticism. The doctrine of infallibility is a less violent hypothesis than this sacrifice either of faith or of charity. It secures the object, while it gives definiteness and force to the matter, of the Revelation.

10.

8. I have called the doctrine of Infallibility an hypothesis: let it be so considered for the sake of argument, that is, let it be considered to be a mere position, supported by no direct evidence, but required by the facts of the case, and reconciling them with each other. That hypothesis is indeed, in matter of fact, maintained and acted on in the largest portion of Christendom, and from time immemorial; but let this coincidence be accounted for by the need. Moreover, it is not a naked or isolated fact, but the animating principle of a large scheme of doctrine which the need itself could not simply create; but again, let this system be merely called its development. Yet even as an hypothesis, which has been held by one out of various communions, it may

not be lightly put aside. Some hypothesis, this or that, all parties, all controversialists, all historians must adopt, if they would treat of Christianity at all. . . . The question is, which of all these theories is the simplest, the most natural, the most persuasive. Certainly the notion of development under infallible authority is not a less grave winning hypothesis, than the chance and coincidence of events, or the Oriental Philosophy, or the working of Antichrist, to account for the rise of Christianity and the formation of its theology.

SECTION III
THE EXISTING DEVELOPMENTS OF DOCTRINE THE PROBABLE FULFILMENT OF THAT EXPECTATION

I have been arguing, in respect to the revealed doctrine, given to us from above in Christianity, first, that, in consequence of its intellectual character, and as passing through the minds of so many generations of men, and as applied by them to so many purposes, and as investigated so curiously as to its capabilities, implications, and bearings, it could not but grow or develope, as time went on, into a large theological system; – next, that, if development must be, then, whereas Revelation is a heavenly gift, He who gave it virtually has not given it, unless He has also secured it from perversion and corruption, in all such development as comes upon it by the necessity of its nature or, in other words, that that intellectual action through successive generations, which is the organ of development, must, so far forth as it can claim to have been put in charge of the Revelation, be in its determinations infallible.

Passing from these two points, I come next to the question whether in the history of Christianity there is any fulfilment of such anticipation as I have insisted on, whether in matter-of-fact doctrines, rites, and usages have grown up round the Apostolic Creed and have interpenetrated its Articles, claiming to be part of Christianity and looking like those additions which we are in search of. The answer is, that such additions there are, and that they are found just where they might be expected, in the authoritative seats and homes of old tradition, the Latin and Greek Churches. Let me enlarge on this point.

2.

I observe, then, that, if the idea of Christianity, as originally given to us from heaven, cannot but contain much which will be only partially recognized by us as included in it and only held by us unconsciously; and if again, Christianity being from heaven, all that is necessarily involved in it, and is evolved from it, is from heaven, and if, on the other hand, large accretions actually do exist, professing to be its true and legitimate results, our first impression naturally is, that these must be the very developments which they profess to be. Moreover, the very scale on which they have been made, their high antiquity yet present promise, their gradual formation yet precision, their harmonious order, dispose the imagination most forcibly towards the belief that a teaching so consistent with itself, so well balanced, so young and so old, not obsolete after so many centuries, but vigorous and progressive still, is the very development contemplated in the Divine Scheme. These doctrines are members of one family, and suggestive, or correlative, or confirmatory, or illustrative of each other. One furnishes evidence to another, and all to each of them; if this is proved, that becomes probable; if this and that are both probable, but for different reasons, each adds to the other its own probability. The Incarnation is the antecedent of the doctrine of Mediation, and the archetype both of the Sacramental principle and of the merits of Saints. From the doctrine of Mediation follow the Atonement, the Mass, the merits of Martyrs and Saints, their invocation and *cultus*. From the Sacramental principle come the Sacraments properly so called; the unity of the Church, and the Holy See as its type and centre; the authority of Councils; the sanctity of rites; the veneration of holy places, shrines, images, vessels, furniture, and vestments. Of the Sacraments, Baptism is developed into Confirmation on the one hand; into Penance, Purgatory, and Indulgences on the other; and the Eucharist into the Real Presence, adoration of the Host, Resurrection of the body, and the virtue of relics. Again, the doctrine of the Sacraments leads to the doctrine of Justification; Justification to that of Original Sin; Original Sin to the merit of Celibacy. Nor do these separate developments stand independent of each other, but by cross relations they are connected, and grow together while they grow from one. The Mass and Real Presence are parts of one; the veneration of Saints and their relics are parts of one; their intercessory power and the Purgatorial State, and again the Mass and that State are correlative, Celibacy is the characteristic mark of Monachism and of the Priesthood. You must accept the whole or reject the whole; attenuation does but enfeeble, and amputation mutilate. It is trifling to receive all but something which is as integral as any other portion; and, on the other hand, it is a solemn thing to accept any part, for, before you know where you are, you may be carried on by a stern logical necessity to accept the whole.

3.

Next, we have to consider that from first to last other developments there are none, except those which have possession of Christendom; none, that is, of prominence and permanence sufficient to deserve the name. In early times the heretical doctrines were confessedly barren and short-lived, and could not stand their ground against Catholicism. As to the medieval period I am not aware that the Greeks present more than a negative opposition to the Latins. And now in like manner the Tridentine Creed is met by no rival developments; there is no antagonist system. Criticisms, objections, protests, there are in plenty, but little of positive teaching anywhere; seldom an attempt on the part of any opposing school to master its own doctrines, to investigate their sense and bearing, to investigate their sense and bearing, to determine their relation to the decrees of Trent and their distance from them. And when at any time this attempt is by chance in any measure made, then an incurable contrariety does but come to view between portions of the theology thus developed, and a war of principles; an impossibility moreover of reconciling that theology with the general drift of the formularies in which its elements occur, and a consequent appearance of unfairness and sophistry in adventurous persons who aim at forcing them into consistency; and, further, a prevalent understanding of the truth of this representation, authorities keeping silence, eschewing a hopeless enterprise and discouraging it in others, and the people plainly intimating that they think both doctrines and usage, antiquity and development, of very little matter at all; and, lastly, the evident despair of even the better sort of men, who, in consequence, when they set great schemes on foot, as for the conversion of the heathen world, are afraid to agitate the question of the doctrines to which it is to be converted, lest through the opened door they should lose what they have, instead of gaining what they have not. To the weight of recommendation which this contrast throws upon the developments commonly called Catholic, must be added the argument which arises from the coincidence of their consistency and permanence, with their claim of an infallible sanction, – a claim, the existence of which, in some quarter or other of the Divine Dispensation, is, as we have already seen, antecedently probable. All these things being considered, I think few persons will deny the very strong presumption which exists, that, if there must be and are in fact developments in Christianity, the doctrines propounded by successive Popes and Councils, through so many ages, are they.

4.

A further presumption in behalf of these doctrines arises from the general opinion of the world about them. Christianity being one, all its doctrines are necessarily developments of one, and, if so, are of necessity consistent with each other, or form a whole. Now the world fully enters into this view of those well-known developments which claim the name of Catholic. It allows them that title, it considers them to belong to one family, and refers them to one theological system. It is scarcely necessary to set about proving what is urged by their opponents even more strenuously than by their champions. Their opponents avow that they protest, not against this doctrine or that, but against one and all; and they seem struck with wonder and perplexity, not to say with awe, at a consistency which they feel to be superhuman, though they would not allow it to be divine. The system is confessed on all hands to bear a character of integrity and indivisibility upon it, both at first view and on inspection. ... This, I say, is no private judgment of this man or that, but the common opinion and experience of all countries. The two great divisions of religion feel it, Roman Catholic and Protestant, between whom the controversy lies, feel it; philosophers feel it. A school of divines there is, I grant, dear to memory, who have not felt it; and their exception will have its weight, – till we reflect that the particular theology which they advocate has not the prescription of success, never has been realized in fact, or, if realized for a moment, had no stay; moreover, that, when it has been enacted by human authority, it has scarcely travelled beyond the paper on which it was printed, or out of the legal forms in which it was embodied. But, putting the weight of these revered names at the highest, they do not constitute more than an exception to the general rule, such as is found in every subject that comes into discussion.

5.

And this general testimony to the oneness of Catholicism extends to its past teaching relatively to its present, as well as to the portions of its present teaching one with another. No one doubts, with such exception as has just been allowed, that the Roman Catholic communion of this day is the successor and representative of the Medieval Church, or that the Medieval Church is the legitimate heir of the Nicene; even allowing that it is a question whether a line cannot be drawn between the Nicene Church and the Church which preceded it. On the whole, all parties will agree that, of all existing systems, the present communion of Rome is the nearest approximation in fact to the Church of the Fathers, possible though some may think it, to be nearer still to that Church on paper. Did St. Athanasius or St. Ambrose come suddenly to life, it cannot be doubted what communion he would take to be his own. All surely will agree that these Fathers, with whatever opinions of their own, whatever protests, if we will, would find themselves more at home with such men as St. Bernard or Sr. Ignatius Loyola, or with the lonely priest in his lodging, or the holy sisterhood of mercy, or the unlettered crowd before the altar, than with the teachers or with the members of any other creed. And may we not add, that were those same Saints, who once sojourned, one in exile, one on embassy, at Treves, to come more northward still, and to travel until they reached another fair city, seated among groves, green meadows, and calm streams, the holy brothers would turn from many a high aisle and solemn cloister which they found there, and ask the way to some small chapel where mass was said in the populous alley or forlorn suburb? And, on the other hand, can any one who has but heard his name, and cursorily read his history, doubt for one instant how, in turn, the people of England, "we, our princes, our priests, and our prophets," Lords and Commons, Universities, Ecclesiastical Courts, marts of commerce, great towns, country parishes, would deal with Athanasius, – Athanasius, who spent his long years in fighting against sovereigns for a theological term? (*Dev.* 55–68, 71–81, 85–98)

V
GENUINE DEVELOPMENTS CONTRASTED WITH CORRUPTIONS

I have been engaged in drawing out the positive and direct argument in proof of the intimate connexion, or rather oneness, with primitive Apostolic teaching, of the body of doctrine known at this day by the name of Catholic, and professed substantially both by Eastern and Western Christendom. That faith is undeniably the historical continuation of the religious system, which bore the name of Catholic in the eighteenth century, in the seventeenth, in the sixteenth, and so back in every preceding century, till we arrive at the first; – undeniably the successor, the representative, the heir of the religion of Cyprian, Basil, Ambrose and Augustine. The only question that can be raised is whether the said Catholic faith, as now held, is logically, as well as historically, the representative of the ancient faith. This then is the subject, to which I have as yet addressed myself, and I have maintained that modern Catholicism is nothing else but simply the legitimate growth and complement, that is, the natural and necessary development, of the doctrine of the early church, and that its divine authority is included in the divinity of Christianity.

2.

So far I have gone, but an important objection presents itself for distinct consideration. It may be said in answer to me that it is not enough that a certain large system of doctrine, such as that which goes by the name of Catholic, should admit of being referred to beliefs, opinions, and usages which prevailed among the first Christians, in order to my having a logical right to include a reception of the later teaching in the reception of the earlier; that an intellectual development may be in one sense natural, and yet untrue to its original, as diseases come of nature, yet are the destruction, or rather the negation of health; that the causes which stimulate the growth of ideas may also disturb and deform them; and that Christianity might indeed have been intended by its Divine Author for a wide expansion of the ideas proper to it, and yet this great benefit hindered by the evil birth of cognate errors which acted as its counterfeit; in a word that what I have called developments in the Roman Church are nothing more or less than what used to be called her corruptions; and that new names do not destroy old grievances.

This is what may be said, and I acknowledge its force: it becomes necessary in consequence to assign certain characteristics of faithful developments, which none but faithful developments have, and the presence of which serves as a test to discriminate between them and corruptions. This I at once proceed to do, and I shall begin by determining what a corruption is, and why it cannot rightly be called, and how it differs from, a development.

3.

To find then what a corruption or perversion of the truth is, let us inquire what the word means, when used literally of material substances. Now it is plain, first of all, that a corruption is a word attaching to organized matters only; a stone may be crushed to powder, but it cannot be corrupted. Corruption, on the contrary, is the breaking up of life preparatory to its termination. This resolution of a body into its component parts is the stage before its dissolution; it begins when life has reached its perfection, and it is the sequel, or rather the continuation, of that process towards perfection, being at the same time the reversal and undoing of what want before. Till this point of regression is reached, the body has a function of its own, and a direction and aim in its action, and a nature with laws; these it is now losing; and the traits and tokens of former years; and with them its vigour and powers of nutrition, of assimilations, and of self-reparation.

4.

Taking this analogy as a guide, I venture to set down seven Notes of varying cogency, independence and applicability, to discriminate healthy developments of an idea from its state of corruption and decay, as follows: – There is no corruption if it retains one and the same type, the same principles, the same organization; if its beginnings anticipate its subsequent phases, and its later phenomena protect and subserve its earlier; if it has a power of assimilation and revival, and a vigorous action from first to last. On these tests I shall now enlarge, nearly in the order in which I have enumerated them.

SECTION I
FIRST NOTE OF A GENUINE DEVELOPMENT. PRESERVATION OF TYPE

This is readily suggested by the analogy of physical growth, which is such that the parts and proportions of the developed form, however altered, correspond to those which belong to its rudiments. The adult animal has the same make, as it had on its birth; young birds do not grow into fishes, nor does the child degenerate into the brute, wild or domestic, of which he is by inheritance lord. . . .

However . . . this unity of type, characteristic as it is of faithful developments, must not be pressed to the extent of denying all variation, nay, considerable alteration of proportion and relation, as time goes on, in the parts or aspects of an idea. Great changes in outward appearance and internal harmony occur in the instance of the animal creation itself. The fledged bird differs much from its rudimental form in the egg. The butterfly is the development, but not in any sense the image, of the grub. . . .

More subtle still and mysterious are the variations which are consistent or not inconsistent with identity in political and religious developments. . . .

The same man may run through various philosophies or beliefs, which are in themselves irreconcilable, without inconsistency, since in him they may be nothing more than accidental instruments or expressions of what he is inwardly from first to last. The political doctrines of the modern Tory resemble those of the primitive Whig; yet few will deny that the Whig and Tory characters have each a discriminating type. Calvinism has changed into Unitarianism: yet this need not be called a corruption, even if it be not strictly speaking, a development. . . .

The history of national character supplies an analogy, rather than an instance strictly in point; yet there is so close a connexion between the development of minds and of ideas that it is allowable to refer to it here. Thus we find England of old the most loyal supporter and England of late the most jealous enemy, of the Holy See. As a great a change is exhibited in France, once the eldest born of the Church and the flower of her knighthood, now democratic and lately infidel. Yet, in neither nation, can these great changes be well called corruptions. . . .

And, in like manner, ideas may remain, when the expression of them is indefinitely varied; and we cannot determine whether a professed development is truly such or not, without some further knowledge than an experience of the mere fact of this variation. Nor will our instinctive feelings serve as a criterion. It must have been an extreme shock to St. Peter to be told he must slay and eat beasts, unclean as well as clean, though such a command was implied already in that faith which he held and taught; a shock which a single effort, or a short period, or the force of reason would not suffice to overcome. Nay, it may happen that a representation which varies from its original may be felt as more true and faithful than one which has more pretensions to be exact. So it is with many a portrait which is not striking: at first look, of course, it disappoints us; but when we are familiar with it, we see in it what we could not see at first, and prefer it, not to a perfect likeness, but to many a sketch which is so precise as to be a caricature.

On the other hand, real perversions and corruptions are often not so unlike externally to the doctrine from which they come, as are changes which are consistent with it and true developments. When Rome changed from a Republic to an Empire, it was a real alteration of polity, or what may be called a corruption; yet in appearance the change was small. The old office or functions of government remained: it was only that the Imperator, or Commander in Chief, concentrated them in his own person. Augustus was Consul and Tribune, Supreme Pontiff and Censor, and the Imperial rule was, in the words of Gibbon "an absolute monarchy disguised by the forms of a commonwealth."On the other hand, when the dissimulation of Augustus was exchanged for the ostentation of Dioclesian, the real alteration of constitution was trivial, but the appearance of change was great. Instead of plain Consul, Censor, and Tribune, Dioclesian became Dominus or King, assumed the diadem, and throw around him the forms of a court.

Nay, one cause of corruption in religion is the refusal to follow the course of doctrine as it moves on, and an obstinacy in the notions of the past. Certainly: as we see conspicuously in the history of the chosen race. The Samaritans who refused to add the Prophets to the Law, and the Sadducees who denied a truth which was covertly taught in the Book of Exodus, were in appearance only faithful adherents to the primitive doctrine. Our Lord found His people precisians in their obedience to the letter; He condemned them for not being led on to its spirit, that is, to its developments. The Gospel is the development of the Law; yet what difference seems wider than that which separates the unbending rule of Moses from the "grace and truth"which "came by Jesus Christ?". . .

An idea then does not always bear about it the same external image; this circumstance, however, has no force to weaken the argument for its substantial identity, as drawn from its external sameness, when such sameness remains. On the contrary, for that very reason, *unity of type* becomes so much the surer guarantee of the healthiness and soundness of developments, when it is persistently preserved in spite of their number or importance.

SECTION II
SECOND NOTE. CONTINUITY OF PRINCIPLES

As in mathematical creations figures are formed on distinct formulæ, which are the laws under which they are developed, so it is in ethical and political subjects. Doctrines expand variously according to the mind, individual or social, into which they are received; and the peculiarities of the recipient are the regulating power, the law, the organization, or, as it may be called, the form of the development. The life of doctrines may be said to consist in the law or principle which they embody.

Principles are abstract and general, doctrines relate to facts; doctrines develope, and principles at first sight do not; doctrines grow and are enlarged, principles are permanent; doctrines are intellectual, and principles are more immediately ethical and practical. Systems live in principles and represent doctrines. Personal responsibility is a principle, the Being of a God is a Doctrine; from that doctrine all theology has come in due course, whereas that principle is not clearer under the Gospel than in paradise, and depends, not on belief in an Almighty Governor, but on conscience.

Yet the difference between the two sometimes merely exists in our mode of viewing them; and what is a doctrine in one philosophy is a principle in another. Personal responsibility may be made a doctrinal basis, and develope into Arminianism or Pelagianism. Again, it may be discussed whether infallibility is a principle or a doctrine of the Church of Rome, and dogmatism a principle or doctrine of Christianity. Again, consideration for the poor is a doctrine of the Church considered as a religious body, and a principle when she is viewed as a political power.

Doctrines stand to principles, as definitions to the axioms and postulates of mathematics. Thus the 15th and 17th propositions of Euclid's book I. are developments, not of the three first axioms, which are required in the proof, but of the definition of a right angle. Perhaps the perplexity, which arises in the mind of a beginner, on learning the early propositions of the second book, arises from these being more prominently exemplifications of axioms than developments of definitions. He looks for developments from the definition of the rectangle, and finds but various particular cases of the general truth, that "the whole is equal to its parts."

It might be expected that the Catholic principles would be later in development than the Catholic doctrines, inasmuch as they lie deeper in the mind, and are assumptions rather than objective professions. This has been the case. The Protestant controversy has mainly turned, or is turning, on one or other of the principles of Catholicity; and to this day the rule of Scripture Interpretation, the doctrine of Inspiration, the relation of Faith to Reason, moral responsibility, private judgment, inherent grace, the seat of infallibility, remain, I suppose, more or less undeveloped, or, at least, undefined, by the Church.

Doctrines stand to principles, if it may be said without fancifulness, as fecundity viewed relatively to generation, though this analogy must not be strained. Doctrines are developed by the operation of principles, and develope variously according to those principles. Thus a belief in the transitiveness of worldly goods leads the Epicurean to enjoyment, and the ascetic to mortification; and, from their common doctrine of the sinfulness of matter, the Alexandrian Gnostics became sensualists, and the Syrian devotees. The same philosophical elements, received into a certain sensibility or insensibility to sin and its consequences, leads one mind to the Church of Rome; another to what, for want of a better word, may be called Germanism.

Again, religious investigation sometimes is conducted on the principle that it is a duty ''to follow and speak the truth,'' which really means that it is no duty to fear error, or to consider what is safest, or to shrink from scattering doubts, or to regard the responsibility of misleading; and thus it terminates in heresy or infidelity, without any blame to religious investigation in itself.

Again, to take a different subject, what constitutes a chief interest of dramatic compositions and tales, is to use external circumstances, which may be considered their law of development, as a means of bringing out into different shapes, and showing under new aspects, the personal peculiarities of character, according as either those circumstances or those peculiarities vary in the case ot the personages introduced.

Principles are popularly said to develope when they are but exemplified; thus the various sects of Protestantism, unconnected as they are with each other, are called developments of the principle of Private Judgment, of which really they are but applications and results.

A development, to be faithful, must retain both the doctrine and the principle with which it started. Doctrine without its correspondent principle remains barren, if not lifeless, of which the Greek Church seems an instance; or it forms those hollow professions which are familiarly called ''shams,'' as a zeal for an established Church and its creed on merely conservative or temporal motives. Such, too, was the Roman Constitution between the reigns of Augustus and Dioclesian.

On the other hand, principle without its corresponding doctrine may be considered as the state of religious minds in the heathen world, viewed relatively to Revelation; that is, of the "church of God who are scattered abroad."

Pagans may have, heretics cannot have, the same principles as Catholics; if the latter have the same, they are not real heretics, but in ignorance. Principle is a better test of heresy than doctrine. Heretics are true to their principles, but change to and fro, backwards and forwards, in opinion; for very opposite doctrines may be exemplifications of the same principle. Thus the Antiochenes and other heretics sometimes were Arians, sometimes Sabellians, sometimes Nestorians, sometimes Monophysites, as if at random, from fidelity to their common principle, that there is no mystery in theology. Thus Calvinists become Unitarians from the principle of private judgment. The doctrines of heresy are accidents and soon run to an end; its principles are everlasting.

This, too, is often the solution of the paradox "Extremes meet," and of the startling reactions which take place in individuals; viz., the presence of some one principle or condition, which is dominant in their minds from first to last. If one of two contradictory alternatives be necessarily true on a certain hypothesis, then the denial of the one leads, by mere logical consistency and without direct reasons, to a reception of the other. Thus the question between the Church of Rome and Protestantism falls in some minds into the proposition, "Rome is either the pillar and ground of the Truth or she is Antichrist;" in proportion, then, as they revolt from considering her the latter are they compelled to receive her as the former. Hence, too, men may pass from infidelity to Rome, and from Rome to infidelity, from a conviction in both courses that there is no tangible intellectual position between the two.

Protestantism, viewed in its more Catholic aspect, is doctrine without active principle; viewed in its heretical it is active principle without doctrine. Many of its speakers, for instance, use eloquent and glowing language about the Church and its characteristics; some of them do not realize what they say, but use high words and general statements about "the faith," and "primitive truth," and "schism," and "heresy," to which they attach no definite meaning; while others speak of "unity," "universality," and "Catholicity," and use the words in their own sense and for their own ideas. . . .

SECTION III
THIRD NOTE. POWER OF ASSIMILATION

In the physical world, whatever has life is characterized by growth, so that in no respect to grow is to cease to live. It grows by taking into its own substance external materials; and this absorption or assimilation is completed when the materials appropriated come to belong to it or enter into its unity. Two things cannot become one, except there be a power of assimilation in one or the other. Sometimes assimilation is effected only with an effort; it is possible to die of repletion, and there are animals who lie torpid for a time under the contest between the foreign substance and the assimilating power. And different food is proper for different recipients.

This analogy may be taken to illustrate certain peculiarities in the growth or development in ideas, which were noticed in the first Chapter. It is otherwise with mathematical and other abstract creations, which, like the soul itself, are solitary and self-dependent; but doctrines and views which relate to man are not placed in a void, but in the crowded world, and make way for themselves by interpenetration, and develope by absorption. Facts and opinions, which have hitherto been regarded in other relations and grouped round other centres, henceforth are gradually attracted to a new influence and subjected to a new sovereign. They are modified, laid down afresh, thrust aside, as the case may be. A new element of order and composition has come among them; and its life is proved by this capacity of expansion, without disarrangement or dissolution. An eclectic, conservative, assimilating, healing, moulding process, a unitive power, is of the essence, and a third test, of a faithful development.

Thus, a power of development is a proof of life, not only in its essay, but especially in its success; for a mere formula either does not expand or is shattered in expanding. A living idea becomes many, yet remains one.

The attempt at development shows the presence of a principle, and its success the presence of an idea. Principles stimulate thought, and an idea concentrates it.

The idea never was that throve and lasted, yet, like mathematical truth, incorporated nothing from external sources. So far from the fact of such incorporation implying corruption, as is sometimes supposed, development is a process of incorporation. . . .

The stronger and more living is an idea, that is, the more powerful hold it exercises on the minds of men, the more able is it to dispense with safeguards, and trust to itself against the danger of corruption. As strong frames exult in their agility, and healthy constitutions throw off ailments, so parties or schools that live can afford to be rash, and will sometimes be betrayed into extravagances, yet are brought right by their inherent vigour. On the other hand, unreal systems are commonly decent externally. Forms, subscriptions, or Articles of religion are indispensable when the principle of life is weakly. Thus Presbyterianism has maintained its original theology in Scotland where legal subscriptions are enforced, while it has run into Arianism or Unitarianism where that protection is away. We have yet to see whether the Free Kirk can keep its present theological ground. The Church of Rome can consult expedience more freely than other bodies, as trusting to her living tradition, and is sometimes thought to disregard principle and scruple, when she is but dispensing with forms. Thus Saints are often characterized by acts which are not pattern for others; and the most gifted men are, by reason of their very gifts, sometimes led into fatal inadvertences. Hence vows are the wise defence of unstable virtue, and general rules the refuge of feeble authority.

And so much may suffice on the *unitive power* of faithful developments, which constitutes their third characteristic.

SECTION IV
FOURTH NOTE. LOGICAL SEQUENCE

Logic is the organization of thought, and, as being such, is a security for the faithfulness of intellectual developments; and the necessity of using it is undeniable as far as this, that its rules must not be transgressed. That it is not brought into exercise in every instance of doctrinal development is owing to the varieties of mental constitution, whether in communities or in individuals, with whom great truths or seeming truths are lodged. The question indeed may be asked whether a development can be other in any case than a logical operation; but, if by this is meant a conscious reasoning from premises to conclusion, of course the answer must be in the negative. An idea under one or other of its aspects grows in the mind by remaining there; it becomes familiar and distinct, and is viewed in its relations; it leads to other aspects, and these again to others, subtle, recondite, original, according to the character, intellectual and moral, of the recipient; and thus a body of thought is gradually formed without his recognizing what is going on within him. And all this while, or at least from time to time, external circumstances elicit into formal statement the thoughts which are coming into being in the depths of his mind; and soon he has to begin to defend them; and then again a further process must take place, of analyzing his statements and ascertaining their dependence one on another. And thus he is led to regard as consequences, and to trace to principles, what hitherto he has discerned by a moral perception, and adopted on sympathy; and logic is brought in to arrange and inculcate what no science was employed in gaining.

And so in the same way, such intellectual processes, as are carried on silently and spontaneously in the mind of a party or school, of necessity come to light at a later date, and are recognized, and their issues are scientifically arranged. And then logic has the further function of propagation; analogy, the nature of the case, antecedent probability, application of principles, congruity, expedience, being some of the methods of proof by which the development is continued from mind to mind and established in the faith of the community.

Yet even then the analysis is not made on a principle, or with any view to its whole course and finished results. Each argument is brought for an immediate purpose; minds develop step by step, without looking behind them or anticipating their goal, and without either intention or promise of forming a system. Afterwards, however, this logical character which the whole wears becomes a test that the process has been a true development, not a perversion or corruption, from its evident naturalness; and in some cases from the gravity, distinctness, precision, and majesty of its advance, and the harmony of its proportions, like the tall growth, and graceful branching, and rich foliage, of some vegetable production. . . .

At the same time it may be granted that the spontaneous process which goes on within the mind itself is higher and choicer than that which is logical; for the latter, being scientific, is common property, and can be taken and made use of by minds who are personally strangers, in any true sense, both to the ideas in question and to their development.

Thus, the holy Apostles would without words know all the truths concerning the high doctrines of theology, which controversialists after then have piously and charitably reduced to formulæ, and developed through argument. Thus, St. Justin or St. Irenæus might be without any digested ideas of Purgatory or Original Sin, yet have an intense feeling, which they had not defined or located, both of the fault of our first nature and the responsibilities of our nature regenerate. Thus St. Antony said to the philosophers who came to mock him, ''He whose mind is in health does not need letters;'' and St. Ignatius Loyola, while yet an unlearned neophyte, was favoured with transcendent perceptions of the Holy Trinity during his penance at Manresa. Thus St. Athanasius himself is more powerful in statement and exposition than in proof; while in Bellarmine we find the whole series of doctrines carefully drawn out, duly adjusted with one another, and exactly analyzed by one. . . .

SECTION V
FIFTH NOTE. ANTICIPATION OF ITS FUTURE

Since, when an idea is living, that is, influential and effective, it is sure to develope according to its own nature, and the tendencies, which are carried out on the long run, may under favourable circumstances show themselves early as well as late, and logic is the same in all ages, instances of a development which is to come, though vague and isolated, may occur from the very first, though a lapse of time be necessary to bring them to perfection. And since developments are in great measure only aspects of the idea from which they proceed, and all of them are natural consequences of it, it is often a matter of accident in what order they are carried out in individual minds; and it is in no wise strange that here and there definite specimens of advanced teaching should very early occur, which in the historical course are not found till a late day. The fact, then of such early or recurring intimations of tendencies which afterwards are fully realized, is a sort of evidence that those later and more systematic fulfilments are only in accordance with the original idea. . . .

SECTION VI
SIXTH NOTE. CONSERVATIVE ACTION UPON ITS PAST

As developments which are preceded by definite indications have a fair presumption in their favour, so those which do but contradict and reverse the course of doctrine which has been developed before them, and out of which they spring, are certainly corrupt; for a corruption is a development in that very stage in which it ceases to illustrate, and begins to disturb, the acquisitions gained in its previous history. . . .

A true development, then, may be described as one which is conservative of the course of antecedent developments being really those antecedents and something besides them; it is an addition which illustrates, not obscures, corroborates, not corrects, the body of thought from which it proceeds; and this is its characteristic as contrasted with a corruption.

For instance, a gradual conversion from a false to a true religion plainly, has much of the character of a continuous process, or a development, in the mind itself, even when the two religions, which are the limits of its course, are antagonists. Now let it be observed, that such a change consists in addition and increase chiefly, not in destruction. . . .

When Roman Catholics are accused of substituting another Gospel for the primitive Creed, they answer that they hold, and can show that they hold, the doctrines of the Incarnation and Atonement, as firmly as any Protestant can state them. To this it is replied that they do certainly profess them, but that they obscure and virtually annul them by their additions; that the *cultus* of St. Mary and the Saints is no development of the truth, but a corruption and a religious mischief to those doctrines of which it is the corruption, because it draws away the mind and

heart from Christ. But they answer that, so far from this, it sub-
serves, illustrates, protects the doctrine of our Lord's loving kind-
ness and mediation. Thus the parties in controversy join issue
on the common ground, that a developed doctrine which
reverses the course of development which has preceded it, is
no true development but a corruption; also, that what is corrupt
acts as an element of unhealthiness towards what is sound. . . .

SECTION VII

SEVENTH NOTE. CHRONIC VIGOUR

Since the corruption of an idea, as far as the appearance goes,
is a sort of accident or affection of its development, being the
end of a course, and a transition-state leading to a crisis, it is,
as has been observed above, a brief and rapid process. While
ideas live in men's minds, they are ever enlarging into fuller
development: they will not be stationary in their corruption any
more than before it ; and dissolution is that further state to which
corruption tends. Corruption cannot, therefore, be of long standing; and thus *duration* is another test of a faithful development. . . .

The course of heresies is always short; it is an intermediate
state between life and death, or what is like death; or, if it does
not result in death, it is resolved into some new, perhaps
opposite, course of error, which lays no claim to be connected
with it. And in this way indeed, but in this way only, an heretical
principle will continue in life many years, first running one way,
then another. . . .

It is true that decay, which is one form of corruption, is slow;
but decay is a state in which there is no violent or vigorous
action at all, whether of a conservative or a destructive character,
the hostile influence being powerful enough to enfeeble the functions of life, but not to quicken its own process. And thus we
see opinions, usages, and systems, which are of venerable and
imposing aspect, but which have no soundness within them,
and keep together from a habit of consistence, or from dependence on political institutions; or they become almost peculiarities of a country, or the habits of a race, or the fashions of society.
And then, at length, perhaps, they go off suddenly and die out
under the first rough influence from without. Such are the super-

stitions which pervade a population, like some ingrained dye or inveterate odour, and which at length come to an end, because nothing lasts for ever, but which run no course, and have no history; such was the established paganism of classical times, which was the fit subject of persecution, for its first breath made it crumble and disappear. Such apparently is the state of the Nestorian and Monophysite communions; such might have been the condition of Christianity had it been absorbed by the feudalism of the middle ages; such too is that Protestantism, or (as it sometimes calls itself) attachment to the Establishment, which is not unfrequently the boast of the respectable and wealthy among ourselves.

Whether Mahometanism external to Christendom, and the Greek Church within it, fall under this description is yet to be seen. Circumstances can be imagined which would even now rouse the fanaticism of the Moslem; and the Russian despotism does not meddle with the usages, though it may domineer over the priesthood, of the national religion.

Thus, while a corruption is distinguished from decay by its energetic action, it is distinguished from a development by its *transitory character*.

Such are seven out of various Notes, which may be assigned, of fidelity in the development of an idea. The point to be ascertained is the unity and identify of the idea with itself through all stages of its development first to last, and these are seven tokens that it may rightly be accounted one and the same all along. To guarantee its own substantial unity, it must be seen to be one in type, one in its system of principles, one in its unitive power towards externals, one in its logical consecutiveness, one in the witness of its early phases to its later, one in the protection which its later extend to its earlier, and one in its union of vigour with continuance, that is, in its tenacity.

(*Dev.* 169–82, 185–6, 188–92, 195–6, 199–200, 202–6)

5

LAITY*

ON CONSULTING THE FAITHFUL IN MATTERS OF DOCTRINE

"On Consulting the Faithful in Matters of Doctrine" was published in the July number of the Rambler. *In October it was denounced to Rome by Bishop Brown of Newport for allegedly saying that the Church had fallen into error during the Arian heresy. Newman himself held that he had not been guilty of implying formal heresy on the part of the teaching Church, but merely of pointing out that at a particular point in history a majority of the bishops had in fact failed temporarily to uphold the orthodox faith. The failure of Cardinal Wiseman, the Archbishop of Westminster, to send on to Newman the list of passages the Roman authorities found objectionable meant that Newman was never able to defend or explain the meaning of what he had been trying to say. Rome for its part thought that he had deliberately refused either to justify or to retract the offending parts of the article. The result was a deep suspicion of him in the Roman Curia, which was not dispelled for many years. The article was eventually republished over a hundred years later in book form in 1961 (edited with an introduction by John Coulson) on the eve of the Second Vatican Council, which more than vindicated Newman's position on the ecclesial importance of the laity. And so the article which cost Newman so much trouble in his own lifetime has become a minor classic of theology.*

ON CONSULTING THE FAITHFUL IN MATTERS OF DOCTRINE

A question has arisen among persons of theological knowledge and fair and candid minds, about the wording and the sense of passage in the *Rambler* for May. It admits to my own mind of so clear and satisfactory an explanation, that I should think it unnecessary to intrude myself, an anonymous person,

*See also above, p. 42.

between the conductors and readers of this Magazine, except that, as in dogmatic works the replies made to objections often contain the richest matter, so here too, plain remarks on a plain subject may open to the minds of others profitable thoughts, which are more due to their own superior intelligence than to the very words of the writer.

The *Rambler*, then, has these words at p. 122: ''In the preparation of a dogmatic definition, the faithful are consulted, as lately in the instance of the Immaculate Conception.'' Now two questions bearing upon doctrines have been raised on this sentence, putting aside the question of fact as regards the particular instance cited, which must follow the decision on the doctrinal questions: viz. first, whether it can, with doctrinal correctness, be said that an *appeal* to the faithful is one of the preliminaries of a definition of doctrine; and secondly, granting that the faithful are taken into account, still, whether they can correctly be said to be *consulted*. I shall remark on both these points, and I shall begin with the second.

Now doubtless, if a divine were expressing himself formally, and in Latin, he would not commonly speak of the laity being ''consulted'' among the preliminaries of a dogmatic definition, because the technical, or even scientific, meaning of the word ''consult'' is to ''consul *with*,'' or to ''take *counsel*.'' But the English word ''consult'', in its popular and ordinary use, is not so precise and narrow in its meaning; it is doubtless a word expressive of trust and deference, but not of submission. It includes the idea of inquiring into a matter of *fact*, as well as asking a judgment. Thus we talk of ''consulting our barometer'' about the weather: – the barometer only attests the *fact* of the state of the atmosphere. In like manner, we may consult a watch or a sun-dial about the time of day. A physician consults the pulse of his patient; but not in the same sense in which his patient consults *him*. It is but an index of the state of his health. Ecclesiastes says, ''Qui *observat* ventum, non seminat;'' we might translate it, ''he who consults'', without meaning that we ask the wind's opinion. This being considered, it was, I conceive, quite allowable for a writer, who was not teaching or treating theology, but, as it were, conversing, to say, as in the passage in question, ''In the preparation of a dogmatic definition, the faithful are consulted." Doubtless their advice, their opinion, their judgment on the question of definition is not asked; but the matter of fact, viz. their belief, *is* sought for, as a testimony to that apostolical tradition, on which alone any doctrine whatsoever can be defined. In like manner, we may "consult" the liturgies or the rites of the Church; not that they speak, not that they can taken any part whatever in the definition, for they are documents or customs; but they are witnesses to the antiquity or universality of the doctrines which they contain, and about which they are "consulted". And, in like manner, I certainly understood the writer in the *Rambler* to mean (and I think any lay reader might so understand him) that the *fidelium sensus* and *consensus* is a branch of evidence which it is natural or necessary for the Church to regard and consult, before she proceeds to any definition, from its intrinsic cogency; and by consequence, that it ever has been so regarded and consulted. And the writer's use of the word "opinion" in the foregoing sentence, and his omission of it in the sentence in question, seemed to show that, though the two cases put therein were analogous, they were not identical.

Having said as much as this, I go further, and maintain that the word "consulted", used as it was used, was in no respect unadvisable, except so far as it distressed any learned and good men, who identified it with the Latin. I might, indeed, even have defended the word as it was used, in the Latin sense of it. . . . But in my bountifulness I will give up this use of the word as untheological; still I will maintain that the true theological sense is unknown to all *but* theologians. Accordingly, the use of it in the *Rambler* was in no sense dangerous to any lay reader, who, if he knows Latin, still is not called upon, in the structure of his religious ideas, to draw those careful lines and those fine distinctions, which in theology itself are the very means of anticipating and repelling heresy. The laity would not have a truer, or a clearer, or a different view of the doctrine itself, though the sentence had run, "in the preparation of a dogmatic decree, *regard* is had to the sense of the faithful'; or, "there is an *appeal* to the general voice of the faithful'; or, " *inquiry* is made into the belief of the Christian people'; or, "the definition is not made without a previous *reference* to what the faithful will think of it and say to it'; or though any other form of words had been used, stronger or weaker, expressive of the same general idea, viz. that *the sense of the faithful is not left out of the question* by the Holy See among the preliminary acts of defining a doctrine. . . .

Then follows the question, Why? and the answer is plain, viz. because the body of the faithful is one of the witnesses to the fact of the tradition of revealed doctrine, and because their *consensus* through Christendom is the voice of the Infallible Church.

I think I am right in saying that the tradition of the Apostles, committed to the whole Church in its various constituents and functions *per modum unius*, manifests itself variously at various times: sometimes by the mouth of the episcopacy, sometimes by the doctors, sometimes by the people, sometimes by liturgies, rites, ceremonies, and customs, by events, disputes, movements, and all those other phenomena which are comprised under the name of history. It follows that none of these channels of tradition may be treated with disrespect; granting at the same time fully, that the gift of discerning, discriminating, defining, promulgating, and enforcing any portion of that tradition resides solely in the *Ecclesia docens*.

One man will lay more stress on one aspect of doctrine, another on another; for myself, I am accustomed to lay great stress on the *consensus fidelium* . . . as a compensation for whatever deficiency there might be of patristical testimony in behalf of various point of the Catholic dogma. . . .

. . . I will set down the various ways in which theologians put before us the bearing of the Consent of the faithful upon the manifestation of the tradition of the Church. Its *consensus* is to be regarded: 1. as a testimony to the fact of the apostolical dogma; 2. as a sort of instinct or phronema deep in the bosom of the mystical body of Christ; 3. as a direction of the Holy Ghost; 4. as an answer to its prayer; 5. as a jealousy of error, which it at once feels as a scandal . . .

It is not a little remarkable, that, though, historically speaking, the fourth century is the age of doctors, illustrated, as it was, by the saints Athanasius, Hilary, the two Gregories, Basil, Chrysostom, Ambrose, Jerome, and Augustine, and all of these saints bishops also, except one, nevertheless in that very day the divine tradition committed to the infallible Church was proclaimed and maintained far more by the faithful than by the Episcopate.

Here, of course, I must explain: – in saying this, then, undoubtedly I am not denying that the great body of the Bishops were in their internal belief orthodox; nor that there were numbers of clergy who stood by the laity, and acted as their centres and guides; nor that the laity actually received their faith, in the first instance, from the Bishops and clergy; nor that some portions of the laity were ignorant, and other portions at length corrupted by the Arian teachers, who got possession of the sees and ordained an heretical clergy; – but I mean still, that in that time of immense confusion the divine dogma of our Lord's divinity was proclaimed, enforced, maintained, and (humanly speaking) preserved, far more by the ''Ecclesia docta'' than by the ''Ecclesia docens''; that the body of the episcopate was unfaithful to its commission, while the body of the laity was faithful to its baptism; that at one time the Pope, at other times the patriarchal, metropolitan, and other great sees, at other times general councils, said what they should not have said, or did what obscured and compromised revealed truth; while, on the other hand, it was the Christian people who, under Providence, were the ecclesiastical strength of Anthanasius, Hilary, Eusebius of Vercellae, and other great solitary confessors, who would have failed without them.

I see, then, in the Arian history a palmary example of a state of the Church, during which, in order to know the tradition of the Apostles, we must have recourse to the faithful; for I fairly own, that if I go to writers, since I must adjust the letter of Justin, Clement, and Hippolytus with the Nicene Doctors, I get confused; and what revives and reinstates me, as far as history goes, is the faith of the people. For I argue that, unless they had been catechised, as St. Hilary says, in the orthodox faith from the time of their baptism, they never could have had that horror, which they show, of the heterodox Arian doctrine. Their voice, then, is the voice of tradition; and the instance comes to us with still greater emphasis, when we consider – 1. that it occurs in the very beginning of the history of the ''Ecclesia docens'', for there can scarcely be said to be any history of her teaching till the age of martyrs was over; 2. that the doctrine in controversy was so momentous, being the very foundation of the Christian system; 3. that the state of controversy and disorder lasted over the long space of sixty years; and 4. that it involved serious persecutions, in life, limb, and property, to the faithful whose loyal perseverance decided it.

... [On the other hand] there was a temporary suspense of the functions of the "Ecclesia docens." The body of Bishops failed in their confession of the faith. They spoke variously, one against another; there was nothing, after Nicaea, of firm, unvarying, consistent testimony, for nearly sixty years. There were untrustworthy Councils, unfaithful Bishops; there was weakness, fear of consequences, misguidance, delusion, hallucination, endless, hopeless, extending itself into nearly every corner of the Catholic Church. The comparatively few who remained faithful were discredited and driven into exile; the rest were either deceivers or were deceived. ...

... I am not supposing that such times as the Arian will ever come again. As to the present, certainly, if there ever was an age which might dispense with the testimony of the faithful, and leave the maintenance of the truth to the pastors of the Church, it is the age in which we live. Never was the Episcopate of Christendom so devoted to the Holy See, so religious, so earnest in the discharge of its special duties, so little disposed to innovate, so superior to the temptation of theological sophistry. And perhaps this is the reason why the "consensus fidelium" has, in the minds of many, fallen into the background. Yet each constituent portion of the Church has its proper functions, and no portion can safely be neglected. Though the laity be but the reflection or echo of the clergy in matters of faith, yet there is something in the "pastorum et fidelium *conspiratio*", which is not in the pastors alone. The history of the definition of the Immaculate Conception shows us this; and it will be one among the blessings which the Holy Mother, who is the subject of it, will gain for us, in repayment of the definition, that by that very definition we are all reminded of the part which the laity have had in the preliminaries of its promulgation. ...

... I think certainly that the *Ecclesia docens* is more happy when she has such enthusiastic partisans about her as are here represented, than when she cuts off the faithful from the study of her divine doctrines and the sympathy of her divine contemplations, and requires from them a *fides implicita* in her word, which in the educated classes will terminate in indifference, and in the poorer in superstition.

(*Rambler*, July 1859).

6

THE MAGISTERIUM AND
THEOLOGIANS*

APOLOGIA PRO VITA SUA

*At the end of December 1863 Newman was sent (anonymously) a
copy of an issue of* Macmillan's Magazine, *which contained a review
by the novelist Charles Kingsley that included the famous jibe,
"Truth, for its own sake, had never been a virtue with the Roman
clergy. Father Newman informs us that it need not, and on the whole
ought not to be . . ." The ensuing correspondence with the ultra-Pro-
testant Kingsley was the controversy out of which the* Apologia pro
vita Sua *was born. Newman felt that the only way he could refute
Kingsley's aspersions on his integrity, suspicions which he knew were
shared by many of his Protestant countrymen, was to tell the story of
his religious development and how he had come to be converted to
the Roman Catholic Church. In a sense Kingsley's accusation was a
godsend: it gave Newman the opportunity to reply fully for the first
time to all the many attacks which had followed his conversion in 1845.*

The book that was entitled Apologia pro Vita Sua: Being a Reply
to a Pamphlet entitled "What, then, Does Dr. Newman Mean?"
*appeared first in the form of eight parts or pamphlets in 1864. The
second edition, simply called* History of My Religious Opinions,
*appeared in 1865 and replaced the original two polemical first parts
with a brief preface. The third and definitive edition of 1873 restored
not only the original title but also some of the controversial material
in a new enlarged preface; the 1865 title was replaced by the original
title but retained as a sub-title.*

*Newman completed the story of his Anglican life at the end of
the fourth chapter, and in the final fifth chapter he offered a general
defence of Catholicism. It is from this chapter, called "Position of
my Mind since 1845", that the following extract is taken.*

APOLOGIA PRO VITA SUA

CHAPTER V
POSITION OF MY MIND SINCE 1845

From the time that I became a Catholic, of course I have no

*See also above, p. 44.

further history of my religious opinions to narrate. In saying this, I do not mean to say that my mind has been idle, or that I have given up thinking on theological subjects; but that I have had no variations to record, and have had no anxiety of heart whatever. I have been in perfect peace and contentment; I never have had one doubt. I was not conscious to myself, on my conversion, of any change, intellectual or moral, wrought in my mind. I was not conscious of firmer faith in the fundamental truths of Revelation, or of more self-command; I had not more fervour; but it was like coming into port after a rough sea; and my happiness on that score remains to this day without interruption.

Nor had I any trouble about receiving those additional articles, which are not found in the Anglican Creed. Some of them I believed already, but not any one of them was a trial to me. I made a profession of them upon my reception with the greatest ease, and I have the same ease in believing them now. I am far of course from denying that every article of the Christian Creed, whether as held by Catholics or by Protestants, is beset with intellectual difficulties; and it is simple fact, that, for myself, I cannot answer those difficulties. Many persons are very sensitive of the difficulties of Religion; I am as sensitive of them as any one; but I have never been able to see a connexion between apprehending those difficulties, however keenly, and multiplying them to any extent, and on the other hand doubting the doctrines to which they are attached. Ten thousand difficulties do not make one doubt, as I understand the subject; difficulty and doubt are incommensurate. There of course may be difficulties in the evidence; but I am speaking of difficulties intrinsic to the doctrines themselves, or to their relations with each other. A man may be annoyed that he cannot work out a mathematical problem, of which the answer is or is not given to him, without doubting that it admits of an answer, or that a certain particular answer is the true one. Of all points of faith, the being of a God is, to my own apprehension, encompassed with most difficulty, and yet borne in upon our minds with most power.

People say that the doctrine of Transubstantiation is difficult to believe; I did not believe the doctrine till I was a Catholic. I had no difficulty in believing it, as soon as I believed that the Catholic Roman Church was the oracle of God, and that she had declared this doctrine to be part of the original revelation.

It is difficult, impossible, to imagine, I grant; – but how is it difficult to believe? Yet Macaulay thought it so difficult to believe, that he had need of a believer in it of talents as eminent as Sir Thomas More, before he could bring himself to conceive that the Catholics of an enlightened age could resist "the overwhelming force of the argument against it". "Sir Thomas More", he says, "is one of the choice specimens of wisdom and virtue; and the doctrine of transubstantiation is a kind of proof charge. A faith which stands that test, will stand any test." But for myself, I cannot indeed prove it, I cannot tell how it is; but I say, "Why should it not be? What's to hinder it? What do I know of substance or matter? just as much as the greatest philosophers, and that is nothing at all'; – so much is this the case, that there is a rising school of philosophy now, which considers phenomena to constitute the whole of our knowledge in physics. The Catholic doctrine leaves phenomena alone. It does not say that the phenomena go; on the contrary, it says that they remain; nor does it say that the same phenomena are in several places at once. It deals with what no one on earth knows any thing about, the material substances themselves. And, in like manner, of that majestic Article of the Anglican as well as of the Catholic Creed, – the doctrine of the Trinity in Unity. What do I know of the Essence of the Divine Being? I know that my abstract idea of three is simply incompatible with my idea of one; but when I come to the question of concrete fact, I have no means of proving that there is not a sense in which one and three can equally be predicated of the Incommunicable God.

But I am going to take upon myself the responsibility of more than the mere Creed of the Church; as the parties accusing me are determined I shall do. They say, that now, in that I am a Catholic, though I may not have offences of my own against honesty to answer for, yet, at least, I am answerable for the offences of others, of my co-religionists, of my brother priests, of the Church herself. I am quite willing to accept the responsibility; and, as I have been able, as I trust, by means of a few words, to dissipate, in the minds of all those who do not begin with disbelieving me, the suspicion with which so many Protestants start, in forming their judgment of Catholics, viz. that our Creed is actually set up in inevitable superstition and hypocrisy, as the original sin of Catholicism; so now I will proceed, as before, identifying myself with the Church and vindicating it, – not of course denying the enormous mass of sin and error which exists of necessity in that world-wide multiform Communion, – but going to the proof of this one point, that its system is in no sense dishonest, and that therefore the upholders and teachers of that system, as such, have a claim to be acquitted in their own persons of that odious imputation.

Starting then with the being of a God, (which, as I have said, is as certain to me as the certainty of my own existence, though when I try to put the grounds of that certainty into logical shape I find a difficulty in doing so in mood and figure to my satisfaction,) I look out of myself into the world of men, and there I see a sight which fills me with unspeakable distress. The world seems simply to give the lie to that great truth, of which my whole being is so full; and the effect upon me is, in consequence, as a matter of necessity, as confusing as if it denied that I am in existence myself. If I looked into a mirror, and did not see my face, I should have the sort of feeling which actually comes upon me, when I look into this living busy world, and see no reflexion of its Creator. This is, to me, one of those great difficulties of this absolute primary truth, to which I referred just now. Were it not for this voice, speaking so clearly in my conscience and my heart, I should be an atheist, or a pantheist, or a polytheist when I looked into the world. I am speaking for myself only; and I am far from denying the real force of the arguments in proof of a God, drawn from the general facts of human society and the course of history, but these do not warm me or enlighten me; they do not take away the winter of my desolation, or make the buds unfold and the leaves grow within me, and my moral being rejoice. The sight of the world is nothing else than the prophet's scroll, full of ''lamentations, and mourning, and woe''.

To consider the world in its length and breadth, its various history, the many races of man, their starts, their fortunes, their mutual alienation, their conflicts; and then their ways, habits, governments, forms of worship; their enterprises, their aimless courses, their random achievements and acquirements, the impotent conclusion of long-standing facts, the tokens so faint and broken of a superintending design, the blind evolution of what turn out to be great powers or truths, the progress of things, as if from unreasoning elements, not towards final causes, the greatness and littleness of man, his far-reaching aims, his short duration, the curtain hung over his futurity, the disappointments of life, the defeat of good, the success of evil, physical pain, mental anguish, the prevalence and intensity of sin, the pervading idolatries, the corruptions, the dreary hopeless irreligion, that condition of the whole race, so fearfully yet exactly described in the Apostle's words, "having no hope and without God in the world", – all this is a vision to dizzy and appal; and inflicts upon the mind the sense of a profound mystery, which is absolutely beyond human solution.

What shall be said to this heart-piercing, reason-bewildering fact? I can only answer, that either there is no Creator, or this living society of men is in a true sense discarded from His presence. Did I see a boy of good make and mind, with the tokens on him of a refined nature, cast upon the world without provision, unable to say whence he came, his birth-place or his family connexions, I should conclude that there was some mystery connected with his history, and that he was one, of whom, from one cause or other, his parents were ashamed. Thus only should I be able to account for the contrast between the promise and the condition of his being. And so I argue about the world; – if there be a God, since there is a God, the human race is implicated in some terrible aboriginal calamity. It is out of joint with the purposes of its Creator. This is a fact, a fact as true as the fact of its existence; and thus the doctrine of what is theologically called original sin becomes to me almost as certain as that the world exists, and as the existence of God.

And now, supposing it were the blessed and loving will of the Creator to interfere in this anarchical condition of things, what are we to suppose would be the methods which might be necessarily or naturally involved in His purpose of mercy? Since the world is in so abnormal a state, surely it would be no surprise to me, if the interposition were of necessity equally extraordinary – or what is called miraculous. But that subject does not directly come into the scope of my present remarks. Miracles as evidence, involve a process of reason, or an argument; and of course I am thinking of some mode of interference which does not immediately run into argument. I am rather asking what must be the face-to-face antagonist, by which to with-stand and baffle the fierce energy of passion and the all-corrod-ing, all-dissolving scepticism of the intellect in religious inquiries? I have no intention at all of denying, that truth is the real object of our reason, and that, if it does not attain to truth, either the premiss or the process is in fault; but I am not speaking here of right reason, but of reason as it acts in fact and concretely in fallen man. I know that even the unaided rea-son, when correctly exercised, leads to a belief in God, in the immortality of the soul, and in a future retribution; but I am considering the faculty of reason actually and historically; and in this point of view, I do not think I am wrong in saying that its tendency is towards a simple unbelief in matters of religion. No truth, however sacred, can stand against it, in the long run; and hence it is that in the pagan world, when our Lord came, the last traces of the religious knowledge of former times were all but disappearing from those portions of the world in which the intellect had been active and had had a career.

And in these latter days, in like manner, outside the Catholic Church things are tending, – with far greater rapidity than in that old time from the circumstance of the age, – to atheism in one shape or other. What a scene, what a prospect, does the whole of Europe present at this day! and not only Europe, but every government and every civilization through the world, which is under the influence of the European mind! Especially, for it most concerns us, how sorrowful, in the view of religion, even taken in its most elementary, most attenuated form, is the spectacle presented to us by the educated intellect of England, France, and Germany! Lovers of their country and of their race, religious men, external to the Catholic Church, have attempted various expedients to arrest fierce wilful human nature in its onward course, and to bring it into subjection. The necessity of some form of religion for the interests of humanity, has been generally acknowledged: but where was the concrete representa-tive of things invisible, which would have the force and the toughness necessary to be a breakwater against the deluge? Three centuries ago the establishment of religion, material, legal, and social, was generally adopted as the best expedient for the purpose, in those countries which separated from the Catholic Church; and for a long time it was successful; but now the crevices of those establishments are admitting the enemy. Thirty years ago, education was relied upon: ten years ago there was a hope that wars would cease for ever, under the influence of commercial enterprise and the reign of the useful and fine arts; but will any one venture to say that there is any thing any where on this earth, which will afford a fulcrum for us, whereby to keep the earth from moving onwards?

The judgment, which experience passes whether on establishments or on education, as a means of maintaining religious truth in this anarchical world, must be extended even to Scripture, though Scripture be divine. Experience proves surely that the Bible does not answer a purpose for which it was never intended. It may be accidentally the means of the conversion of individuals; but a book, after all, cannot make a stand against the wild living intellect of man, and in this day it begins to testify, as regards its own structure and contents, to the power of that universal solvent, which is so successfully acting upon religious establishments.

Supposing then it to be the Will of the Creator to interfere in human affairs, and to make provisions for retaining in the world a knowledge of Himself, so definite and distinct as to be proof against the energy of human scepticism, in such a case, – I am far from saying that there was no other way, – but there is nothing to surprise the mind, if He should think fit to introduce a power into the world, invested with the prerogative of infallibility in religious matters. Such a provision would be a direct, immediate, active, and prompt means of withstanding the difficulty; it would be an instrument suited to the need; and, when I find that this is the very claim of the Catholic Church, not only do I feel no difficulty in admitting the idea, but there is a fitness in it, which recommends it to my mind. And thus I am brought to speak of the Church's infallibility, as a provision, adapted by the mercy of the Creator, to preserve religion in the world, and to restrain that freedom of thought, which of course in itself is one of the greatest of our natural gifts, and to rescue it from its own suicidal excesses. And let it be observed that, neither here nor in what follows, shall I have occasion to speak directly of Revelation in its subject-matter, but in reference to the sanction which it gives to truths which may be known independently of it, – as it bears upon the defence of natural religion.

I say, that a power, possessed of infallibility in religious teaching, is happily adapted to be a working instrument, in the course of human affairs, for smiting hard and throwing back the immense energy of the aggressive, capricious, untrustworthy intellect: – and in saying this, as in the other things that I have to say, it must still be recollected that I am all along bearing in mind my main purpose, which is a defence of myself.

I am defending myself here from a plausible charge brought against Catholics, as will be seen better as I proceed. The charge is this: – that I, as a Catholic, not only make profession to hold doctrines which I cannot possibly believe in my heart, but that I also believe in the existence of a power on earth, which at its own will imposes upon men any new set of credenda, when it pleases, by a claim to infallibility; in consequence, that my own thoughts are not my own property; that I cannot tell that tomorrow I may not have to give up what I hold to-day, and that the necessary effect of such a condition of mind must be a degrading bondage, or a bitter inward rebellion relieving itself in secret infidelity, or the necessity of ignoring the whole subject of religion in a sort of disgust, and of mechanically saying every thing that the Church says, and leaving to others the defence of it. As then I have above spoken of the relation of my mind towards the Catholic Creed, so now I shall speak of the attitude which it takes up in the view of the Church's infallibility.

And first, the initial doctrine of the infallible teacher must be an emphatic protest against the existing state of mankind. Man had rebelled against his Maker. It was this that caused the divine interposition: and to proclaim it must be the first act of the divinely-accredited messenger. The Church must denounce rebellion as of all possible evils the greatest. She must have no terms with it; if she would be true to her Master, she must ban and anathematize it. This is the meaning of a statement of mine which has furnished matter for one of those special accusations to which I am at present replying: I have, however, no fault at all to confess in regard to it; I have nothing to withdraw, and in consequence I here deliberately repeat it. I said, ''The Catholic Church holds it better for the sun and moon to drop from heaven, for the earth to fail, and for all the many millions on it to die of starvation in extremest agony, as far as temporal affliction goes, than that one soul, I will not say, should be lost, but should commit one single venial sin, should tell one wilful untruth, or should steal one poor farthing without excuse." I think the principle here enunciated to be the mere preamble in the formal credentials of the Catholic Church, as an Act of Parliament might begin with a "Whereas". It is because of the intensity of the evil which has possession of mankind, that a suitable antagonist has been provided against it; and the initial act of that divinely-commissioned power is of course to deliver her challenge and to defy the enemy. Such a preamble then gives a meaning to her position in the world, and an interpretation to her whole course of teaching and action.

In like manner she has ever put forth, with most energetic distinctness, those other great elementary truths, which either are an explanation of her mission or give a character to her work. She does not teach that human nature is irreclaimable, else wherefore should she be sent? not, that it is to be shattered and reversed, but to be extricated, purified, and restored; not, that it is a mere mass of hopeless evil, but that it has the promise upon it of great things, and even now, in its present state of disorder and excess, has a virtue and a praise proper to itself. But in the next place she knows and she preaches that such a restoration, as she aims at effecting in it, must be brought about, not simply through certain outward provisions of preaching and teaching, even though they be her own, but from an inward spiritual power or grace imparted directly from above, and of which she is the channel. She has it in charge to rescue human nature from its misery, but not simply by restoring it on its own level, but by lifting it up to a higher level than its own. She recognizes in it real moral excellence though degraded, but she cannot set it free from earth except by exalting it towards heaven. It was for this end that a renovating grace was put into her hands; and therefore from the nature of the gift, as well as from the reasonableness of the case, she goes on, as a further point, to insist, that all true conversion must begin with the first springs of thought, and to teach that each individual man must be in his own person one whole and perfect temple of God, while he is also one of the living stones which build up a visible religious community. And thus the distinctions between nature and grace, and between outward and inward religion, become two further articles in what I have called the preamble of her divine commission.

Such truths as these she vigorously reiterates, and pertinaciously inflects upon mankind; as to such she observes no half-measures, no economical reserve, no delicacy or prudence. "Ye must be born again," is the simple, direct form of words which she uses after her Divine Master: "your whole nature must be re-born; your passions, and your affections, and your aims, and your conscience, and your will, must all be bathed in a new element, and reconsecrated to your Maker, – and, the last not the least, your intellect." It was for repeating these points of her teaching in my own way, that certain passages of one of my Volumes have been brought into the general accusation which has been made against my religious opinions. The writer has said that I was demented if I believed, and unprincipled if I did not believe, in my own statement, that a lazy, ragged, filthy, story-telling beggar-woman, if chaste, sober, cheerful, and religious, had a prospect of heaven, such as was absolutely closed to an accomplished statesman, or lawyer, or noble, be he ever so just, upright, generous, honourable, and conscientious, unless he had also some portion of the divine Christian graces; – yet I should have thought myself defended from criticism by the words which our Lord used to the chief priests, "The publicans and harlots go into the kingdom of God before you." And I was subjected again to the same alternative of imputations, for having ventured to say that consent to an unchaste wish was indefinitely more heinous than any lie viewed apart from its causes, its motives, and its consequences: though a lie, viewed under the limitation of these conditions, is a random utterance, an almost outward act, not directly from the heart, however disgraceful and despicable it may be, however prejudicial to the social contract, however deserving of public reprobation; whereas we have the express words of our Lord to the doctrine that "whoso looketh on a woman to lust after her, hath committed adultery with her already in his heart". On the strength of these texts, I have surely as much right to believe in these doctrines which have caused so much surprise, as to believe in original sin, or that there is a supernatural revelation, or that a Divine Person suffered, or that punishment is eternal.

Passing now from what I have called the preamble of that

grant of power, which is made to the Church, to that power itself, Infallibility, I premise two brief remarks: – 1. on the one hand, I am not here determining any thing about the essential seat of that power, because that is a question doctrinal, not historical and practical; 2. nor, on the other hand, am I extending the direct subject-matter, over which that power of Infallibility has jurisdiction, beyond religious opinion: – and now as to the power itself.

This power, viewed in its fulness, is as tremendous as the giant evil which has called for it. It claims, when brought into exercise but in the legitimate manner, for otherwise of course it is but quiescent, to know for certain the very meaning of every portion of that Divine Message in detail, which was committed by our Lord to His Apostles. It claims to know its own limits, and to decide what it can determine absolutely and what it cannot. It claims, moreover, to have a hold upon statements not directly religious, so far as this, – to determine whether they indirectly relate to religion, and, according to its own definitive judgment, to pronounce whether or not, in a particular case, they are simply consistent with revealed truth. It claims to decide magisterially, whether as within its own province or not, that such and such statements are or are not prejudicial to the Depositum of faith, in their spirit or in their consequences, and to allow them, or condemn and forbid them, accordingly. It claims to impose silence at will on any matters, or controversies, of doctrine, which on its own ipse dixit, it pronounces to be dangerous, or inexpedient, or inopportune. It claims that, whatever may be the judgment of Catholics upon such acts, these acts should be received by them with those outward marks of reverence, submission, and loyalty, which Englishmen, for instance, pay to the presence of their sovereign, without expressing any criticism on them on the ground that in their matter they are inexpedient, or in their manner violent or harsh. And lastly, it claims to have the right of inflicting spiritual punishment, of cutting off from the ordinary channels of the divine life, and of simply excommunicating, those who refuse to submit themselves to its formal declarations. Such is the infallibility lodged in the Catholic Church, viewed in the concrete, as clothed and surrounded by the appendages of its high sovereignty: it is, to repeat what I said above, a supereminent prodigious power sent upon earth to encounter and master a giant evil.

And now, having thus described it, I profess my own absolute submission to its claim. I believe the whole revealed dogma as taught by the Apostles, as committed by the Apostles to the Church, and as declared by the Church to me. I receive it, as it is infallibly interpreted by the authority to whom it is thus committed, and (implicitly) as it shall be, in like manner, further interpreted by that same authority till the end of time. I submit, moreover, to the universally received traditions of the Church, in which lies the matter of those new dogmatic definitions which are from time to time made, and which in all times are the clothing and the illustration of the Catholic dogma as already defined. And I submit myself to those other decisions of the Holy See, theological or not, through the organs which it has itself appointed, which, waiving the question of their infallibility, on the lowest ground come to me with a claim to be accepted and obeyed. Also, I consider that, gradually and in the course of ages, Catholic inquiry has taken certain definite shapes, and has thrown itself into the form of a science, with a method and a phraseology of its own, under the intellectual handling of great minds, such as St. Athanasius, St. Augustine, and St. Thomas; and I feel no temptation at all to break in pieces the great legacy of though thus committed to us for these latter days.

All this being considered as the profession which I make ex animo, as for myself, so also on the part of the Catholic body, as far as I know it, it will at first sight be said that the restless intellect of our common humanity is utterly weighed down, to the repression of all independent effort and action whatever, so that, if this is to be the mode of bringing it into order, it is brought into order only to be destroyed. But this is far from the result, far from what I conceive to be the intention of that high Providence who has provided a great remedy for a great evil, – far from borne out by the history of the conflict between Infallibility and Reason in the past, and the prospect of it in the future. The energy of the human intellect "does from opposition grow"; it thrives and is joyous, with a tough elastic strength, under the terrible blows of the divinely-fashioned weapon, and is never so much itself as when it has lately been overthrown. It is the custom with Protestant writers to consider that, whereas there are two great principles in action in the history of religion, Authority and Private Judgment, they have all the Private Judgment to themselves, and we have the full inheritance and the superincumbent oppression of Authority. But this is not so; it is the vast Catholic body itself, and it only, which affords an arena for both combatants in that awful, never-dying duel. It is necessary for the very life of religion, viewed in its large operations and its history, that the warfare should be incessantly carried on. Every exercise of Infallibility is brought out into act by an intense and varied operation of the Reason, both as its ally and as its opponent, and provokes again, when it has done its work, a re-action of Reason against it; and, as in a civil polity the State exists and endures by means of the rivalry and collision, the encroachments and defeats of its constituent parts, so in like manner Catholic Christendom is no simple exhibition of religious absolutism, but presents a continuous picture of Authority and Private Judgment alternately advancing and retreating as the ebb and flow of the tide; – it is a vast assemblage of human beings with wilful intellects and wild passions, brought together into one by the beauty and the Majesty of a Superhuman Power, – into what may be called a large reformatory or training-school, not as if into a hospital or into a prison, not in order to be sent to bed, not be buried alive, but (if I may change my metaphor) brought together as if into some moral factory, for the melting, refining, and moulding, by an incessant, noisy process, of the raw material of human nature, so excellent, so dangerous, so capable of divine purposes.

St. Paul says in one place that his Apostolical power is given him to edification, and not to destruction. There can be no better account of the Infallibility of the Church. It is a supply for a need, and it does not go beyond that need. Its object is, and its effect also, not to enfeeble the freedom or vigour of human thought in religious speculation, but to resist and control its extravagance. What have been its great works? All of them in the distinct province of theology: – to put down Arianism, Eutychianism, Pelagianism, Manichaeism, Lutheranism, Jansenism. Such is the broad result of its action in the past; – and now as to the securities which are given us that so it ever will act in time to come.

First, Infallibility cannot act outside of a definite circle of thought, and it must in all its decisions, or definitions, as they are called, profess to be keeping within it. The great truths of the moral law, of natural religion, and of Apostolical faith, are both its boundary and its foundation. It must not go beyond them, and it must ever appeal to them. Both its subject-matter, and its articles in that subject-matter, are fixed. And it must ever profess to be guided by Scripture and by tradition. It must refer to the particular Apostolic truth which it is enforcing, or (what is called) defining. Nothing, then, can be presented to me, in time to come, as part of the faith, but what I ought already to have received, and hitherto have been kept from receiving (if so) merely because it has not been brought home to me. Nothing can be imposed upon me different in kind from what I hold already, – much less contrary to it. The new truth which is promulgated, if it is to be called new, must be at least homogeneous, cognate, implicit, viewed relatively to the old truth. It must be what I may even have guessed, or wished, to be included in the Apostolic revelation; and at least it will be of such a character, that my thoughts readily concur in it or coalesce with it, as soon as I hear it. Perhaps I and others actually have always believed it, and the only question which is now decided in my behalf, is, that I have henceforth the satisfaction of having to believe, that I have only been holding all along what the Apostles held before me.

Let me take the doctrine which Protestants consider our greatest difficulty, that of the Immaculate Conception. Here I entreat the reader to recollect my main drift, which is this. I have no difficulty in receiving the doctrine; and that, because it so intimately harmonizes with that circle of recognized dogmatic truths, into which it has been recently received; – but if I have no difficulty, why may not another have no difficulty also? why may not a hundred? a thousand? Now I am sure that Catholics in general have not any intellectual difficulty at all on the subject of the Immaculate Conception; and that there is no reason why they should. Priests have no difficulty. You tell me that they ought to have a difficulty; – but they have not. Be large-minded enough to believe, that men may reason and feel very differently from yourselves; how is it that men, when left to themselves, fall into such various forms of religion, except that there are various types of mind among them, very distinct from each other? From my testimony then about myself, if you believe it, judge of others also who are Catholics: we do not find the difficulties which you do in the doctrines which we hold; we have no intellectual difficulty in that doctrine in particular, which you call a novelty of this day. We priests need not be hypocrites, though we be called upon to believe in the Immaculate Conception. To that large class of minds, who believe in Christianity after our manner, – in the particular temper, spirit, and light, (whatever word is used,) in which Catholics believe it, – there is no burden at all in holding that the Blessed Virgin was conceived without original sin; indeed, it is a simple fact to say, that Catholics have not come to believe it because it is defined, but that it was defined because they believed it.

So far from the definition in 1854 being a tyrannical infliction on the Catholic world, it was received every where on its promulgation with the greatest enthusiasm. It was in consequence of the unanimous petition, presented from all parts of the Church to the Holy See, in behalf of an *ex cathedrâ* declaration that the doctrine was Apostolic, that it was declared so to be. I never heard of one Catholic having difficulties in receiving the doctrine, whose faith on other grounds was not already suspicious. Of course there were grave and good men, who were made anxious by the doubt whether it could be formally proved to be Apostolical either by Scripture or tradition, and who accordingly, though believing it themselves, did not see how it could be defined by authority and imposed upon all Catholics as a matter of faith; but this is another matter. The point in question is, whether the doctrine is a burden. I believe it to be none. So far from it being so, I sincerely think that St. Bernard and St. Thomas, who scrupled at it in their day, had they lived into this, would have rejoiced to accept it for its own sake. Their difficulty, as I view it, consisted in matters of words, ideas, and arguments. They thought the doctrine inconsistent with other doctrines; and those who defended it in that age had not that precision in their view of it, which has been attained by means of the long disputes of the centuries which followed. And in this want of precision lay the difference of opinion, and the controversy.

Now the instance which I have been taking suggests another remark; the number of those (so called) new doctrines will not oppress us, if it takes eight centuries to promulgate even one of them. Such is about the length of time through which the preparation has been carried on for the definition of the Immaculate Conception. This of course is an extraordinary case; but it is difficult to say what is ordinary, considering how few are the formal occasions on which the voice of Infallibility has been solemnly lifted up. It is to the Pope in Ecumenical Council that we look, as to the normal seat of Infallibility: now there have been only eighteen such Councils since Christianity was, – an average of one to a century, – and of these Councils some passed no doctrinal decree at all, others were employed on only one, and many of them were concerned with only elementary points of the Creed. The Council of Trent embraced a large field of doctrine certainly; but I should apply to its Canons a remark contained in that University Sermon of mine, which has been so ignorantly criticized in the Pamphlet which has been the occasion of this Volume; – I there have said that the various verses of the Anthanasian Creed are only repetitions in various shapes of one and the same idea; and in like manner, the Tridentine Decrees are not isolated from each other, but are occupied in bringing out in detail, by a number of separate declarations, as if into bodily form, a few necessary truths. I should make the same remark on the various theological censures, promulgated by Popes, which the Church has received, and on their dogmatic decisions generally. I own that at first sight those decisions seem from their number to be a greater burden on the faith of individuals than are the Canons of Councils; still I do not believe that in matter of fact they are so at all, and I give this reason for it: – it is not that a Catholic, layman or priest, is indifferent to the subject, or, from a sort of recklessness, will accept any thing that is placed before him, or is willing, like a lawyer, to speak according to his brief, but that in such condemnations the Holy See is engaged, for the most part, in repudiating one or two great lines of error, such as Lutheranism or Jansenism, principally ethical not doctrinal, which are divergent from the Catholic mind, and that it is but expressing what any good Catholic, of fair abilities, though unlearned, would say himself, from common and sound sense, if the matter could be put before him.

Now I will go on in fairness to say what I think is the great trial to the Reason, when confronted with that august prerogative of the Catholic Church, of which I have been speaking. I enlarged just now upon the concrete shape and circumstances, under which pure infallible authority presents itself to the Catholic. That authority has the prerogative of an indirect jurisdiction on subject-matters which lie beyond its own proper limits, and it most reasonably has such a jurisdiction. It could not act in its own province, unless it had a right to act out of it. It could not properly defend religious truth, without claiming for that truth what may be called its *pomœria*; or, to take another illustration, without acting as we act, as a nation, in claiming as our own, not only the land on which we live, but what are called British waters. The Catholic Church claims, not only to judge infallibly on religious questions, but to animadvert on opinions in secular matters which bear upon religion, on matters of philosophy, of science, of literature, of history, and it demands our submission to her claim. It claims to censure books, to silence authors, and to forbid discussions. In this province, taken as a whole, it does not so much speak doctrinally, as enforce measures of discipline. It must of course be obeyed without a word, and perhaps in process of time it will tacitly recede from its own injunctions. In such cases the question of faith does not come in at all; for what is matter of faith is true for all times, and never can be unsaid. Nor does it at all follow, because there is a gift of infallibility in the Catholic Church, that therefore the parties who are in possession of it are in all their proceedings infallible. "O, it is excellent", says the poet, "to have a giant's strength, but tyrannous, to use it like a giant." I think history supplies us with instances in the Church, where legitimate power has been harshly used. To make such admission is no more than saying that the divine treasure, in the words of the Apostle, is "in earthen vessels'; nor does it follow that the substance of the acts of the ruling power is not right and expedient, because its manner may have been faulty. Such high authorities act by means of instruments; we know how such instruments claim for themselves the name of their principals, who thus get the credit of faults which really are not theirs. But granting all this to an extent greater than can with any show of reason be imputed to the ruling power in the Church, what difficulty is there in the fact of this want of prudence or moderation more than can be urged, with far greater justice, against Protestant communities and institutions? What is there in it to make us hypocrites, if it has not that effect upon Protestants? We are called upon, not to profess any thing, but to submit and be silent, as Protestant Churchmen have before now obeyed the royal command to abstain from certain theological question. Such injunctions as I have been contemplating are laid merely upon our actions, not upon our thoughts. How, for instance, does it tend to make a man a hypocrite, to be forbidden to publish a libel? his thoughts are as free as before: authoritative prohibitions may tease and irritate, but they have no bearing whatever upon the exercise of reason.

So much at first sight; but I will go on to say further, that, in spite of all that the most hostile critic may urge about the encroachments or severities of high ecclesiastics, in times past, in the use of their power, I think that the event has shown after all, that they were mainly in the right, and that those whom they were hard upon were mainly in the wrong. I love, for instance, the name of Origen: I will not listen to the notion that so great a soul was lost; but I am quite sure that, in the contest between his doctrine and followers and the ecclesiastical power, his opponents were right, and he was wrong. Yet who can speak with patience of his enemy and the enemy of St. John Chrysostom, that Theophilus, bishop of Alexandria? who can admire or revere Pope Vigilius? And here another consideration presents itself to my thoughts. In reading ecclesiastical history, when I was an Anglican, it used to be forcibly brought home to me, how the initial error of what afterwards became heresy was the urging forward some truth against the prohibition of authority at an unseasonable time. There is a time for every thing, and many a man desires a reformation of an abuse, or the fuller development of a doctrine, or the adoption of a particular policy, but forgets to ask himself whether the right time for it is come: and, knowing that there is no one who will be doing any thing towards its accomplishment in his own lifetime unless he does it himself, he will not listen to the voice of authority, and he spoils a good work in his own century, in order that another man, as yet unborn, may not have the opportunity of bringing it happily to perfection in the next. He may seem to the world to be nothing else than a bold champion for the truth and a martyr to free opinion, when he is just one of those persons whom the competent authority ought to silence; and, though the case may not fall within that subject-matter in which that authority is infallible, or the formal conditions of the exercise of that gift may be wanting, it is clearly the duty of authority to act vigorously in the case. Yet its act will go down to posterity as an instance of a tyrannical interference with private judgment, and of the silencing of a reformer, and of a base love of corruption or error; and it will show still less to advantage, if the ruling power happens in its proceedings to evince any defect of prudence or consideration. And all those who take the part of that ruling authority will be considered as time-servers, or indifferent to the cause of uprightness and truth; while, on the other hand, the said authority may be accidentally supported by a violent ultra party, which exalts opinions into dogmas, and has it principally at heart to destroy every school of thought but its own.

Such a state of things may be provoking and discouraging at the time, in the case of two classes of persons; of moderate men who wish to make differences in religious opinion as little as they fairly can be made; and of such as keenly perceive, and are honestly eager to remedy, existing evils, – evils, of which divines in this or that foreign country know nothing at all, and which even at home, where they exist, it is not every one who has the means of estimating. This is a state of things both of past time and of the present. We live in a wonderful age; the enlargement of the circle of secular knowledge just now is simply a bewilderment, and the more so, because it has the promise of continuing, and that with greater rapidity, and more signal results. Now these discoveries, certain or probable, have in matter of fact an indirect bearing upon religious opinions, and the question arises how are the respective claims of revelation and of natural science to be adjusted. Few minds in earnest can remain at ease without some sort of rational grounds for their religious belief; to reconcile theory and fact is almost an instinct of the mind. When then a flood of facts, ascertained or suspected, comes pouring in upon us, with a multitude of others in prospect, all believers in Revelation, be they Catholic or not, are roused to consider their bearing upon themselves, both for the honour of God, and from tenderness for those many souls who, in consequence of the confident tone of the schools of secular knowledge, are in danger of being led away into a bottomless liberalism of thought.

I am not going to criticize here that vast body of men, in the mass, who at this time would profess to be liberals in religion; and who look towards the discoveries of the age, certain or in progress as their informants, direct or indirect, as to what they shall think about the unseen and the future. The Liberalism which gives a colour to society now, is very different from that character of thought which bore the name thirty or forty years ago. Now it is scarcely a party; it is the educated lay world. When I was young, I knew the word first as giving name to a periodical, set up by Lord Byron and others. Now, as then, I have no sympathy with the philosophy of Byron. Afterwards, Liberalism was the badge of a theological school, of a dry and repulsive character, not very dangerous in itself, though dangerous as opening the door to evils which it did not itself either anticipate or comprehend. At present it is nothing else than that deep, plausible scepticism, of which I spoke above, as being the development of human reason, as practically exercised by the natural man.

The Liberal religionists of this day are a very mixed body, and therefore I am not intending to speak against them. There may be, and doubtless is, in the hearts of some or many of them a real antipathy or anger against revealed truth, which it is distressing to think of. Again; in many men of science or literature there may be an animosity arising from almost a personal feeling; it being a matter of party, a point of honour, the excitement of a game, or a satisfaction to the soreness or annoyance occasioned by the acrimony or narrowness of apologists for religion, to prove that Christianity or that Scripture is untrustworthy. Many scientific and literary men, on the other hand, go on, I am confident, in a straightforward impartial way, in their own province and on their own line of thought, without any disturbance from religious difficulties in themselves, or any wish at all to give pain to others by the result of their investigations. It would ill become me, as if I were afraid of truth of any kind, to blame those who pursue secular facts, by means of the reason which God has given them, to their logical conclusions: or to be angry with science, because religion is bound in duty to take cognizance of its teaching. But putting these particular classes of men aside, as having no special call on the sympathy of the Catholic, of course he does most deeply enter into the feelings of a fourth and large class of men, in the educated portions of society, of religious and sincere minds, who are simply perplexed, – frightened or rendered desperate, as the case may be, – by the utter confusion into which late discoveries or speculations have thrown their most elementary ideas of religion. Who does not feel for such men? who can have one unkind thought of them? I take up in their behalf St. Augustine's beautiful words, ''Illi in vos saeviant'', &c. Let them be fierce with you who have no experience of the difficulty with which error is discriminated from truth, and the way of life is found amid the illusions of the world. How many a Catholic has in his thoughts followed such men, many of them so good, so true, so noble! how often has the wish risen in his heart that some one from among his own people should come forward as the champion of revealed truth against its opponents! Various persons, Catholic and Protestant, have asked me to do so myself; but I had several strong difficulties in the way. One of the greatest is this, that at the moment it is so difficult to say precisely what it is that is to be encountered and overthrown. I am far from denying that scientific knowledge is really growing, but it is by fits and starts; hypotheses rise and fall; it is difficult to anticipate which of them will keep their ground, and what the state of knowledge in relation to them will be from year to year. In this condition of things, it has seemed to me to be very undignified for a Catholic to commit himself to the work of chasing what might turn out to be phantoms, and, in behalf of some special objections, to be ingenious in devising a theory, which, before it was completed, might have to give place to some theory newer still, from the fact that those former objections had already come to nought under the uprising of others. It seemed to be specially a time, in which Christians had a call to be patient, in which they had no other way of helping those who were alarmed, than that of exhorting them to have a little faith and fortitude, and to ''beware'', as the poet says, ''of dangerous steps''. This seemed so clear to me, the more I thought of the matter, as to make me surmise, that, if I attempted what had so little promise in it, I should find that the highest Catholic Authority was against the attempt, and that I should have spent my time and my thought, in doing what either it would be imprudent to bring before the public at all, or what, did I do so, would only complicate matters further which were already complicated, without my interference, more than enough. And I interpret recent acts of that authority as fulfilling my expectation; I interpret them as tying the hands of a controversialist, such as I should be, and teaching us that true wisdom, which Moses inculcated on his people, when the Egyptians were pursuing them, "Fear ye not, stand still; the Lord shall fight for you, and ye shall hold your peace." And so far from finding a difficulty in obeying in this case, I have cause to be thankful and to rejoice to have so clear a direction in a matter of difficulty.

But if we would ascertain with correctness the real course of a principle, we must look at it at a certain distance, and as history represents it to us. Nothing carried on by human instruments, but has its irregularities, and affords ground for criticism, when minutely scrutinized in matters of detail. I have been speaking of that aspect of the action of an infallible authority, which is most open to invidious criticism from those who view it from without; I have tried to be fair, in estimating what can be said to its disadvantage, as witnessed at a particular time in the Catholic Church, and now I wish its adversaries to be equally fair in their judgment upon its historical character. Can, then, the infallible authority, with any show of reason, be said in fact to have destroyed the energy of the Catholic intellect? Let is be observed, I have not here to speak of any conflict which ecclesiastical authority has had with science, for this simple reason, that conflict there has been none; and that, because the secular sciences, as they now exist, are a novelty in the world, and there has been no time yet for a history of relations between theology and these new methods of knowledge, and indeed the Church may be said to have kept clear of them, as is proved by the constantly cited case of Galileo. Here "exceptio probat regulam": for it is the one stock argument. Again, I have not to speak of any relations of the Church to the new sciences, because my simple question all along has been whether the assumption of infallibility by the proper authority is adapted to make me a hypocrite, and till that authority passes decrees on pure physical subjects and calls on me to subscribe them, (which it never will do, because it has not the power,) it has no tendency to interfere by any of its acts with my private judgment on those points. The simple question is, whether authority has so acted upon the reason of individuals, that they can have no opinion of their own, and have but an alternative of slavish superstition or secret rebellion of heart; and I think the whole history of theology puts an absolute negative upon such a supposition.

It is hardly necessary to argue out so plain a point. It is individuals, and not the Holy See, that have taken the initiative, and given the lead to the Catholic mind, in theological inquiry. Indeed, it is one of the reproaches urged against the Roman Church, that it has originated nothing, and has only served as a sort of *remora* or break in the development of doctrine. And it is an objection which I really embrace as a truth; for such I conceive to be the main purpose of its extraordinary gift. It is said, and truly, that the Church of Rome possessed no great mind in the whole period of persecution. Afterwards for a long while, it has not a single doctor to show; St. Leo, its first, is the teacher of one point of doctrine; St. Gregory, who stands at the very extremity of the first age of the Church, has no place in dogma or philosophy. The great luminary of the western world, is, as we know, St. Augustine; he, no infallible teacher, has formed the intellect of Christian Europe; indeed to the African Church generally we must look for the best early exposition of Latin ideas. Moreover, of the African divines, the first in order of time, and not the least influential, is the strong-minded and heterodox Tertullian. Nor is the Eastern intellect, as such, without its share in the formation of the Latin teaching. The free thought of Origen is visible in the writings of the Western Doctors, Hilary and Ambrose; and the independent mind of Jerome has enriched his own vigorous commentaries on Scripture, from the stores of the scarcely orthodox Eusebius. Heretical questionings have been transmuted by the living power of the Church into salutary truths. The case is the same as regards the Ecumenical Councils. Authority in its most imposing exhibition, grave bishops, laden with the traditions and rivalries of particular nations or places, have been guided in their decisions by the commanding genius of individuals, sometimes young and of inferior rank. Not that uninspired intellect overruled the superhuman gift which was committed to the Council, which would be a self-contradictory assertion, but that in that process of inquiry and deliberation, which ended in an infallible enunciation, individual reason was paramount. Thus Malchion, a mere presbyter, was the instrument of the great Council of Antioch in the third century in meeting and refuting, for the assembled Fathers, the heretical Patriarch of that see. Parallel to this instance is the influence, so well known, of a young deacon, St. Athanasius, with the 318 Fathers at Nicaea. In mediaeval times we read of St. Anselm at Bari, as the champion of the Council there held, against the Greeks. At Trent, the writings of St. Bonaventura, and, what is more to the point, the address of a Priest and theologian, Salmeron, had a critical effect on some of the definitions of dogma. In some of these cases the influence might be partly moral, but in others it was that of a discursive knowledge of ecclesiastical writers, a scientific acquaintance with theology, and a force of thought in the treatment of doctrine.

There are of course intellectual habits which theology does not tend to form, as for instance the experimental, and again the philosophical; but that is because it is theology, not because of the gift of infallibility. But, as far as this goes, I think it could be shown that physical science on the other hand, or again mathematical, affords but an imperfect training for the intellect. I do not see then how any objection about the narrowness of theology comes into our question, which simply is, whether the belief in an infallible authority destroys the independence of the mind; and I consider that the whole history of the Church, and especially the history of the theological schools, gives a negative to the accusation. There never was a time when the intellect of the educated class was more active, or rather more restless, than in the middle ages. And then again all through Church history from the first, how slow is authority in interfering! Perhaps a local teacher, or a doctor in some local school, hazards a proposition, and a controversy ensues. It smoulders or burns in one place, no one interposing; Rome simply lets it alone. Then it comes before a Bishop; or some priest, or some professor in some other seat of learning takes it up; and then there is a second stage of it. Then it comes before a University, and it may be condemned by the theological faculty. So the controversy proceeds year after year, and Rome is still silent. An appeal perhaps is next made to a seat of authority inferior to Rome; and then at last after a long while it comes before the supreme power.

Meanwhile, the question has been ventilated and turned over and over again, and viewed on every side of it, and authority is called upon to pronounce a decision, which has already been arrived at by reason. But even then, perhaps the supreme authority hesitates to do so, and nothing is determined on the point for years: or so generally and vaguely, that the whole controversy has to be gone through again, before it is ultimately determined. It is manifest how a mode of proceeding, such as this, tends not only to the liberty, but to the courage, of the individual theologian or controversialist. Many a man has ideas, which he hopes are true, and useful for his day, but he is not confident about them, and wishes to have them discussed. He is willing, or rather would be thankful, to give them up, if they can be proved to be erroneous or dangerous, and by means of controversy he obtains his end. He is answered, and he yields; or on the contrary he finds that he is considered safe. He would not dare to do this, if he knew an authority, which was supreme and final, was watching every word he said, and made signs of assent or dissent to each sentence, as he uttered it. Then indeed he would be fighting, as the Persian soldiers, under the lash, and the freedom of his intellect might truly be said to be beaten out of him. But this has not been so: – I do not mean to say that, when controversies run high, in schools or even in small portions of the Church, an interposition may not advisably take place; and again, questions may be of that urgent nature, that an appeal must, as a matter of duty, be made at one to the highest authority in the Church; but if we look into the history of controversy, we shall find, I think, the general run of things to be such as I have represented it. Zosimus treated Pelagius and Coelestius with extreme forbearance; St. Gregory VII. was equally indulgent with Berengarius: – by reason of the very power of the Popes they have commonly been slow and moderate in their use of it.

And here again is a further shelter for the legitimate exercise of the reason: – the multitude of nations which are within the fold of the Church will be found to have acted for its protection, against any narrowness, on the supposition of narrowness, in the various authorities at Rome, with whom lies the practical decision of controverted questions. How have the Greek traditions been respected and provided for in the later Ecumenical

Councils, in spite of the countries that held them being in a state of schism! There are important points of doctrine which have been (humanly speaking) exempted from the infallible sentence, by the tenderness with which its instruments, in framing it, have treated the opinions of particular places. Then, again, such national influences have a providential effect in moderating the bias which the local influences of Italy may exert upon the See of St. Peter. It stands to reason that, as the Gallican Church has in it a French element, so Rome must have in it an element of Italy; and it is no prejudice to the zeal and devotion with which we submit ourselves to the Holy See to admit this plainly. It seems to me, as I have been saying, that Catholicity is not only one of the notes of the church, but, according to the divine purposes, one of its securities. I think it would be a very serious evil, which Divine Mercy avert! that the Church should be contracted in Europe within the range of particular nationalities. It is a great idea to introduce Latin civilization into America, and to improve the Catholics there by the energy of French devotedness; but I trust that all European races will ever have a place in the Church, and assuredly I think that the loss of the English, not to say the German element, in its composition has been a most serious misfortune. And certainly, if there is one consideration more than another which should make us English grateful to Pius the Ninth, it is that, by giving us a Church of our own, he has prepared the way for our own habits of mind, our own manner of reasoning, our own tastes, and our own virtues, finding a place and thereby a sanctification, in the Catholic Church.

(*Apo.* 214–41)

7

PAPAL INFALLIBILITY*

A LETTER TO THE DUKE OF NORFOLK

A Letter to the Duke of Norfolk was completed on 21 December 1874 after a month's continuous writing and published on 14 January 1875. Newman had actually begun trying to write it five or six weeks previously, but he had found it very hard going. The subject really demanded a whole book, and he felt that unless he was really effective, he would only damage the Catholic cause. The so-called "pamphlet" was actually 150 pages of close print. It took the form of a letter because Newman always found it easier to write when he was addressing a specific person or audience. The extracts here are from sections 5 ("conscience") and 9 ("The Vatican Definition").

§5. CONSCIENCE

It seems, then, that there are extreme cases in which Conscience may come into collision with the word of a Pope, and is to be followed in spite of that word. Now I wish to place this proposition on a broader basis, acknowledged by all Catholics, and, in order to do this satisfactorily . . . I must begin with the Creator and His creature, when I would draw out the prerogatives and the supreme authority of Conscience.

I say, then, that the Supreme Being is of a certain character, which, expressed in human language, we call ethical. He has the attributes of justice, truth, wisdom, sanctity, benevolence and mercy, as eternal characteristics in His nature, the very Law of His being, identical with Himself; and next, when He became Creator, He implanted this Law, which is Himself, in the intelligence of all His rational creatures. The Divine Law, then, is the rule of ethical truth, the standard of right and wrong, a sovereign, irreversible, absolute authority in the presence of men and Angels. . . . This law, as apprehended in the minds of individual

*See also above, p. 51.

men, is called "conscience;" and though it may suffer refraction in passing into the intellectual medium of each, it is not therefore so affected as to lose its character of being the Divine Law, but still has, as such, the prerogative of commanding obedience. . . .

This view of conscience, I know, is very different from that ordinarily taken of it, both by the science and literature, and by the public opinion, of this day. It is founded on the doctrine that conscience is the voice of God, whereas it is fashionable on all hands now to consider it in one way or another a creation of man. Of course, there are great and broad exceptions to this statement. It is not true of many or most religious bodies of men; especially not of their teachers and ministers. When Anglicans, Wesleyans, the various Presbyterian sects in Scotland, and other denominations among us, speak of conscience, they mean what we mean, the voice of God in the nature and heart of man, as distinct from the voice of Revelation. They speak of a principle planted within us, before we have had any training, although training and experience are necessary for its strength, growth, and due formation. They consider it a constituent element of the mind, as our perception of other ideas may be, as our powers of reasoning, as our sense of order and the beautiful, and our other intellectual endowments. They consider it, as Catholics consider it, to be the internal witness of both the existence and the law of God. They think it holds of God, and not of man, as an Angel walking on the earth would be no citizen or dependent of the Civil Power. They would not allow, any more than we do, that it could be resolved into any combination of principles in our nature, more elementary than itself; nay, though it may be called, and is, a law of the mind, they would not grant that it was nothing more; I mean, that it was not a dictate, nor conveyed the notion of responsibility, of duty, of a threat and a promise, with a vividness which discriminated it from all other constituents of our nature.

This, at least, is how I read the doctrine of Protestants as well as of Catholics. The rule and measure of duty is not utility, nor expedience, nor the happiness of the greatest number, nor State convenience, nor fitness, order, and the *pulchrum*. Conscience is not a long-sighted selfishness, nor a desire to be consistent with oneself; but it is a messenger from Him, who, both in nature and in grace, speaks to us behind a veil, and teaches and rules us by His representatives. Conscience is the aboriginal Vicar of Christ, a prophet in its informations, a monarch in its peremptoriness, a priest in its blessings and anathemas, and, even though the eternal priesthood throughout the Church could cease to be, in it the sacerdotal principle would remain and would have a sway.

Words such as these are idle empty verbiage to the great world of philosophy now. All through my day there has been a resolute warfare, I had almost said conspiracy against the rights of conscience, as I have described it. Literature and science have been embodied in great institutions in order to put it down. Noble buildings have been reared as fortresses against that spiritual, invisible influence which is too subtle for science and too profound for literature. Chairs in Universities have been made the seats of an antagonist tradition. Public writers, day after day, have indoctrinated the minds of innumerable readers with theories subversive of its claims. As in Roman times, and in the middle age, its supremacy was assailed by the arm of physical force, so now the intellect is put in operation to sap the foundations of a power which the sword could not destroy. We are told that conscience is but a twist in primitive and untutored man; that its dictate is an imagination; that the very notion of guiltiness, which that dictate enforces, is simply irrational, for how can there possibly be freedom of will, how can there be consequent responsibility, in that infinite eternal network of cause and effect, in which we helplessly lie? and what retribution have we to fear, when we have had no real choice to do good or evil?

So much for philosophers; now let us see what is the notion of conscience in this day in the popular mind. There, no more than in the intellectual world, does "conscience" retain the old, true, Catholic meaning of the word. There too the idea, the presence of a Moral Governor is far away from the use of it, frequent and emphatic as that use of it is. When men advocate the rights of conscience, they in no sense mean the rights of the Creator, nor the duty to Him, in thought and deed, of the creature; but the right of thinking, speaking, writing, and acting, according to their judgment or their humour, without any thought of God at all. They do not even pretend to go by any moral rule, but they demand, what they think is an Englishman's prerogative, for each to be his own master in all things, and to profess what he pleases, asking no one's leave, and accounting priest or preacher, speaker or writer, unutterably impertinent, who dares to say a word against his going to perdition, if he like it, in his own way. Conscience has rights because it has duties; but in this age, with a large portion of the public, it is the very right and freedom of conscience to dispense with conscience, to ignore a Lawgiver and Judge, to be independent of unseen obligations. It becomes a licence to take up any or no religion, to take up this or that and let it go again, to go to church, to go to chapel, to boast of being above all religions and to be an impartial critic of each of them. Conscience is a stern monitor, but in this century it has been superseded by a counterfeit, which the eighteen centuries prior to it never heard of, and could not have mistaken for it, if they had. It is the right of self-will. . . .

So indeed it is; did the Pope speak against Conscience in the true sense of the word, he would commit a suicidal act. He would be cutting the ground from under his feet. His very mission is to proclaim the moral law, and to protect and strengthen that "Light which enlighteneth every man that cometh into the world." On the law of conscience and its sacredness are founded both his authority in theory and his power in fact. Whether this or that particular Pope in this bad world always kept this great truth in view in all he did, it is for history to tell. I am considering here the Papacy in its office and its duties, and in reference to those who acknowledge its claims. They are not bound by the Pope's personal character or private acts, but by his formal teaching. Thus viewing his position, we shall find that it is by the universal sense of right and wrong, the consciousness of transgression, the pangs of guilt, and the dread of retribution, as first principles deeply lodged in the hearts of men, it is thus and only thus, that he has gained his footing in the world and achieved his success. It is his claim to come from the Divine Lawgiver, in order to elicit, protect, and enforce those truths which the Lawgiver has sown in our very nature, it is this and this only that is the explanation of his length of life more than antediluvian. The championship of the Moral Law and of conscience is his *raison d'être*. The fact of his mission is the answer to the complaints of those who feel the insufficiency of the natural light;

and the insufficiency of that light is the justification of his mission.

All sciences, except the science of Religion, have their certainty in themselves; as far as they are sciences, they consist of necessary conclusions from undeniable premises, or of phenomena manipulated into general truths by an irresistible induction. But the sense of right and wrong, which is the first element in religion, is so delicate, so fitful, so easily puzzled, obscured, perverted, so subtle in its argumentative methods, so impressible by education, so biassed by pride and passion, so unsteady in its course, that, in the struggle for existence amid the various exercises and triumphs of the human intellect this sense is at once the highest of all teachers, yet the least luminous; and the Church, the Pope, the Hierarchy are, in the Divine purpose, the supply of an urgent demand. Natural Religion, certain as are its grounds and its doctrines as addressed to thoughtful, serious minds, needs, in order that it may speak to mankind with effect and subdue the world, to be sustained and completed by Revelation.

In saying all this, of course I must not be supposed to be limiting the Revelation of which the Church is the keeper to a mere republication of the Natural Law; but still it is true, that, though Revelation is so distinct from the teaching of nature and beyond it, yet it is not independent of it, nor without relations towards it, but is its complement, reassertion, issue, embodiment, and interpretation. The Pope, who comes of Revelation, has no jurisdiction over Nature. If, under the plea of his revealed prerogatives, he neglected his mission of preaching truth, justice, mercy, and peace, much more if he trampled on the consciences of his subjects, – if he had done so all along, as Protestants say, then he could not have lasted all these many centuries till now, so as to supply a mark for their reprobation. . . .

Such is the relation of the ecclesiastical power to the human conscience: – however, a contrary view may be taken of it. It may be said that no one doubts that the Pope's power rests on those weaknesses of human nature, that religious sense, which in ancient days Lucretius noted as the cause of the worst ills of our race; that he uses it dexterously, forming under shelter of it a false code of morals for his own aggrandisement and tyranny; and that thus conscience becomes his creature and his slave, doing, as if on a divine sanction, his will; so that in the abstract indeed and in idea it is free, but never free in fact, never able to take a flight of its own, independent of him, any more than birds whose wings are clipped; – moreover, that, if it were able to exert a will of its own, then there would ensue a collision more unmanageable than that between the Church and the State, as being in one and the same subject-matter – viz., religion; for what would become of the Pope's "absolute authority," as Mr. Gladstone calls it, if the private conscience had an absolute authority also?

I wish to answer this important objection distinctly.

1. First, I am using the word "conscience" in the high sense in which I have already explained it, – not as a fancy or an opinion, but as a dutiful obedience to what claims to be a divine voice, speaking within us; and that this is the view properly to be taken of it, I shall not attempt to prove here, but shall assume it as a first principle.

2. Secondly, I observe that conscience is not a judgment upon any speculative truth, any abstract doctrine, but bears immediately on conduct, on something to be done or not done. "Conscience," says St. Thomas, "is the practical judgment or dictate of reason, by which we judge what *hic et nunc* is to be done as being good, or to be avoided as evil." Hence conscience cannot come into direct collision with the Church's or the Pope's infallibility; which is engaged on general propositions, and in the condemnation of particular and given errors.

3. Next, I observe that, conscience being a practical dictate, a collision is possible between it and the Pope's authority only when the Pope legislates, or gives particular orders, and the like. But a Pope is not infallible in his laws, nor in his commands, nor in his acts of state, nor in his administration, nor in his public policy. Let it be observed that the Vatican Council has left him just as it found him here. ... What have excommunication and interdict to do with Infallibility? Was St. Peter infallible on that occasion at Antioch when St. Paul withstood him? was St. Victor infallible when he separated from his communion the Asiatic Churches? or Liberius when in like manner he excommunicated Athanasius? And, to come to later times, was Gregory XIII., when he had a medal struck in honour of the Bartholomew massacre? or Paul IV. in his conduct towards Elizabeth? or Sextus

V. when he blessed the Armada? or Urban VIII. when he perse-
cuted Galileo? No Catholic ever pretends that these Popes were
infallible in these acts. Since then infallibility alone could block
the exercise of conscience, and the Pope is not infallible in that
subject-matter in which conscience is of supreme authority, no
dead-lock, such as is implied in the objection which I am answering, can take place between conscience and the Pope.

4. But, of course, I have to say again, lest I should be misunder-
stood, that when I speak of Conscience, I mean conscience truly
so called. When it has the right of opposing the supreme, though
not infallible Authority of the Pope, it must be something more
than that miserable counterfeit which, as I have said above, now
goes by the name. If in a particular case it is to be taken as
a sacred and sovereign monitor, its dictate, in order to prevail
against the voice of the Pope, must follow upon serious thought,
prayer, and all available means of arriving at a right judgment
on the matter in question. And further, obedience to the Pope
is what is called "in possession;" that is, the *onus probandi* of
establishing a case against him lies, as in all cases of exception,
on the side of conscience. Unless a man is able to say to himself,
as in the Presence of God, that he must not, and dare not, act
upon the Papal injunction, he is bound to obey it, and would
commit a great sin in disobeying it. *Primâ facie* it is his bounden
duty, even from a sentiment of loyalty, to believe the Pope right
and to act accordingly. He must vanquish that mean, ungener-
ous, selfish, vulgar spirit of his nature, which, at the very first
rumour of a command, places itself in opposition to the Superior
who gives it, asks itself whether he is not exceeding his right,
and rejoices, in a moral and practical matter to commence with
scepticism. He must have no wilful determination to exercise
a right of thinking, saying, doing just what he pleases, the question of truth and falsehood, right and wrong, the duty if possible
of obedience, the love of speaking as his Head speaks, and of
standing in all cases on his Head's side, being simply discarded.
If this necessary rule were observed, collisions between the
Pope's authority and the authority of conscience would be very
rare. On the other hand, in the fact that, after all, in extraordinary
cases, the conscience of each individual is free, we have a safeguard and security, were security necessary (which is a most
gratuitous supposition), that no Pope ever will be able, as the

objection supposes, to create a false conscience for his own ends. . . .

Thus, if the Pope told the English Bishops to order their priests to stir themselves energetically in favour of teetotalism, and a particular priest was fully persuaded that abstinence from wine, &c, was practically a Gnostic error, and therefore felt he could not so exert himself without sin; or suppose there was a Papal order to hold lotteries in each mission for some religious object, and a priest could say in God's sight that he believed lotteries to be morally wrong, that priest in either of these cases would commit a sin *hic et nunc* if he obeyed the Pope, whether he was right or wrong in his opinion, and, if wrong, although he had not taken proper pains to get at the truth of the matter. . . .

I add one remark. Certainly, if I am obliged to bring religion into after-dinner toasts, (which indeed does not seem quite the thing) I shall drink – to the Pope, if you please, – still, to Conscience first, and to the Pope afterwards. (*Diff.* ii. 246–50, 252–8, 260–1)

§9. THE VATICAN DEFINITION

Now I am to speak of the Vatican definition, by which the doctrine of the Pope's infallibility has become *de fide*, that is, a truth necessary to be believed, as being included in the original divine revelation, for those terms, revelation, *depositum*, dogma, and *de fide*, are correlatives; and I begin with a remark which suggests the drift of all I have to say about it. It is this: – that so difficult a virtue is faith, even with the special grace of God, in proportion as the reason is exercised, so difficult is it to assent inwardly to propositions, verified to us neither by reason nor experience, but depending for their reception on the word of the Church as God's oracle, that she has ever shown the utmost care to contract, as far as possible, the range of truths and the sense of propositions, of which she demands this absolute reception. . . . To co-operate in this charitable duty has been one special work of her theologians, and rules are laid down by herself, by tradition, and by custom, to assist them in the task. She only speaks when it is necessary to speak; but hardly has she spoken out magisterially some great general principle, when she sets her theologians to work to explain her meaning in the concrete, by strict interpretation of its wording, by the illustration of its circumstances, and by the recognition of exceptions, in order to make it as tolerable as possible, and the least of a temptation, to self-willed, independent, or wrongly educated minds. . . .

The Vatican definition, which comes to us in the shape of the Pope's Encyclical Bull called the *Pastor Æternus*, declares that "the Pope has that same infallibility which the Church has' (Romanum Pontificem eâ infallibilitate pollere, quâ divinus Redemptor Ecclesiam suam in definiendâ doctrinâ de fide vel moribus instructam esse voluit.): to determine therefore what is meant by the infallibility of the Pope we must turn first to consider the infallibility of the Church. And again, to determine the character of the Church's infallibility, we must consider what is the characteristic of Christianity, considered as a revelation of God's will.

Our Divine Master might have communicated to us heavenly truths without telling us that they came from Him, as it is commonly thought He has done in the case of heathen nations; but He willed the Gospel to be a revelation acknowledged and authenticated, to be public, fixed, and permanent; and accordingly, as Catholics hold, He framed a Society of men to be its home, its instrument, and its guarantee. The rulers of that Association are the legal trustees, so to say, of the sacred truths which He spoke to the Apostles by word of mouth. As He was leaving them, He gave them their great commission, and bade them "teach" their converts all over the earth, "to observe all things whatever He had commanded them;" and then He added, "Lo, I am with you always, even to the end of the world.'

Here, first, He told them to "teach" His revealed Truth; next, "to the consummation of all things;" thirdly, for their encouragement, He said that He would be with them "all days," all along, on every emergency or occasion, until that consummation. They had a duty put upon them of teaching their Master's words, a duty which they could not fulfil in the perfection which fidelity required, without His help; therefore came His promise to be with them in their performance of it. Nor did that promise of supernatural help end with the Apostles personally, for He adds, "to the consummation of the world," implying that the Apostles would have successors, and engaging that He would be with those successors as He had been with them.

The same safeguard of the Revelation – viz. an authoritative, permanent tradition of teaching, is insisted on by an informant of equal authority with St. Matthew, but altogether independent of him, I mean St. Paul. He calls the Church "the pillar and ground of the Truth;" and he bids his convert Timothy, when he had become a ruler in that Church, to "take heed unto his doctrine," to "keep the deposit" of the faith, and to "commit" the things which he had heard from himself "to faithful men who should be fit to teach others."

This is how Catholics understand the Scripture record, nor does it appear how it can otherwise be understood; but, when we have got as far as this, and look back, we find that we have by implication made profession of a further doctrine. For, if the Church, initiated in the Apostles and continued in their successors, has been set up for the direct object of protecting, preserving, and declaring the Revelation, and that, by means of the Guardianship and Providence of its Divine Author, we are led on to perceive that, in asserting this, we are in other words asserting, that, so far as the message entrusted to it is concerned, the Church is infallible; for what is meant by infallibility in teaching but that the teacher in his teaching is secured from error? and how can fallible man be thus secured except by a supernatural infallible guidance? And what can have been the object of the words, "I am with you all along to the end," but to give thereby an answer by anticipation to the spontaneous, silent alarm of the feeble company of fishermen and labourers, to whom they were addressed, on their finding themselves laden with superhuman duties and responsibilities?

Such then being, in its simple outline, the infallibility of the Church, such too will be the Pope's infallibility, as the Vatican Fathers have defined it. And if we find that by means of this outline we are able to fill out in all important respects the idea of a Council's infallibility, we shall thereby be ascertaining in detail what has been defined in 1870 about the infallibility of the Pope. With an attempt to do this I shall conclude.

1. The Church has the office of teaching, and the matter of that teaching is the body of doctrine, which the Apostles left behind them as her perpetual possession. If a question arises as to what the Apostolic doctrine is on a particular point, she has infallibility promised to her to enable her to answer correctly.

And, as by the teaching of the Church is understood, not the teaching of this or that Bishop, but their united voice, and a Council is the form the Church must take, in order that all men may recognize that in fact she is teaching on any point in dispute, so in like manner the Pope must come before us in some special form or posture, if he is to be understood to be exercising his teaching office, and that form is called *ex cathedra*. This term is most appropriate, as being on one occasion used by our Lord Himself. When the Jewish doctors taught, they placed themselves in Moses' sect, and spoke *ex cathedra*; and then, as He tells us, they were to be obeyed by their people, and that, whatever were their private lives or characters. "The Scribes and Pharisees," He says, "are seated on the chair of Moses: all things therefore whatsoever they shall say to you, observe and do; but according to their works do you not, for they say and do not.'

2. The forms, by which a General Council is identified as representing the Church herself, are too clear to need drawing out; but what is to be that moral *cathedra*, or teaching chair, in which the Pope sits, when he is to be recognized as in the exercise of his infallible teaching? the new definition answers this question. He speaks *ex cathedra*, or infallibly, when he speaks, first, as the Universal Teacher; secondly, in the name and with the authority of the Apostles; thirdly, on a point of faith or morals; fourthly, with the purpose of binding every member of the Church to accept and believe his decision. . . .

5. Nor is a Council infallible, even in the prefaces and introductions to its definitions. There are theologians of name . . . who contend that even those most instructive *capitula* passed in the Tridentine Council, from which the Canons, with anathemas are drawn up, are not portions of the Church's infallible teaching; and the parallel introductions prefixed to the Vatican anathemas have an authority not greater nor less than that of those capitula.

6. Such passages, however, as these are too closely connected with the definitions themselves, not to be what is sometimes called, by a *catachresis*, "proximum fidei;" still, on the other hand, it is true also that, in those circumstances and surroundings of formal definitions, which I have been speaking of, whether on the part of a Council or a Pope, there may be not only no exercise of an infallible voice, but actual error. . . .

This remark and several before it will become intelligible if we consider that neither Pope nor Council are on a level with the Apostles. To the Apostles the whole revelation was given, by the Church it is transmitted; no simply new truth has been given to us since St. John's death; the one office of the Church is to guard "that noble deposit" of truth, as St. Paul speaks to Timothy, which the Apostles bequeathed to her, in its fulness and integrity. Hence the infallibility of the Apostles was of a far more positive and wide character than that needed by and granted to the Church. We call it, in the case of the Apostles, inspiration; in the case of the Church, *assistentia*.

Of course there is a sense of the word "inspiration" in which it is common to all members of the Church, and therefore especially to its Bishops, and still more directly to those rulers, when solemnly called together in Council, after much prayer throughout Christendom, and in a frame of mind especially serious and earnest by reason of the work they have in hand. The Paraclete certainly is ever with them, and more effectively in a Council ... but I speak of the special and promised aid necessary for their fidelity to Apostolic teaching; and, in order to secure this fidelity, no inward gift of infallibility is needed, such as the Apostles had, no direct suggestion of divine truth, but simply an external guardianship, keeping them off from error (as a man's good Angel, without at all enabling him to walk, might, on a night journey, keep him from pitfalls in his way), a guardianship, saving them, as far as their ultimate decisions are concerned, from the effects of their inherent infirmities, from any chance of extravagance, of confusion of thought, of collision with former decisions or with Scripture, which in seasons of excitement might reasonably be feared. ...

But since the process of defining truth is human, it is open to the chance of error; what Providence has guaranteed is only this, that there should be no error in the final step, in the resulting definition or dogma.

7. Accordingly, all that a Council, and all that the Pope, is infallible in, is the direct answer to the special question which he happens to be considering; his prerogative does not extend beyond a power, when in his *Cathedra*, of giving that very answer truly. ...

8. This rule is so strictly to be observed that, though dogmatic statements are found from time to time in a Pope's Apostolic

Letters, &c., yet they are not accounted to be exercises of his infallibility if they are said only *obiter* – by the way, and without direct intention to define. . . .

9. Another limitation is given in Pope Pius's own conditions, set down in the *Pastor Æternus*, for the exercise of infallibility: viz., the proposition defined will be without any claim to be considered binding on the belief of Catholics, unless it is referable to the Apostolic *depositum*, through the channel either of Scripture or Tradition; and, though the Pope is the judge whether it is so referable or not, yet the necessity of his professing to abide by this reference is in itself a certain limitation of his dogmatic action. A Protestant will object indeed that, after his distinctly asserting that the Immaculate Conception and the Papal Infallibility are in Scripture and Tradition, this safeguard against erroneous definitions is not worth much, nor do I say that it is one of the most effective: but anyhow, in consequence of it, no Pope any more than a counsel, could, for instance, introduce Ignatius's Epistles into the Canon of Scripture; – and, as to his dogmatic condemnation of particular books, which, of course, are foreign to the *depositum*, I would say, that, as to their false doctrine there can be no difficulty in condemning that, by means of that Apostolic deposit; nor surely in his condemning the very wording, in which they convey it, when the subject is carefully considered. For the Pope's condemning the language, for instance, of Jansenius is a parallel act to the Church's sanctioning the word "Consubstantial," and if a Council and the Pope were not infallible so far in their judgment of language, neither Pope nor Council could draw up a dogmatic definition at all, for the right exercise of words is involved in the right exercise of thought.

10. And in like manner, as regards the precepts concerning moral duties, it is not in every such precept that the Pope is infallible.[17] As a definition of faith must be drawn from the Apostolic *depositum* of doctrine, in order that it may be considered an exercise of infallibility, whether in the Pope or a Council, so too a precept of morals, if it is to be accepted as from an infallible voice, must be drawn from the Moral law, that primary revelation to us from God.

That is, in the first place, it must relate to things in themselves good or evil. If the Pope prescribed lying or revenge, his command would simply go for nothing, as if he had not issued it, because he has no power over the Moral Law. If he forbade his flock to eat any but vegetable food, or to dress in a particular fashion (questions of decency and modesty not coming into the question), he would also be going beyond the province of faith, because such a rule does not relate to a matter in itself good or bad. But if he gave a precept all over the world for the adoption of lotteries instead of tithes or offerings, certainly it would be very hard to prove that he was contradicting the Moral Law, or ruling a practice to be in itself good which was in itself evil; and there are few persons but would allow that it is at least doubtful whether lotteries are abstractedly evil, and in a doubtful matter the Pope is to be believed and obeyed.

However, there are other conditions besides this, necessary for the exercise of Papal infallibility, in moral subjects: – for instance, his definition must relate to things necessary for salvation. No one would so speak of lotteries, nor of a particular dress, nor of a particular kind of food; – such precepts, then, did he make them, would be simply external to the range of his prerogative.

And again, his infallibility in consequence is not called into exercise, unless he speaks to the whole world; for, if his precepts, in order to be dogmatic, must enjoin what is necessary to salvation, they must be necessary for all men. Accordingly orders which issue from him for the observance of particular countries, or political or religious classes, have no claim to be the utterances of his infallibility. If he enjoins upon the hierarchy of Ireland to withstand mixed education, this is no exercise of his infallibility.

It may be added that the field of morals contains so little that is unknown and unexplored, in contrast with revelation and doctrinal fact, which form the domain of faith, that it is difficult to say what portions of moral teaching in the course of 1800 years actually have proceeded from the Pope, or from the Church, or where to look for such. Nearly all that either oracle has done in this respect, has been to condemn such propositions as in a moral point of view are false, or dangerous or rash; and these condemnations, besides being such as in fact will be found to command the assent of most men, as soon as heard, do not necessarily go so far as to present any positive statements for universal acceptance.

11. With the mention of condemned propositions I am brought to another and large consideration, which is one of the best illustrations that I can give of that principle of minimizing so necessary, as I think, for a wise and cautious theology: at the same time I cannot insist upon it in the connexion into which I am going to introduce it, without submitting myself to the correction of divines more learned than I can pretend to be myself.

The infallibility, whether of the Church or of the Pope, acts principally or solely in two channels, in direct statements of truth, and in the condemnation of error. The former takes the shape of doctrinal definitions, the latter stigmatizes propositions as heretical, next to heresy, erroneous, and the like. In each case the Church, as guided by her Divine Master, has made provision for weighing as lightly as possible on the faith and conscience of her children.

As to the condemnation of propositions all she tells us is, that the thesis condemned when taken as a whole, or, again, when viewed in its context, is heretical, or blasphemous, or impious, or whatever like epithet she affixes to it. We have only to trust her so far as to allow ourselves to be warned against the thesis, or the work containing it. Theologians employ themselves in determining what precisely it is that is condemned in that thesis or treatise; and doubtless in most cases they do so with success; but that determination is not *de fide*; all that is of faith is that there is in that thesis itself, which is noted, heresy or error, or other like peccant matter, as the case may be, such, that the censure is a peremptory command to theologians, preachers, students, and all other whom it concerns, to keep clear of it. But so light is this obligation, that instances frequently occur, when it is successfully maintained by some new writer, that the Pope's act does not imply what it has seemed to imply, and questions which seemed to be closed, are after a course of years re-opened. In discussions such as these, there is a real exercise of private judgment and an allowable one; the act of faith, which cannot be superseded or trifled with, being, I repeat, the unreserved acceptance that the thesis in question is heretical, or the like, as the Pope or the Church has spoken of it.

In these cases which in a true sense may be called the Pope's *negative* enunciations, the opportunity of a legitimate minimizing lies in the intensely concrete character of the matters condemned;

in his affirmative enunciations a like opportunity is afforded by their being more or less abstract. Indeed, excepting such as relate to persons, that is, to the Trinity in Unity, the Blessed Virgin, the Saints, and the like, all the dogmas of Pope or of Council are but general, and so far, in consequence, admit of exceptions in their actual application, – these exceptions being determined either by other authoritative utterances, or by the scrutinizing vigilance, acuteness, and subtlety of the *Schola Theologorum*.

One of the most remarkable instances of what I am insisting on is found in a dogma, which no Catholic can ever think of disputing, viz., that "Out of the Church, and out of the faith, is no salvation." Not to go to Scripture, it is the doctrine of St. Ignatius, St. Irenæus, St. Cyprian in the first three centuries, as of St. Augustine and his contemporaries in the fourth and fifth. It can never be other than an elementary truth of Christianity; and the present Pope has proclaimed it as all Popes, doctors, and bishops before him. But that truth has two aspects, according as the force of the negative falls upon the "Church" or upon the "salvation." The main sense is, that there is no other communion or so-called Church, but the Catholic, in which are stored the promises, the sacraments, and other means of salvation; the other and derived sense is, that no one can be saved who is not *in* that one and only Church. But it does not follow, because there is no Church but one, which has the Evangelical gifts and privileges to bestow, that therefore no one can be saved without the intervention of that one Church. ... it is possible to belong to the soul of the Church without belonging to the body; and, at the end of 1800 years, it has been formally and authoritatively put forward by the present Pope (the first Pope, I suppose, who has done so), on the very same occasion on which he has repeated the fundamental principle of exclusive salvation itself. ...

Another instance of a similar kind is suggested by the general acceptance in the Latin Church, since the time of St. Augustine, of the doctrine of absolute predestination, as instanced in the teaching of other great saints beside him, such as St. Fulgentius, St. Prosper, St. Gregory, St. Thomas, and St. Buonaventure. Yet in the last centuries a great explanation and modification of this doctrine has been effected by the efforts of the Jesuit School, which have issued in the reception of a distinction between predestination to grace and predestination to glory; and a consequent admission of the principle that, though our own works do not avail for bringing us under the action of grace here, that does not hinder their availing, when we are in a state of grace, for our attainment of eternal glory hereafter. Two saints of late centuries, St. Francis de Sales and St. Alfonso, seemed to have professed this less rigid opinion, which is now the more common doctrine of the day.

Another instance is supplied by the Papal decisions concerning Usury. Pope Clement V., in the Council of Vienne, declares, "If any one shall have fallen into the error of pertinaciously presuming to affirm that usury is no sin, we determine that he is to be punished as a heretic." However, in the year 1831 the Sacred *Pœnitentiaria* answered an inquiry on the subject, to the effect that the Holy See suspended its decision on the point, and that a confessor who allowed of usury was not to be disturbed, "non esse inquietandum." Here again a double aspect seems to have been realized of the idea intended by the word *usury*. . . .

These instances out of many similar are sufficient to show what caution is to be observed, on the part of private and unauthorized persons, in imposing upon the consciences of others any interpretation of dogmatic enunciations which is beyond the legitimate sense of the words, inconsistent with the principle that all general rules have exceptions, and unrecognized by the Theological *Schola*.   (*Diff.* ii. 320–38)

8

THE TRIPLE OFFICE OF THE CHURCH*

PREFACE TO THE VIA MEDIA

At the end of November 1876 Newman began to compile the two volumes of a work to be called The Via Media. *The second volume was to consist of various tracts and letters he had published as an Anglican, while the first volume was to be the third edition of the* Lectures on the Prophetical Office. *The new preface to this first volume was to be his last great contribution to ecclesiology. It was published in August 1877.*

3.

... from the nature of the case, such an apparent contrariety between word and deed, the abstract and the concrete, could not but take place, supposing the Church to be gifted with those various prerogatives, and charged with those independent and conflicting duties, which Anglicans, as well as ourselves, recognize as belonging to her. Her organization cannot be otherwise than complex, considering the many functions which she has to fulfil, the many aims to keep in view, the many interests to secure, – functions, aims, and interests, which in their union and divergence remind us of the prophet's vision of the Cherubim, in whom "the wings of one were joined to the wings of another," yet "they turned not, when they went, but every one went straight forward." Or, to speak without figure, we know in matters of this world, how difficult it is for one and the same man to satisfy independent duties and incommensurable relations; to act at once as a parent and a judge, as a soldier and a minister of religion, as a philosopher and a statesman, as a courtier or a politician and a Catholic; the rules of conduct in these various positions being so distinct, and the obligations so contrary. Prudent men keep clear, if they can, of such perplexi-

---

*See also above, p. 57.

ties; but as to the Church, gifted as she is with grace up to the measure of her responsibilities, if she has on her an arduous work, it is sufficient to refer to our Lord's words, "What is impossible with men, is possible with God," in order to be certain (in spite of appearances) of her historical uprightness and consistency. At the same time it may undeniably have happened before now that her rulers and authorities, as men, on certain occasions have come short of what was required of them, and have given occasion to criticism, just or unjust, on account of the special antagonisms or compromises by means of which her many-sided mission under their guidance has been carried out.

4.

With this introduction I remark as follows: – When our Lord went up on high, He left His representative behind Him. This was Holy Church, His mystical Body and Bride, a Divine Institution, and the shrine and organ of the Paraclete, who speaks through her till the end comes. She, to use an Anglican poet's words, is "His very self below," as far as men on earth are equal to the discharge and fulfilment of high offices, which primarily and supremely are His.

These offices, which specially belong to Him as Mediator, are commonly considered to be three; He is Prophet, Priest, and King; and after His pattern, and in human measure, Holy Church has a triple office too; not the Prophetical alone and in isolation, as these Lectures virtually teach, but three offices, which are indivisible, though diverse, viz. teaching, rule, and sacred ministry. This then is the point on which I shall now insist, the very title of the Lectures I am to criticize suggesting to me how best to criticize them.

I will but say in passing, that I must not in this argument be supposed to forget that the Pope, as the Vicar of Christ, inherits these offices and acts for the Church in them. This is another matter; I am speaking here of the Body of Christ, and the sovereign Pontiff would not be the visible head of that Body, did he not first belong to it. He is not himself the Body of Christ, but the chief part of the Body; I shall have quite opportunities enough in what is to come to show that I duly bear him in mind.

Christianity, then, is at once a philosophy, a political power, and a religious rite: as a religion, it is Holy; as a philosophy, it is Apostolic; as a political power, it is imperial, that is, One and Catholic. As a religion, its special centre of action is pastor and flock; as a philosophy, the Schools; as a rule, the Papacy and its Curia.

Though it has exercised these three functions in substance from the first, they were developed in their full proportions one after another, in a succession of centuries; first, in the primitive time it was recognized as a worship, springing up and spreading in the lower ranks of society, and among the ignorant and dependent, and making its power felt by the heroism of its Martyrs and confessors. Then it seized upon the intellectual and cultivated class, and created a theology and schools of learning. Lastly it seated itself, as an ecclesiastical polity, among princes, and chose Rome for its centre.

Truth is the guiding principle of theology and theological inquiries; devotion and edification, of worship; and of government, expedience. The instrument of theology is reasoning; of worship, our emotional nature; of rule, command and coercion. Further, in man as he is, reasoning tends to rationalism; devotion to superstition and enthusiasm; and power to ambition and tyranny.

Arduous as are the duties involved in these three offices, to discharge one by one, much more arduous are they to administer, when taken in combination. Each of the three has its separate scope and direction; each has its own interests to promote and further; each has to find room for the claims of the other two; and each will find its own line of action influenced and modified by the others, nay, sometimes in a particular case the necessity of the others converted into a rule of duty for itself.

5.

"Who," in St. Paul's words, "is sufficient for these things?" Who, even with divine aid, shall successfully administer offices so independent of each other, so divergent, and so conflicting? What line of conduct, except on the long, the very long run, is at once edifying, expedient, and true? Is it not plain, that, if one determinate course is to be taken by the Church, acting at once in all three capacities, so opposed to each other in their idea, that course must, as I have said, be deflected from the line which would be traced out by any one of them, if viewed by itself, or else the requirements of one or two sacrificed to the interests of the third? What, for instance, is to be done in a case when to enforce a theological point, as the Schools determine it, would make a particular population less religious, not more so, or cause riots or risings? Or when to defend a champion of ecclesiastical liberty in one country would encourage an Anti-Pope, or hazard a general persecution, in another? or when either a schism is to be encountered or an opportune truth left undefined?

All this was foreseen certainly by the Divine Mind, when He committed to His Church so complex a mission; and, by promising her infallibility in her formal teaching, He indirectly protected her from serious error in worship and political action also. This aid, however, great as it is, does not secure her from all dangers as regards the problem which she has to solve; nothing but the gift of impeccability granted to her authorities would secure them from all liability to mistake in their conduct, policy, words and decisions, in her legislative and her executive, in ecclesiastical and disciplinarian details; and such a gift they have not received. In consequence, however well she may perform her duties on the whole, it will always be easy for her enemies to make a case against her, well founded or not, from the action or inter-action, or the chronic collisions or contrasts, or the temporary suspense or delay, of her administration, in her three several departments of duty, – her government, her devotions, and her schools, – from the conduct of her rulers, her divines, her pastors, or her people.

It is this difficulty lying in the nature of the case, which supplies the staple of those energetic charges and vivid pictures of the inconsistency, double-dealing, and deceit of the Church of Rome, as found in Protestant writings ...

7.

I am to apply then the doctrine of the triple office of the Church in explanation of this phenomenon, which gives so much offence to Protestants; and I begin by admitting the general truth of the facts alleged against us; – at the same time in the passages just quoted there is one misconception of fact which needs to be corrected before I proceed. The Author of them ascribes the corruptions and other scandals, which he laments in the action of the Church, to the Schools; but ambition, craft, cruelty, and superstition are not commonly the characteristic of theologians, and the natural and proper function of the Schools lies and has lain in forming those abstract decrees which the Author considers to be the least blamable portion of Roman teaching. Nor, again, is it even accurate to say, as he does, that those so-called corruptions are at least the result and development of those abstract decrees: on the contrary, they bear on their face the marks of having a popular or a political origin, and in fact theology, so far from encouraging them, has restrained and corrected such extravagances as have been committed, through human infirmity, in the exercise of the regal and sacerdotal powers; nor is religion ever in greater danger than when, in consequence of national or international troubles, the Schools of theology have been broken up and ceased to be.

And this will serve as a proposition with which to begin. I say, then, Theology is the fundamental and regulating principle of the whole Church system. It is commensurate with Revelation, and Revelation is the initial and essential idea of Christianity. It is the subject-matter, the formal cause, the expression, of the Prophetical Office, and, as being such, has created both the Regal Office and the Sacerdotal. And it has in a certain sense a power of jurisdiction over those offices, as being its own creations, theologians being ever in request and in employment in keeping within bounds both the political and popular elements in the Church's constitution, – elements which are far more congenial than itself to the human mind, are far more liable to excess and corruption, and are ever struggling to liberate themselves from those restraints which are in truth necessary for their well-being. On the one hand Popes, such as Liberius, Vigilius, Boniface VIII., and Sixtus V., under secular inducements of the moment, seem from time to time to have been wishing, though unsuccessfully, to venture beyond the lines of theology; and on the other hand, private men of an intemperate devotion are from time to time forming associations, or predicting events, or imagining miracles, so unadvisedly as to call for the interference of the Index or Holy Office. It is not long since the present Pope in his exercise of the Prophetical Office, warned the faithful against putting trust in certain idle prophecies which were in circulation, disallowed a profession of miracles, and forbade some new and extravagant titles which had been given to the Blessed Virgin.

8.

Yet theology cannot always have its own way; it is too hard, too intellectual, too exact, to be always equitable, or to be always compassionate; and it sometimes has a conflict or overthrow, or has to consent to a truce or a compromise, in consequence of the rival force of religious sentiment or ecclesiastical interests; and that, sometimes in great matters, sometimes in unimportant. . . .

Now it is well known that Bellarmine has written on Justification, and of course in his treatise he insists, as a theologian must, on the doctrine of merit; but it also happens he is led on, as if he was praying or preaching or giving absolution, to drop some few words, beyond the limits of his science, about his own or his brethren's unworthiness and need of pardon and grace. That is, he has happened to let his devout nature betray itself between the joints of his theological harness. . . .

Again, I have already referred to the dilemma which has occurred before now in the history of the Church, when a choice had to be made between leaving a point of faith at a certain moment undefined, and indirectly opening the way to some extended and permanent schism. Here her Prophetical function is impeded for a while in its action, perhaps seriously, by the remonstrances of charity and of the spirit of peace.

In another familiar instance which may be given, the popular and scholastic elements in the Church seem to change parts, and theology to be kind and sympathetic and religion severe. I mean, whereas the whole School with one voice speaks of freedom of conscience as a personal prerogative of each individual, on the other hand the vow of obedience may sometimes in particular cases be enforced by Religious Superiors in some lesser matter to the conceivable injury of such sacred freedom of thought.

Another instance of collision in a small matter is before us just at this time, the theological and religious element of the Church being in antagonism with the political. Humanity, a sense of morality, hatred of a special misbelief, views of Scripture prophecy, a feeling of brotherhood with Russians, Greeks, and Bulgarians, though schismatics, have determined some of us against the Turkish cause; and a dread lest Russia, if successful, should prove a worse enemy to the Church than Turks can be, determines others of us in favour of it.

9.

But I will come to illustrations which involve more difficult questions. Truth is the principle on which all intellectual, and therefore all theological inquiries proceed, and is the motive power which gives them effect; but the principle of popular edification, quickened by a keen sensitiveness of the chance of scandals, is as powerful as Truth, when the province is Religion. To the devotional mind what is new and strange is as repulsive, often as dangerous, as falsehood is to the scientific. Novelty is often error to those who are unprepared for it, from the refraction with which it enters into their conceptions. Hence popular ideas on religion are practically a match for the clearest *dicta*, deductions, and provisos of the Schools, and will have their way in cases when the particular truth, which is the subject of them, is not of vital or primary importance. Thus, in a religion, which embraces large and separate classes of adherents, there always is of necessity to a certain extent an exoteric and an esoteric doctrine.

The history of the Latin versions of the Scriptures furnishes a familiar illustration of this conflict between popular and educated faith. The Gallican version of the Psalter, St. Jerome's earlier work, got such possession of the West, that to this day we use it instead of his later and more correct version from the Hebrew. Devotional use prevailed over scholastic accuracy in a matter of secondary concern. . . . A parallel anxiety for the same reason is felt at this time within the Anglican communion, upon the proposal to amend King James's Translation of the Scriptures.

10.

Here we see the necessary contrast between religious inquiry or teaching, and investigation in purely secular matters. Much is said in this day by men of science about the duty of honesty in what is called the pursuit of truth, – by "pursuing truth" being meant the pursuit of facts. It is just now reckoned a great moral virtue to be fearless and thorough in inquiry into facts; and, when science crosses and breaks the received path of Revelation, it is reckoned a serious imputation upon the ethical character of religious men, whenever they show hesitation to shift at a minute's warning their position, and to accept as truths shadowy views at variance with what they have ever been taught and have held. But the contrast between the cases is plain. The love and pursuit of truth in the subject-matter of religion, if it be genuine, must always be accompanied by the fear of error, of error which may be sin. An inquirer in the province of religion is under a responsibility for his reasons and for their issue. But, whatever be the real merits, nay, virtues, of inquirers into physical or historical facts, whatever their skill, their acquired caution, their experience, their dispassionateness and fairness of mind, they do not avail themselves of these excellent instruments of inquiry as a matter of conscience, but because it is expedient, or honest, or beseeming, or praiseworthy, to use them; nor, if in the event they were found to be wrong as to their supposed discoveries, would they, or need they, feel aught of the remorse and self-reproach of a Catholic, on whom it breaks that he has been violently handling the text of Scripture, misinterpreting it, or superseding it, on an hypothesis which he took to be true, but which turns out to be untenable.

Let us suppose in his defence that he was challenged either to admit or to refute what was asserted, and to do so without delay; still it would have been far better could he have waited awhile, as the event has shown, – nay, far better, even though the assertion has proved true. Galileo might be right in his conclusion that the earth moves; to consider him a heretic might have been wrong; but there was nothing wrong in censuring abrupt, startling, unsettling, unverified disclosures, if such they were, disclosures at once uncalled for and inopportune, at a time when the limits of revealed truth had not as yet been ascertained. A man ought to be very sure of what he is saying, before he risks the chance of contradicting the word of God. It was safe, not dishonest, to be slow in accepting what nevertheless turned out to be true. Here is an instance in which the Church obliges Scripture expositors, at a given time or place, to be tender of the popular religious sense.

11.

I have been led on to take a second view of this matter. That jealousy of originality in the matter of religion, which is the instinct of piety, is, in the case of questions which excite the popular mind, the dictate of charity also. Galileo's truth is said to have shocked and scared the Italy of his day. It revolutionized the received system of belief as regards heaven, purgatory, and hell, to say that the earth went round the sun, and it forcibly imposed upon categorical statements of Scripture, a figurative interpretation. Heaven was no longer above, and earth below; the heavens no longer literally opened and shut; purgatory and hell were not for certain under the earth. The catalogue of theological truths was seriously curtailed. Whither did our Lord go on His ascension? If there is to be a plurality of worlds, what is the special importance of this one? and is the whole visible universe with its infinite spaces, one day to pass away? We are used to these questions now, and reconciled to them; and on that account are no fit judges of the disorder and dismay, which the Galilean hypothesis would cause to good Catholics, as far as they became cognizant of it, or how necessary it was in charity, especially then, to delay the formal reception of a new interpretation of Scripture, till their imaginations should gradually get accustomed to it.

12.

As to the particular measures taken at the time with this end, I neither know them accurately, nor have I any anxiety to know them. They do not fall within the scope of my argument; I am only concerned with the principle on which they were conducted. All I say is, that not all knowledge is suited to all minds; a proposition may be ever so true, yet at a particular time and place may be "temerarious, offensive to pious ears, and scandalous," though not "heretical" nor "erroneous." It must be recollected what very strong warnings we have from our Lord and St. Paul against scandalizing the weak and unintellectual. The latter goes into detail upon the point. He says, that, true as it may be that certain meats are allowable, this allowance cannot in charity be used in a case in which it would be of spiritual injury to others. "Take care," he says, "that you put not a stumbling-block or a scandal in your brother's way;" "destroy not the work of God for meat;" "it is good to abstain from everything whereby thy brother is offended, or scandalized, or made weak; there is not knowledge in every one," but "take heed lest your liberty become a stumbling-block to the weak." "All things are lawful to me, but not all edify; do not eat for his sake who spoke of it, and for conscience sake, conscience, not thine own, but the other's."[18]

Now, while saying this, I know well that "all things have their season," and that there is not only "a time to keep silence," but "a time to speak," and that, in some states of society, such as our own, it is the worst charity, and the most provoking, irritating rule of action, and the most unhappy policy, not to speak out, not to suffer to be spoken out, all that there is to say. Such speaking out is under such circumstances the triumph of religion, whereas concealment, accommodation, and evasion is to co-operate with the spirit of error; – but it is not always so. There are times and places, on the contrary, when it is the duty of a teacher, when asked, to answer frankly as well as truly, though not even then to say more than he need, because learners will but misunderstand him if he attempts more, and therefore it is wiser and kinder to let well alone, than to attempt what is better. I do not say that this is a pleasant rule of conduct, and that it would not be a relief to most men to be rid of its necessity, – and for this reason, if for no other, because it is so difficult to apply it aright, so that St. Paul's precept may be interpreted in a particular case as the warrant for just contrary courses of action, – but still, it can hardly be denied that there is a great principle in what he says, and a great duty in consequence.

13.

In truth we recognize the duty of concealment, or what may be called evasion, not in religious matters only, but universally. It is very well for sublime sciences, which work out their problems apart from the crowding and jostling, the elbowing and the toe-treading of actual life, to care for nobody and nothing but themselves, and to preach and practise the cheap virtue of devotion to what they call truth, meaning of course facts; but a liberty to blurt out all things whatever without self-restraint is not only forbidden by the Church, but by Society at large; of which such liberty, if fully carried out, would certainly be the dissolution. Veracity, like other virtues, lies in a mean. Truth indeed, but not necessarily the whole truth, is the rule of Society. Every class and profession has its secrets; the family lawyer, the medical adviser, the politician, as well as the priest. The physician often dares not tell the whole truth to his patient about his case, knowing that to do so would destroy his chance of recovery. Statesmen in Parliament, I suppose, fight each other with second-best arguments, the real reasons for the policy which they are respectively advocating being, as each is conscious to each, not these, but reasons of state, secrets whether of her Majesty's Privy Council or of diplomacy. As to the polite world, which, to be sure, is in itself not much of an authority, I think an authoress of the last century illustrates in a tale how it would not hold together, if every one told the whole truth to every one, as to what he thought of him. From the time that the Creator clothed Adam, concealment is in some sense the necessity of our fall.

14.

This, then, is one cause of that twofold or threefold aspect of the Catholic Church, which I have set myself to explain. Many popular beliefs and practices have, in spite of theology, been suffered by Catholic prelates, lest, "in gathering up the weeds," they should "root up the wheat with them." We see the operation of this necessary economy in the instance of the Old Covenant, in the gradual disclosures made, age after age, to the chosen people. The most striking of these accommodations is the long sufferance of polygamy, concubinage, and divorce. As to divorce, our Lord expressly says to the Pharisees, that "Moses, by reason of the hardness of their hearts, permitted them to put away their wives;" yet this was a breach of a natural and primeval law, which was in force at the beginning as directly and unequivocally as the law against fratricide. St. Augustine seems to go further still, as if not only a tacit toleration of an imperfect morality was observed towards Israel by his Divine Governor, but positive commands were issued in accordance with that state of imperfection in which the people lay. . . .

This indeed is the great principle of Economy, as advocated in the Alexandrian school, which is in various ways sanctioned in Scripture. In some fundamental points indeed, in the Unity and Omnipotence of God, the Mosaic Law, so tolerant of barbaric cruelty, allowed of no condescension to the ethical state of the times; indeed the very end of the Dispensation was to denounce idolatry, and the sword was its instrument of denunciation; but where the mission of the chosen people was not directly concerned, and amid the heathen populations, even idolatry itself was suffered with something of a Divine sanction, as if a deeper sentiment might lie hid under it. Thus Joseph in the time of the Patriarchs had a divining cup and married the daughter of the Priest of Heliopolis. Jonah in a later time was sent to preach penance to the people of Nineveh, but without giving them a hint, or being understood by them to say, that they must abandon their idols; while the sailors, among whom the Prophet had previously been thrown, though idolaters, recognized with great devotion and religious fear the Lord God of heaven and earth. Again, when Balaam had built his seven altars and offered his sacrifices, and prepared his divinations, it is significantly said, that "the Lord *met* him, and put a word in his mouth," yet without any rebuke of his idolatry and magic. And when Naaman asked forgiveness of God if he "bowed down in the temple of Remmon," the Prophet said no more than "Go in peace." And St. Paul tells both the rude and the cultivated idolaters of Lystra and Athens, that God, in times past, while He gave all nations proofs of His Providence, "suffered them to walk in their own ways," and "winked at the times of their ignorance."

15.

From the time that the Apostles preached, such toleration in primary matters of faith and morals is at an end as regards Christendom. Idolatry is a sin against light; and, while it would involve heinous guilt, or rather is impossible, in a Catholic, it is equally inconceivable in even the most ignorant sectary who claims the Christian name; nevertheless, the principle and the use of the Economy has a place, and is a duty still among Catholics, though not as regards the first elements of Revelation. We have still, as Catholics, to be forbearing and to be silent in many cases, amid the mistakes, excesses, and superstitions of individuals and of classes of our brethren, which we come across. Also in the case of those who are not Catholic, we feel it a duty sometimes to observe the rule of silence, even when so serious a truth as the "Extra Ecclesiam nulla salus" comes into consideration. This truth, indeed, must ever be upheld, but who will venture to blame us, or reproach us with double-dealing, for holding it to be our duty, though we thus believe, still, in a case when a Protestant, near death and to all appearance in good faith, is sure, humanly speaking, not to accept Catholic truth, if urged upon him, to leave such a one to his imperfect Christianity, and to the mercy of God, and to assist his devotions as far as he will let us carry him, rather than to precipitate him at such a moment into controversy which may ruffle his mind, dissipate his thoughts, unsettle such measure of faith as he has, and rouse his slumbering prejudices and antipathies against the Church? Yet this might be represented as countenancing a double aspect of Catholic doctrine and as evasive and shuffling, theory saying one thing, and practice sanctioning another.

16.

I shelter what I go on to say of the Church's conduct occasionally towards her own children, under this rule of her dealing with strangers: – The rule is the same in its principle as that of Moses or St. Paul, or the Alexandrians, or St. Augustine, though it is applied to other subject-matters. Doubtless, her abstract standard of religion and morals in the Schools is higher than that which we witness in her children in particular countries or at particular times; but doubtless also, she, like the old prophets before her, from no fault of hers, is not able to enforce it. Human nature is in all ages one and the same: as it showed itself in the Israelites, so it shows itself in the world at large now, though one country may be better than another. At least, in some countries, truth and error in religion may be so intimately connected as not to admit of separation. I have already referred to our Lord's parable of the wheat and the cockle. For instance, take the instance of relics; modern divines and historians may have proved that certain recognized relics, though the remains of some holy man, still do not certainly belong to the Saint to whom they are popularly appropriated; and in spite of this, a bishop may have sanctioned a public veneration of them, which has arisen out of this unfounded belief. And so again, without pledging himself to the truth of the legend of a miracle attached to a certain crucifix or picture, he may have viewed with tolerance, nay, with satisfaction, the overflowing popular devotion towards our Lord or the Blessed Virgin, of which that legend is the occasion. He is not sure it is true, and he does not guarantee its truth; he does but approve and praise the devotional enthusiasm of the people, which the legendary fact has awakened. Did indeed their faith and devotion towards Christ rise simply out of that legend, if they made Him their God because something was said to have taken place which had not taken place, then no honest man, who was simply aware of this, could take any part in the anniversary outburst of rejoicing; but he knows that miracles are wrought in the Church in every age, and, if he is far from certain that this was a miracle, he is not certain that it was not; and his case would be somewhat like French ecclesiastics in the beginning of the century, if Napoleon ordered a Te Deum for his victory at Trafalgar, – they might have shrewd suspicions about the fact, but they would not see their way not to take part in a national festival. Such may be the feeling under which the Church takes part in popular religious manifestations without subjecting them to theological and historical criticism; she is in a choice of difficulties; did she act otherwise, she would be rooting up the wheat with the intruding weeds; she would be "quenching the smoking flax," and endangering the faith and loyalty of a city or a district, for the sake of an intellectual precision which was quite out of place and was not asked of her.

The difficulty of course is to determine the point at which such religious manifestations become immoderate, and an allowance of them wrong; it would be well, if all suspicious facts could be got rid of altogether. Their tolerance may sometimes lead to pious frauds, which are simply wicked. An ecclesiastical superior certainly cannot sanction alleged miracles or prophecies which he knows to be false, or by his silence connive at a tradition of them being started among his people. Nor can he be dispensed of the duty, when he comes into an inheritance of error or superstition, which is immemorial, of doing what he can to alleviate and dissipate it, though to do this without injury to what is true and good, can after all be only a gradual work. Errors of fact may do no harm, and their removal may do much.

17.

As neither the local rulers nor the pastors of the Church are impeccable in act nor infallible in judgment, I am not obliged to maintain that all ecclesiastical measures and permissions have ever been praiseworthy and safe precedents. But as to the mere countenancing of superstitions, it must not be forgotten, that our Lord Himself, on one occasion, passed over the superstitious act of a woman who was in great trouble, for the merit of the faith which was the real element in it. She was under the influence of what would be called, were she alive now, a "corrupt" religion, yet she was rewarded by a miracle. She came behind our Lord and touched Him, hoping "virtue would go out of Him," without His knowing it. She paid a sort of fetish reverence to the hem of His garment; she stole, as she considered, something from Him, and was much disconcerted at being found out. When our Lord asked who had touched Him, "fearing and trembling," says St. Mark, "knowing what was done in her, she came and fell down before Him, and told Him all the truth," as if there were anything to tell to the All-knowing. What was our Lord's judgment on her? "Daughter, thy faith hath made thee whole; go in peace." Men talk of our double aspect now; has not the first age a double aspect? Do not such incidents in the Gospel as this, and the miracle on the swine, the pool of Bethesda, the restoration of the servant's ear, the changing water into wine, the coin in the fish's mouth, and the like, form an aspect of Apostolic Christianity very different from that presented by St. Paul's Pastoral Epistles and the Epistle General of St. John? Need men wait for the Medieval Church in order to make their complaint that the theology of Christianity does not accord with its religious manifestations?

18.

This woman, who is so prominently brought before us by three evangelists, doubtless understood that, if the garment had virtue, this arose from its being Christ's; and so a poor Neapolitan crone, who chatters to the crucifix, refers that crucifix in her deep mental consciousness to an original who once hung upon a cross in flesh and blood; but if, nevertheless she is puzzle-headed enough to assign virtue to it in itself, she does no more than the woman in the Gospel, who preferred to rely for a cure on a bit of cloth, which was our Lord's, to directly and honestly addressing Him. Yet He praised her before the multitude, praised her for what might, not without reason, be called an idolatrous act; for in His new law He was opening the meaning of the word "idolatry," and applying it to various sins, to the adoration paid to rich men, to the thirst after gain, to ambition, and the pride of life, idolatries worse in His judgment than the idolatry of ignorance, but not commonly startling or shocking to educated minds.

And may I not add that this aspect of our Lord's teaching is quite in keeping with the general drift of His discourses? Again and again He insists on the necessity of faith; but where does He insist on the danger of superstition, an infirmity, which, taking human nature as it is, is the sure companion of faith, when vivid and earnest? Taking human nature as it is, we may surely concede a little superstition, as not the worst of evils, if it be the price of making sure of faith. Of course it need not be the price; and the Church, in her teaching function, will ever be vigilant against the inroad of what is a degradation both of faith and of reason: but considering, as Anglicans will allow, how intimately the sacramental system is connected with Christianity, and how feeble and confused is at present the ethical intelligence of the world at large, it is a distant day, at which the Church will find it easy, in her oversight of her populations, to make her Sacerdotal office keep step with her Prophetical. Just now I should be disposed to doubt whether that nation really had the faith, which is free in all its ranks and classes from all kinds and degrees of what is commonly considered superstition.

19.

Worship, indeed, being the act of our devotional nature, strives hard to emancipate itself from theological restraints. Theology did not create it, but found it in our hearts, and used it. And it has many shapes and many objects, and, moreover, these are not altogether unlawful, though they be many. Undoubtedly the first and most necessary of all religious truths is the Being, Unity, and Omnipotence of God, and it was the primary purpose and work of Revelation to enforce this. But did not that first truth involve in itself and suggest to the mind with a sympathetic response a second truth, namely, the existence of other beings besides the Supreme? and that for the very reason that He was Unity and Perfection, – I mean, a whole world, though to us unknown, – in order to people the vast gulf which separates Him from man? And, when our Lord came and united the Infinite and Finite, was it not natural to think, even before Revelation spoke out, that He came to be "the First born of many brethren," all crowned after His pattern with glory and honour? As there is an instinctive course of reasoning which leads the mind to acknowledge the Supreme God, so we instinctively believe in the existence of beings short of Him, though at the same time far superior to ourselves, beings unseen by us, and yet about us and with relations to us. And He has by His successive revelations confirmed to us the correctness of our anticipation. He has in fact told us of the myriads of beings, good and evil, spirits as God is, friendly or hostile to us, who are round about us; and, moreover, by teaching us also the immortality of man, He sets before us a throng of innumerable souls, once men, who are dead neither to God nor to us, and, who, as having been akin to us, suggest to us, when we think of them, and seem to sanction, acts of mutual intercourse.

20.

Revelation in this matter does but complete what Nature has begun. It is difficult to deny that polytheism is a natural sentiment corrupted. Its radical evil is, not the belief in many divine intelligences, but its forgetfulness of their Creator, the One Living Personal God who is above them all, – that is, its virtual Atheism. First secure in the mind and heart of individuals, in the popular intelligence, a lively faith and trust in Him, and then the *cultus* of Angels and Saints, though ever to be watched with jealousy by theologians, because of human infirmity and perverseness, is a privilege, nay a duty, and has a normal place in revealed Religion. . . .

21.

Here at last I come to the point, which has been the drift of these remarks. The primary object of Revelation was to recall men from idolizing the creature. The Israelites had the mission of effecting this by the stern and pitiless ministry of the sword. The Christian Church, after the pattern of our Lord's gentleness, has been guided to an opposite course. Moses on his death was buried by Divine Agency, lest, as the opinion has prevailed, a people, who afterwards offered incense to the brazen serpent which he set up, should be guilty of idolatry towards his dead body. But Christians, on the contrary, have from the first cherished and honoured with a special *cultus* the memories of the Martyrs, who had shed their blood for Christ, and have kept up a perpetual communion with all their brethren departed by their prayers and by masses for their souls. That is, the Christian Church has understood that her mission was not like that of Moses, to oppose herself to impulses which were both natural and legitimate, though they had been heretofore the instruments of sin, but to do her best, by a right use, to moderate and purify them. Hence, in proportion as the extinction of the old corrupt heathenism made it possible, she has invoked saints, sanctioned the use of their images, and, in the spirit of the Gospels and the Acts, has expected miracles from their persons, garments, relics, and tombs.

This being her mission, not to forbid the memory and veneration of Saints and Angels, but to subordinate it to the worship of the Supreme Creator, it is not wonderful, if she has appeared to lookers-on to be sanctioning and reviving that "old error" which has "passed away;" and that the more so, because she has not been able to do all she could wish against it, and has been obliged at times and in particular cases, as I have said above, as the least of evils, to temporize and compromise, – of course short of any infringement of the Revealed Law or any real neglect of her teaching office. And hence, which is our main subject, there will ever be a marked contrariety between the professions of her theology and the ways and doings of a Catholic country.

22.

It must be recollected, that, while the Catholic Church is ever most precise in her enunciation of doctrine, and allows no liberty of dissent from her decisions, (for on such objective matters she speaks with the authority of infallibility,) her tone is different, in the sanction she gives to devotions, as they are of a subjective and personal nature. Here she neither prescribes measure, nor forbids choice, nor, except so far as they imply doctrine, is she infallible in her adoption or use of them. This is an additional reason why the formal decrees of Councils and statements of theologians differ in their first aspect from the religion of the uneducated classes; the latter represents the wayward popular taste, and the former the critical judgments of clear heads and holy hearts.

  This contrast will be the greater, when, as sometimes happens, ecclesiastical authority takes part with the popular sentiment against a theological decision. Such, we know, was the case, when St. Peter himself committed an error in conduct, in the countenance he gave to the Mosaic rites in consequence of the pressure exerted on him by the Judaic Christians. On that occasion St. Paul withstood him, "because he was to be blamed." A fault, which even the first Pope incurred, may in some other matter of rite or devotion find a place now and then in the history of holy and learned ecclesiastics who were not Popes. Such an instance seems presented to us in the error of judgment which was committed by the Fathers of the Society of Jesus in China, in their adoption of certain customs which they found among the heathen there; and Protestant writers in consequence have noted it as a signal instance of the double-faced conduct of Catholics, as if they were used to present their religion under various aspects according to the expedience of the place or time. But that there is a religious way of thus accommodating ourselves to those among whom we live, and whom it is our duty, if possible, to convert, is plain from St. Paul's own rule of life, considering he "became to the Jews as a Jew, that he might gain the Jews, and to them that were without the law, as if he were without the law, and became all things to all men that he might save all." Or what shall we say to the commencement of St. John's Gospel, in which the Evangelist may be as plausibly represented to have used the language of heathen classics with the purpose of interesting and gaining the Platonizing Jews: as the Jesuits be charged with duplicity and deceit in aiming at the conversion of the heathen in the East by an imitation of their customs. St. Paul on various occasions acts in the same spirit of economy, as did the great Missionary Church of Alexandria in the centuries which followed; its masters did but carry out professedly, a principle of action, of which they considered they found examples in Scripture. Anglicans who appeal to the Ante-nicene period as especially their own, should be tender of the memories of Theonas, Clement, Origen, and Gregory Thaumaturgus.

23.

The mention of missions and of St. Gregory leads me on to another department of my general subject, viz. the embarrassments and difficult questions arising out of the regal office of the Church and her duties to it. It is said of this primitive Father, who was the Apostle of a large district in Asia Minor, that he found in it only seventeen Christians, and on his death left in it only seventeen pagans. This was an enlargement of the Church's territory worthy of a Catholic Bishop, but how did he achieve it? Putting aside the real cause, the Divine blessing, and his gift of miracles, we are told of one special act of his, not unlike that of the Jesuits in the East . . .

At this very time Carnival is allowed, if not sanctioned, by ecclesiastical authorities in the cities of the Continent, while they not only keep away from it themselves but appoint special devotions in the Churches, in order to draw away the faithful from the spiritual dangers attending on it.

24.

St. Gregory was a Bishop as well as a preacher and spiritual guide, so that the economy which is related of him is an act of the regal function of the Church, as well as of her sacerdotal and pastoral. And this indeed attaches to most of the instances which I have been giving above of the Church's moderating or suspending under circumstances the requisitions of her theology. They illustrate at once both these elements of her divinely ordered constitution; for the fear, as already mentioned, of "quenching the smoking flax," which is the attribute of a guide of souls, operated in the same direction as zeal for the extension of Christ's kingdom, in resisting that rigorousness of a logical theology which is more suited for the Schools than for the world. In these cases then the two offices, political and pastoral, have a common interest as against the theological; but this is not always so, and therefore I shall now go on to give instances in which the imperial and political expedience of religion stands out prominent, and both its theological and devotional duties are in the background.

25.

I observe then that Apostolicity of doctrine and Sanctity of worship, as attributes of the Church, are differently circumstanced from her regal autocracy. Tradition in good measure is sufficient for doctrine, and popular custom and conscience for worship, but tradition and custom cannot of themselves secure independence and self-government. The Greek Church shows this, which has lost its political life, while its doctrine, and its ritual and devotional system, have little that can be excepted against. If the Church is to be regal, a witness for Heaven, unchangeable amid secular changes, if in every age she is to hold her own, and proclaim as well as profess the truth, if she is to thrive without or against the civil power, if she is to be resourceful and self-recuperative under all fortunes, she must be more than Holy and Apostolic; she must be Catholic. Hence it is that, first, she has ever from her beginning onwards had a hierarchy and a head, with a strict unity of polity, the claim of an exclusive divine authority and blessing, the trusteeship of the gospel gifts, and the exercise over her members of an absolute and almost despotic rule. And next, as to her work, it is her special duty, as a sovereign State, to consolidate her several portions, to enlarge her territory, to keep up and to increase her various populations in this ever-dying, ever-nascent world, in which to be stationary is to lose ground, and to repose is to fail. It is her duty to strengthen and facilitate the intercourse of city with city, and race with race, so that an injury done to one is felt to be an injury to all, and the act of individuals has the energy and momentum of the whole body. It is her duty to have her eyes upon the movements of all classes in her wide dominion, on ecclesiastics and laymen, on the regular clergy and secular, on civil society, and political movements. She must be on the watch-tower, discerning in the distance and providing against all dangers; she has to protect the ignorant and weak, to remove scandals, to see to the education of the young, to administer temporalities, to initiate, or at least to direct all Christian work, and all with a view to the life, health, and strength of Christianity, and the salvation of souls.

It is easy to understand how from time to time such serious interests and duties involve, as regards the parties who have the responsibility of them, the risk, perhaps the certainty, at least the imputation, of ambition or other selfish motive, and still more frequently of error in judgment, or violent action, or injustice. However, leaving this portion of the subject with this remark, I shall bring what I have to say to an end by putting the Regal office of the Church side by side with the Prophetical, and giving instances of the collisions and compromises which have taken place between them in consequence of their respective duties and interests.

26.

For example: the early tradition of the Church was dissuasive of using force in the maintenance of religion. ... Augustine at first took the same view of duty; but his experience as a Bishop led him to change his mind. Here we see the interests of the

Church, as a regal power, acting as an influence upon his theology.

Again: with a view to the Church's greater unity and strength, Popes, from the time of St. Gregory I., down to the present, have been earnest in superseding and putting away the diversified traditional forms of ritual in various parts of the Church. In this policy ecclesiastical expedience has acted in the subject-matter of theology and worship.

Again: acts simply unjustifiable, such as real betrayals of the truth on the part of Liberius and Honorius, become intelligible, and cease to be shocking, if we consider that those Popes felt themselves to be head rulers of Christendom and their first duty, as such, to be that of securing its peace, union and consolidation. The personal want of firmness or of clear-sightedness in the matter of doctrine, which each of them in his own day evidenced, may have arisen out of his keen sense of being the Ecumenical Bishop and one Pastor of Christ's flock, of the scandal caused by its internal dissensions, and of his responsibility, should it retrograde in health and strength in his day.

27.

The principle, on which these two Popes may be supposed to have acted, not unsound in itself, though by them wrongly applied, I conceive to be this, – that no act could be theologically an error, which was absolutely and undeniably necessary for the unity, sanctity, and peace of the Church; for falsehood never could be necessary for those blessings, and truth alone can be. If one could be sure of this necessity, the principle itself may be granted; though from the difficulty of rightly applying it, it can only be allowed on such grave occasions, with so luminous a tradition, in its flavour, and by such high authorities, as make it safe. If it was wrongly used by the Popes whom I have named, it has been rightly and successfully used by others, in whose decision, in their respective cases, no Catholic has any difficulty in concurring.

28.

I will give some instances of it, and of these the most obvious is our doctrine regarding the Canonization of Saints. The infallibility of the Church must certainly extend to this solemn and public act; and that, because on so serious a matter, affecting the worship of the faithful, though relating to a fact, the Church, (that is, the Pope,) must be infallible. . . .

29.

Again: in like manner, our certainty that the Apostolical succession of Bishops in the Catholic Church has no flaw in it, and that the validity of the Sacraments is secure, in spite of possible mistakes and informalities in the course of 1800 years, rests upon our faith that He who has decreed the end has decreed the means, – that He is always sufficient for His Church, – that, if He has given us a promise ever to be with us, He will perform it.

30.

As regards ordinations made with simony, it seems that Pope Leo IX., on occasion of the ecclesiastical disorders of his time, held a solemn Council, in which judgment was given against the validity of such acts. It seems also that, from certain ecclesiastical difficulties which followed, lying in the region of fact . . . the Pope could not carry out the Synodal act, and was obliged to issue a milder decision instead of it. . . .

Such a mode of resolving a point in theology is intelligible only on the ground laid down above, that a certain quasi-doctrinal conclusion may be in such wise fatal to the constitution, and therefore to the being of the Church, as *ipso facto* to stultify the principles from which it is drawn, it being inconceivable that her Lord and Maker intended that the action of any one of her functions should be the destruction of another. In this case, then, He willed that a point of theology should be determined on its expediency relatively to the Church's Catholicity and the edification of her people, – by the logic of facts, which at times overrides all positive laws and prerogatives, and reaches in its effective force to the very frontiers of immutable truths in religion, ethics, and theology.

271

31.

This instance, in which the motive-cause of the decision ultimately made is so clearly brought out, is confirmed by the parallel case of heretical ordination. For instance, Pope Innocent, in the fourth century, writing to the Bishops of Macedonia, concedes the validity of heretical orders in a certain case specified, declaring the while, that such a concession ran counter to the tradition of the Roman Church. This concession was made in order to put an end to a great scandal . . .

32.

Again, as regards schismatical ordination, as of the Donatists: – on this occasion, Rome stood firm to her traditional view, and Augustine apparently concurred in it; but the African Bishops on the whole were actuated by their sense of the necessity of taking the opposite line, and were afraid of committing themselves to the principle that heresy or schism nullified ordination. They condemned (with the countenance of Augustine) Donatus alone, the author of the schism, but accepted the rest, orders and all, lest remaining outside the Church, they should be a perpetual thorn in her side. . . . This is another instance of the schools giving way to ecclesiastical expedience, and of the interests of peace and unity being a surer way of arriving at a doctrinal conclusion than methods more directly theological.

33.

The considerations which might be urged, in behalf of these irregular ordinations, on the score of expedience, had still greater force when urged in recognition of heretical baptism, which formed the subject of a controversy in the preceding century. Baptism was held to be the entrance to Christianity and its other sacraments, and once a Christian, ever a Christian. It marked and discriminated the soul receiving it from all other souls by a supernatural character, as the owner's name is imprinted on a flock of sheep. Thus heretics far and wide, if baptized, were

children of the Church, and they answered to that title so far
as they were in fact preachers of the truth of Christ to the
heathen; since there is no religious sect without truth in it, and
it would be truth which the heathen had to be taught. That
exuberant birth of strange rites and doctrines, which suddenly
burst into life all round Christianity on its start, is one of the
striking evidences of the wondrous force of the Christian idea,
and of its subtle penetrating influence, when it first fell upon
the ignorant masses: and though many of these sects had little
or no claim to administer a real baptism, and in many or most
the abounding evil that was in them choked the scanty and feeble
good, yet was the Church definitely to reject a baptism simply
on the ground of its not being administered by a Catholic?
Expedience pointed out the duty of acknowledging it in cases
in which our Lord's description of it, when He made it His initia-
tory rite, had been exactly fulfilled, unless indeed Scripture and
Tradition were directly opposed to such a course. To cut off
such cautious baptism from the Church was to circumscribe her
range of subjects, and to impair her catholicity. It was to sacrifice
those, who, though at present blinded by the mist of error, had
enough of truth in their religion, however latent, to leave hope
of their conversion at some future day. The imperial See of Peter,
ever on the watch for the extension of Christ's kingdom, understood this well; and, while its tradition was unfavourable to heretical ordination, it was strong and clear in behalf of the validity
of heretical baptism.

Pope Stephen took this side then in a memorable controversy,
and maintained it against almost the whole Christian world. It
was a signal instance of the triumph, under Divine Providence,
of a high, generous expediency over a conception of Christian
doctrine, which logically indeed seemed unanswerable. One
must grant indeed, as I have said, that he based his decision
upon Tradition, not on expediency, but why was such a Tradition
in the first instance begun? The reason of the Tradition has to
be explained; and, if Stephen is not to have the credit of the
large and wise views which occasioned his conduct, that credit
belongs to the Popes who went before him. . . .

Expedience is an argument which grows in cogency with the
course of years; a hundred and fifty years after St. Stephen,
the ecclesiastical conclusion which he had upheld was accepted

generally by the School of Theologians, in an adhesion to it on the part of St. Augustine.

34.

Lastly, serious as this contrast is between the decision of the Pope and the logic of the above great authors, there was, before and in his time, a change yet greater in the ideas and the tone of the theological schools. . . . I mean that relaxation of the penitential canons, effected by a succession of Popes, which, much as it altered the Church's discipline and the ordinary course of Christian life, still was strictly conformable to the necessities of her prospective state, as our Lord had described it beforehand. As Christianity spread through the various classes of the Pagan Empire, and penetrated into private families, social circles, and secular callings, and was received with temporary or local toleration, the standard of duty amongst its adherents fell; habits and practices of the world found their way into the fold; and scandals became too common to allow of the offenders being cast off by wholesale.

This, I say, was but the fulfilment of our Lord's prophetic announcement, that the kingdom of heaven should be a net, gathering fish of every kind; and how indeed should it be otherwise, if it was to be Catholic, human nature being what it is? Yet, on the other hand, the Sermon on the Mount, and other discourses of our Lord, assigned a very definite standard of morals, and a very high rule of conduct to His people. Under these circumstances, the Holy See and various Bishops took what would be called the laxer side, as being that which charity, as well as expediency suggested, whereas the graver and more strict, as well as the ignorant portion of the Christian community did not understand such a policy, and in consequence there was, in various parts of the world, both among the educated and the uneducated, an indignant rising against this innovation, as it was conceived, of their rulers. . . . The resolution of the difficulties of the problem was found in a clearer recognition of the distinction between precepts and counsels, between mortal sins and venial, and between the two forums of the Church, the external and internal; – also in the development of the doctrine of Purgatory, and in the contemporary rise of the monastic institution, as exhibited in the history of St. Antony and his disciples.

35.

So much on the collision and the adjustment of the Regal or political office of the Church with the Prophetical: that I may not end without an instance of the political in contrast with the Sacerdotal, I will refer to the Labarum of Constantine. The sacred symbol of unresisting suffering, of self-sacrificing love, of life-giving grace, of celestial peace, became in the hands of the first Christian Emperor, with the sanction of the Church, his banner in fierce battle and the pledge of victory for his sword.

36.

To conclude: – whatever is great refuses to be reduced to human rule, and to be made consistent in its many aspects with itself. Who shall reconcile with each other the various attributes of the Infinite God? and, as He is, such in their several degrees are His works. This living world to which we belong, how self-contradictory it is, when we attempt to measure and master its meaning and scope! And how full of incongruities, that is, of mysteries, in its higher and finer specimens, is the soul of man, viewed in its assemblage of opinions, tastes, habits, powers, aims, and doings! We need not feel surprise then, if Holy Church too, the supernatural creation of God, is an instance of the same law, presenting to us an admirable consistency and unity in word and deed, as her general characteristic, but crossed and discredited now and then by apparent anomalies which need, and which claim, at our hands an exercise of faith.

(*Vol* i. xxxviii-xliii, xlvi-lxxi, lxxiii-xciv)

SELECT BIBLIOGRAPHY

Cameron, J. M. "John Henry Newman and the Tractarian Movement". *Nineteenth Century Religious Thought in the West*, vol. 2, ed. Ninian Smart, John Clayton, Steven T. Katz, and Patrick Sherry. Cambridge: Cambridge University Press, 1985.

Chadwick, Owen. *From Bossuet to Newman: The Idea of Doctrinal Development*. Cambridge: Cambridge University Press, 1957.

Coulson, John. *Newman and the Common Tradition: A Study of the Church and Society*. Oxford: Clarendon Press, 1970.

Coulson, John, and Allchin, A. M., eds. *The Rediscovery of Newman: An Oxford Symposium*. London: Sheed and Ward, 1967.

Dessain, Charles Stephen. *John Henry Newman*. London: Nelson, 1966.

Jenkins, Hilary. "Religion and Secularism: The Contemporary Significance of Newman's Thought". *Modes of Thought: Essays on Thinking in Western and non-Western Societies*, ed. Robin Horton and Ruth Finnegan. London: Faber, 1973.

Ker, Ian. *John Henry Newman: A Biography*. Oxford: Clarendon Press, 1988.

Ker, Ian. *The Achievement of John Henry Newman*. Notre Dame: Notre Dame University Press; London: Collins, 1990.

Lash, Nicholas. *Change in Focus: A Study of Doctrinal Change and Continuity*, chs. 9, 10. London: Sheed and Ward, 1973.

Lash, Nicholas. *Newman on Development: The Search for an Explanation in History*. London: Sheed and Ward, 1975.

Miller, Edward Jeremy. *John Henry Newman on the Idea of Church*. Shepherdstown, W. Virginia: Patmos Press, 1987.

Misner, Paul. "Newman's Concept of Revelation and the Development of Doctrine'. *The Heythrop Journal* XI (1970).

Misner, Paul. *Papacy and Development: Newman and the Primacy of the Pope*. Leiden: Brill, 1976.

Selby, Robin C. *The Principle of Reserve in the Writings of John Henry Cardinal Newman*. Oxford: Clarendon Press, 1975.

Sykes, Stephen. *The Identity of Christianity*, ch. 5. Philadelphia: Fortress Press, 1984.

Walgrave, J.-H., OP. *Newman the Theologian: The Nature of Belief and Doctrine as exemplified in his Life and Works*, trans. A.V. Littledale. London: 1960.

Walgrave, Jan Hendrik. *Unfolding Revelation: The Nature of Doctrinal Development*, ch. 9. Philadelphia: Fortress Press, 1972.

NOTES TO THE INTRODUCTION

[1] *GA* 43.
[2] *Apo.* 15.
[3] *AW* 150, 268.
[4] *LD* xxxi. 31.
[5] *AW* 150, 29.
[6] *AW* 169.
[7] *Apo.* 17–19.
[8] *AW* 79–80, 166, 172.
[9] *Apo.* 19–20.
[10] *AW* 73–4, 77–9; *Apo.* 21–2.
[11] *AW* 203–4.
[12] *AW* 83.
[13] *AW* 78.
[14] *Apo.* 23.
[15] *Apo.* 25–6.
[16] *Apo.* 35.
[17] *Apo.* 29.
[18] *Apo.* 34.
[19] *AW* 96.
[20] *LD* ii. 43.
[21] *Ari.* 26–7.
[22] *Ari.* 361–2.
[23] *Ari.* 147–8, 274.
[24] *Ari.* 36–7.
[25] *Ari.* 145–6.
[26] *Ari.* 80–2, 84–5.
[27] *Ess.* i. 31–4, 36, 95–6, 41–2.
[28] See Ian Ker, *John Henry Newman: A Biography* (Oxford: Clarendon Press, 1988), pp. 110–11.
[29] *VM* i. 5–7.
[30] *VM* i. 26–7, 245, 150.
[31] *VM* i. 28–9, 159, 239.
[32] *VM* i. 31–4, 281.
[33] *VM* i. 244.
[34] *VM* i. 49, 51, 56, 71, 107.
[35] *VM* i. 38.
[36] *VM* i. 250–2.
[37] *VM* i. 286.
[38] *VM* i. 189, 203, 209.
[39] *VM* i. 217, 232.
[40] *VM* i. 199, 201–2.
[41] See Ker, *John Henry Newman: A Biography*, p. 137.
[42] *Jfc.* p. v.
[43] *Jfc.* 2.
[44] *Jfc.* 8–9.
[45] *Jfc.* 11–13.
[46] *Jfc.* 19.
[47] *Jfc.* 21.
[48] *Jfc.* 23.
[49] *Jfc.* 24.
[50] *Jfc.* 26.
[51] *Jfc.* 27–8.
[52] *Jfc.* 30–1, 34.
[53] *Jfc.* 36–7, 61.
[54] *Jfc.* 56.
[55] *Jfc.* 263–6.
[56] *Jfc.* 65.
[57] *Jfc.* 72–3.
[58] *Jfc.* 78.
[59] *Jfc.* 81.
[60] *Jfc.* 96, 99, 174.
[61] *Jfc.* 136–8.
[62] *Jfc.* 154.
[63] *Jfc.* 243, 303, 266.
[64] *Jfc.* 313–14.
[65] *Jfc.* 319.
[66] *Jfc.* 316.
[67] *Jfc.* 317–18.
[68] *Jfc.* 323–8.
[69] *Jfc.* 330.
[70] *Jfc.* 332–3.
[71] *Jfc.* 336–7.
[72] *Jfc.* 339–41.
[73] *Jfc.* 57.
[74] *LD* iv. 180.
[75] *VM* i. 40.
[76] *Apo.* 105.

[77] *Apo.* 108.

[78] *US* 320–1, 323.

[79] *US* 331–2, 336–7, 339, 342.

[80] *Apo.* 205, 211.

[81] *Dev.* 29–30, 5.

[82] *Dev.* 38.

[83] *Dev.* 171.

[84] *Dev.* 100.

[85] *Apo.* 108.

[86] *Apo.* 110–12.

[87] *Diff.* i. 379.

[88] Jaroslav Pelikan, *Development of Christian Doctrine: Some Historical Prolegomena* (New Haven and London: Yale University Press, 1969), 3.

[89] Owen Chadwick, *From Bossuet to Newman: The Idea of Doctrinal Development* (Cambridge: Cambridge University Press, 1957), 157–60, 195. For this and similar criticisms, see Ian T. Ker, ''Newman's Theory – Development or Continuing Revelation?'' *Newman and Gladstone Centennial Essays*, ed. James D. Bastable (Dublin: Veritas Publications, 1978), 143–59.

[90] *LD*, xxv. 418.

[91] *US* 321.

[92] *Dev.* 191–2.

[93] *Dev.* 52–3.

[94] *TP* ii. 156–9.

[95] *LD* xix. 135.

[96] *LD* xix. 141.

[97] *Cons.* 54–5.

[98] *Cons.* 63.

[99] *Cons.* 72.

[100] *Cons.* 75–6, 77, 106.

[101] For the details, see Ian Ker, *John Henry Newman: A Biography* (Oxford: Clarendon Press, 1988), ch. 14.

[102] *Apo.* 220, 224–6.

[103] *Apo.* 226, 229–31.

[104] *Apo.* 232, 237–8.

[105] *Apo.* 238–40.

[106] *Diff.* ii. 372.

[107] *LD* xxv. 71.

[108] *Diff.* ii. 335, 337, 330.

[109] *LD* xxv. 284.

[110] *LD* xxv. 447.

[111] *LD* xxvi. 35.

[112] *LD* xxvii. 338.

[113] *Diff.* ii. 280.

[114] *Diff.* ii. 332.

[115] *Diff.* ii. 320–1.

[116] *Diff.* ii. 334.

[117] *Diff.* ii. 307.

[118] *Diff.* ii. 247–50.

[119] *Diff.* ii. 252–4.

[120] For the clarification of this distinction here (although I venture to disagree with his conclusion) I am indebted to John Finnis, ''Conscience in the *Letter to the Duke of Norfolk*'', *Newman After a Hundred Years*, ed. Ian Ker and Alan G. Hill (Oxford: Clarendon Press, 1990).

[121] *Diff.* ii. 256–8.

[122] *Diff.* ii. 261.

[123] *VM* i., pp. xxxvi–xxxvii.

[124] *VM* i., pp. xxviii–xliii.

[125] *VM* i., pp. xlvii–xlviii.

[126] *VM* i., pp. xlviii–l, lii–liv, lvi.

[127] *LD* xxv. 31–2; xxii. 99.

[128] *VM* i., pp. lxvi–lxxi, lxxiv–lxxvi.

[129] *VM* i., pp. lxxx–lxxxi, lxxxvi.

[130] *VM* i., p. xciv.

[131] C. Stephen Dessain, ''Newman's Spirituality: its Value Today'', *English Spiritual Writers*, ed. Charles Davis (New York: Sheed and Ward, 1962), p. 160.

Parts of this introduction appeared in a different form in my *John Henry Newman: A Biography* and *The Achievement of John Henry Newman* (Notre Dame: University of Notre Dame Press; London: Collins, 1990).

NOTES TO THE SELECTED TEXTS

[1] 1 Pet. 1:2; 1 Cor. 6:11; Rom. 8:2,15; John 6:63; Gal. 5:5; Titus 3:5–7.

[2] Rom. 1:11; 6:23; 12:6–18; 1 Cor. 7:7; 12:4, 1 Tim. 4:14; 2 Tim. 1:6; 1 Pet. 4:10.

[3] 2 Cor. 3:8,9.

[4] John 4:10; Acts 2:38.

[5] Heb. 6:4.

[6] The angelic appearances in the Old Testament, to which divine titles are given and divine honour paid, may be taken as an instance of such a presence of Almighty God in a created nature.

[7] John 14:20,21,23; 17:21–23.

[8] 1 John 4:12,16; 3:24; 5:20; 1:3.

[9] 1 John 3:24; 4:13; 2 Cor. 13:14; 1 Cor. 3:16; 6:19; John 14:16–18.

[10] 2 Cor. 6:16; John 7:38,39.

[11] Rev. 3:20.

[12] John 6:51,56; Eph. 5:30; vid. also 2 Pet. 1:4.

[13] Vide Butler's Analogy, part 2, ch. 3.

[14] The controversy between the English Church and the Church of Rome lies, it is presumed, *in the matter of fact*, whether such and such developments are true (e.g. Purgatory a true development of the doctrine of sin after baptism), not in the *principle* of development itself.

[15] John 17:3; Phil. 3:8; 2 Pet. 1:3.

[16] 1 Tim. 3:16; Isa. 59:21.

[17] It is observable that the *Pastor Aeternus* does not speak of ''praecepta'' at all in its definition of the Pope's Infallibility, only of his ''defining doctrine'' and of his ''definitions''.

[18] Vid. also 1 Cor. 3:1,2 and Heb. 5:12–14.